INVESTING IN REAL ESTATE WITH OTHER PEOPLE'S MONEY

Proven Strategies for Turning a Small Investment Into a Fortune

JACK CUMMINGS

McGraw-Hill

New York   Chicago   San Francisco   Lisbon
London   Madrid   Mexico City   Milan   New Delhi
San Juan   Seoul   Singapore   Sydney   Toronto

The *McGraw·Hill* Companies

1 2 3 4 5 6 7 8 9 0   DOC/DOC   0 9 8 7 6 5 4 3

ISBN 0-07-142670-1

This publication is designed to provide accurate and authoritative information in regard to the subject matter covered. It is sold with the understanding that the publisher is not engaged in rendering legal, accounting, or other professional service. If legal advice or other expert assistance is required, the services of a competent professional person should be sought.

> —*From a declaration of principles jointly adopted by a committee of the American Bar Association and a committee of publishers.*

McGraw-Hill books are available at special quantity discounts to use as premiums and sales promotions, or for use in corporate training programs. For more information, please write to the Director of Special Sales, Professional Publishing, McGraw-Hill, Two Penn Plaza, New York, NY 10121-2298. Or contact your local bookstore.

 This book is printed on recycled, acid-free paper containing a minimum of 50% recycled, de-inked fiber.

Library of Congress Cataloging-in-Publication Data

Cummings, Jack.
   Investing in real estate with other people's money : Proven
strategies for turning a small investment into a fortune / by Jack
Cummings.
      p. cm.
Includes bibliographical references and index.
   ISBN 0-07-142670-1 (pbk. : alk. paper)
  1. Real estate investment. 2. Real estate business—Finance. I.
Title.
   HD1382.5.C852 2003
   332.63'24—dc21
                                    2003012978

This book is dedicated to the memory of my father, John William Cummings III. What I learned from him came as a result of his natural ability to be patient, thoughtful of others first and himself last, polite and generous with everyone, and a person with more dignity and humility than I have ever known.

C O N T E N T S

INTRODUCTION

There are 43 exciting, quick-to-read and easy-to-comprehend chapters in this book. One after the other they will build your knowledge of investment strategies and techniques. By the time you have finished this book you will have hundreds of techniques from which to choose for your investment plan. Together this book and the strategies it contains will offer a way for you to become rich investing in real estate. These chapters are designed to transport you into the real estate world where not only can you get rich, but you can also do so using other people's money.

These chapters provide you with true "insider" techniques to purchase real estate in such a way that you maximize your future profits, build solid income-producing real estate, and end your financial problems forever. These same techniques will allow you to sell real estate in tough markets, make a profit even when you sell for less than you paid, and become a confident and respected member of the elite real estate insider community in your investment area.

These chapters and this book are designed to help you become financially independent as quickly as possible. It is my personal goal to help you achieve your financial goals, whether they are to provide for your family in ways you have always wished you could, to send your children to the best schools, to travel now without the worry of an uncertain economic future, or to sleep well at night knowing you are successful in this wonderful investment field. Best of all, this book is dedicated to help you to establish a legacy that you can leave for generations to come.

Is What Everyone Has Told You About Real Estate Wrong?

Here is what you really need to know. Most people have the wrong idea about what it takes to make money—and I mean big money—by investing in real estate. I am constantly surprised at how many common misconceptions there are about what it takes to be a successful real estate investor. One of these is the concept that "location, location, location" are the three most important factors about real estate. Another misconception is that inflation destroys the value of property. Both of these presumed facts are wrong. In this book I will explain why they are wrong, along with other common misconceptions.

To set the stage properly, let me give you some history of my background. I started out, like many real estate brokers, selling houses. I quickly recognized I was better suited for commercial real estate, with a special emphasis in international hotel and development transactions. This early decision was a wise one because it took me down a path that many brokers and investors never see. It provided me with the hands-on education about big money deals that could not be learned at any university. I watched intelligent people lose their shirts while barely literate people cashed in big. I heard every get-rich-quick plan ever devised by man or computer. If it exists in real estate, I have seen it.

In the end I discovered that the secrets to success in any field and in particular real estate are relatively simple. Often they are so simple that people do not believe they actually work. People often want to believe that success is difficult, if not nearly impossible. Why? Because if it is easy, then failing to attain it must be catastrophic to their ego. If it is easy to be successful in real estate there must be something missing. But it is exactly this way with real estate. The secrets *are* simple. But that does not mean they'll be easy to attain or riches will come overnight. Success begins by understanding those secrets and discovering for yourself that they do work. Your job is to fine-tune your ability to implement those secrets effectively. Think of this book as your sharpening agent and your guide to how you can use other people's money to get rich.

The proper place to get started toward your real estate wealth is right here, with this chapter and with this book. By the time you finish this chapter you will have an insight into what it takes and how long it may take you to start building your fortunes using other people's money. I can assure you that you can succeed.

HOW TO BECOME A REAL ESTATE INSIDER

You probably already recognize some of the real estate insiders who live and invest in your community. All you have to do is look at the society pages in the newspaper or attend charity benefits in your community. The "insiders" are there, and often they are not only rich and respected people but also powerful within the community. They are investors and property owners, developers, architects, politicians, lawyers, and others who specialize in real estate matters. It doesn't matter if they are local members of the community or foreign investors, they all have the same thing in common: They have singled out your backyard as a place to make their own fortunes. If you follow their examples, you will shortly be thought of—at least by the other insiders—as a member of their very special club.

In my book *The McGraw-Hill 36-Hour Real Estate Investing Course,* I go into great detail about the plan and roadmap that will drive you to the status of real estate insider. In this chapter I will highlight the essence of this plan and the kind of roads over which you can expect to travel. But first, so that you see what is at the end of this road, let me illustrate the importance of being recognized as a real estate insider. In a long and worthwhile career in real estate I have helped my clients build big fortunes. I have guided them to profits well beyond their dreams. Best of all I have helped them attain their goals and watched while they set even higher ones. As a broker I have participated in over 700 million dollars of transactions for my clients, and I am proud of their success. I will be proud of your success too. The goal of this book is to give you the investment strategies to become wealthy using other people's money when investing in real estate.

In over 40 years of real estate achievements I have become a student of what it takes to short cut the time between thinking about being a real estate investor and becoming rich and financially comfortable by owning real estate. I have studied the mistakes others and I have made along the way. It should not be surprising that I discovered most of those mistakes could have been avoided entirely and all of the negative impacts could have been substantially reduced and even completely eliminated by following a simple plan. That plan is the essence of this book.

When building my own investment portfolio, I have applied this simple plan that has paid off handsomely. My success as an investor has allowed me to surpass my financial goals and to continue as an investor, broker, and advisor in many transactions with and for my clientele of buyers and sellers, as well as to travel extensively around the world.

Your success as a real estate investor will depend on your ability to build your own plan, as each person's goals differ to some degree or other. This book will become your guide to that success. You need not master 100 percent of this book, as you will only need what works for you. The book can be at your side whenever you need to "freshen up" on the different techniques it will provide for you. Look at the following five essentials that you should strive to achieve. Believe me when I tell you that no matter how difficult you may *think* they will be to achieve, they are all within your grasp.

THE FIVE ESSENTIALS TO SUCCESS IN REAL ESTATE INVESTING

1. Be a *real estate insider.*
2. Recognize *real estate opportunities.*
3. Discover the power of using *other people's money.*
4. Learn *buying techniques* that will reduce your risk.
5. Use *selling techniques* that will maximize benefits.

With this book you will learn about these five essentials and expand your knowledge of real estate investing from your present level of investment prowess. However you should keep in mind that while I cover each of these subjects, the main focus of this book is directed toward essentials three, four, and five. Two other books I have authored, *The Real Estate Investor's Answer Book* and *The McGraw-Hill 36-Hour Real Estate Investing Course* focus on the first two essentials listed above. Now we're ready to get started and take a look at these five essentials to success in real estate investing.

Why You Should Become a Real Estate Insider

There are a number of reasons to become a real estate insider, and the benefits are obvious. The key benefit to you, though, is that in attaining this status you start doing things that presently recognized real estate insiders have been doing for years. It's like getting a suntan by simply staying out in the sun or sitting under a sunlamp. Naturally the effort to follow the examples set by real estate insiders is greater than lying in the sun, and it is far more profitable. When you are recognized as a real estate insider, doors will suddenly begin to open for you. Important information you need to make good investment decisions will suddenly come directly to you from the sources of that information. You will build your knowledge of your investment area and enhance your investment skills. As you sharpen your skills, your self-confidence as an investor shines through so that others recognize it. You will be an expert in your community in the very thing you want to do: Invest in and become rich owning real estate.

The Thirteen Steps to Becoming a Real Estate Insider

1. **Start in your own backyard by defining your "investment area."** What this means is choose a geographic area close to where you live or work. This area will become your "investment area" that you learn like the back of your hand. Make sure you start with one city, and do not overlap into others. You may expand your investment area later, but keep in mind that each city will have its own set of "insiders" as well as an entirely different set of rules and regulations. Get one city down pat first. Define your area by getting a city map and drawing a red line around the area of town you want to learn about first. Make sure the area contained within the line is substantial and consists of different kinds of real estate. Do not

limit the area to just single-family homes or commercial areas. You will want to start with an area of 10 to 15 square miles. You can expand later on.

2. **Become a member of a local group or nonsocial club in your area.** Make sure you join a community group within your investment area. Be sure to have a business card that identifies you as "Real Estate Investor." The idea is to become aware of as much about your community as you can and to let the community identify you as one of the real "insiders" in community affairs. I feel strongly about this as a key step. As a real estate investor you are going to profit from the community. In turn you should devote some of your time to that community in as many ways as you can. Over the past 40 years I have participated in and served on many different boards, associations, and civic organizations. I have never felt pressed for time and have always had a good feeling about my accomplishments for my community. You will feel the same. You will discover that it is quick and easy to become a prominent voice in any community association or civic club. All it takes is to be a dependable member who is ready to take on a responsibility within the group.

3. **Tell everyone you meet you are planning to make real estate investments in the area.** Communication is key to networking. The more people you talk to, the more opportunities you may come across. It is okay to let them know you also have another profession if real estate investing is your new venture but establish the fact that real estate is going to be a part of your life.

4. **Send the important people you meet a note with a business card.** Even if you gave them a card when you first met, follow up with another one. Be sure to thank them for the opportunity to meet them. The idea is to let them know you think they are important. If you are sincere about this, they will feel good about you. If you see something about them in local publications or an article you think would be of interest to them, clip it out and send it to them. Never overlook this just because you think other people have done the same thing. The important element here is that you are demonstrating that you recognize them as important. You are building a network of

acquaintances, and from this you will build relationships with any players who may be helpful or critical to your success in real estate investing.

5. **Learn who establishes controls on real estate or plans for its future in your area and take steps to meet them.** The first person to meet with in any area is the mayor of the city and his or her secretary. Take time to establish a personal rapport with the secretary, then personally meet with the mayor. At the end of that meeting, ask the mayor who in these following city departments he or she would recommend you meet: building, planning, and zoning. Get the mayor's business card and write the name of each person on the back (one name per card), and when you meet the person casually hand the official the card and say, "The mayor suggested I meet with you personally." Use this technique with other people you meet and who give you recommendations of other people to meet. The people you meet are important to building your network since they know about the ins and outs of your area. They are the local politicians (city, county, state, federal), the heads of the city and county planning, zoning, and building departments, heads of city and county department of transportation, heads of planning for the school board, utility services, transportation services, and health care, and so on. They are all interested in the future of the community. As a prospective or active real estate investor you want to know as much about the future as you can. The sooner you know where a new hospital, sports arena, or road is to be constructed, the quicker you can assess how that change will affect property values in the area. Some values will go up, others will go down. That is the nature of real estate. The people you are meeting will help you get advanced information on what is going on in the city long before the outsiders catch on.

   One of the quickest ways to find these people is to ask the mayor's secretary how you can get a directory of government officials for the city. Most cities and towns should have this information readily available. Check the city's website or a local phone book. Often local government officials are listed in the front section of the phone book. If none of these resources work, then you may have to check the phone directory for the offices shown above and call for individual names.

6. **Discover what control government has over you and your real estate and who administers those controls.** A key here is to first identify these controls and then find out how—and if—they can be modified. Most of the important controls that cities and counties have fall within the building and zoning areas of government. Zoning ordinances and building codes are generally in flux, that is to say, they often are going through a change. Most cities have separate departments dealing specifically with these rules and regulations. They have staff members who can help to interpret them so don't be bashful about asking a lot of questions if there is anything about those rules and regulations you do not understand.

7. **Learn what the future plans for city development or change are.** Important developments are often discussed years in advance of the general public even hearing about them. Planning departments are found at both county and city levels. Start going to their regular meetings to find out what developments are being discussed or are in progress long before they actually happen. Call the mayor's secretary and ask how you can be put on a mailing list to receive notice of these meetings along with a copy of the agenda.

8. **Attend government meetings and watch the insiders in action.** I have already mentioned the planning meetings, but there are more. City and county commission meetings are important too. New development is discussed at the planning and zoning board meetings, and it is the ideal place to meet the other real estate insiders early in the game. When you are at these meetings, make sure you keep notes of who is doing what. You will discover there are more than two sides to every presentation made and not everyone is in favor or against a project. Best of all you are building your knowledge of how government works and are getting to know the key players— and they are getting to know you.

9. **Learn your investment area like the back of your hand.** Start with a zoning map of the city. You can usually obtain one free from city hall or the zoning department's office. (If they are not free, then be sure to buy one.) Be sure you understand what each zoning is and how it differs from other zonings.

Zoning ordinances control use, and it is use that is key to everything. Remember that "location, location, location" issue? While the location of a property is important, the actual use allowed at a location is the most critical aspect. Zoning will establish whether or not you can put a fast-food operation on that corner or not. But remember zoning can change, and just because there is a fast-food operation at a certain location is no absolute guarantee that the current zoning would allow it to happen again.

On the other hand, it is common for the underlying zoning to allow a greater economic use than what you see. In my backyard, for example, there are large areas of town with small homes built on the lots. A quick check of the zoning map will show you the land is zoned for multifamily dwellings. When you see something like this, you may have just found a gold mine. Old small homes might give way to a cluster of new townhomes at a much greater value. Zoning is one of the issues that you must check before buying any real estate to make sure there are no violations of use.

To get a feel for your area, ride your bike, jog, or just take long walks in different parts of your community. The slow pace provides more time to observe the area in detail. Bring a notepad and pen with you too. When driving from one side of town to another or just going to work, vary your route and take different roads. Real estate is a visual item. By consistently surveying your area, you will recognize the trends and values of the community more quickly, and it will be easier to spot the opportunities in real estate.

10. **Make notes on what is for sale, rent, sold, vacant, and so on.**
The more you know about what is going on the better informed you will be. It's important to invest in what you know, so know your real estate. Be sure to stop in at open houses, even if you have no interest in owning that property. Check out "for rent" properties just to find out what the rental market will support. This information is valuable for buying rental properties for your own investment portfolio. This and the other data you will compile will become a good source for property comparisons later on.

As you continue with this process, you will discover many ways to find critical data on what is going on in the real estate arena. It is relatively easy to check current sales (your realtor can help or go to the tax assessor's web page). Similar houses on similar lots will show you trends in sales. Then check the sales that took place a year or two ago. Were they higher or lower? This is a pattern you should pay attention to. Another effective method of comparison is to see what happens to values when there is a change of infrastructure. Let's say there is a new bridge being built to open up an area. The bridge might be over a river or a highway where there was no previous roadway. If this is happening in your area, find a location where the similar thing happened in the past. Check sale prices before, during, and after the construction of the bridge. What happened there is likely to happen again. Be sure the two areas connected by the bridge in your investment area are similar to the past examples. Clearly a nice residential area buffered by a river from an industrial area is likely to undergo a detrimental impact once there is a direct traffic connection to the industrial area.

11. **Meet with architects, builders, mortgage brokers, and bank presidents doing business in your investment area.** Ask questions and find out who they think you should meet next. Every architect, builder, and lender has a special kind of real estate they like to deal with. Sometimes it is a category of real estate or location within the city. The best way to shortcut the route to success is to find out what the market needs. These people are all some of the best sources for this information. Financing is critical to all of them, and they know that the best loan is obtained when you are dealing with exactly what the lender likes most. Why fight an uphill battle by trying to finance something they do not like?

12. **Introduce yourself to the real estate brokerage community.** By this I mean you should meet realtors. The goal is to let them know you are a real prospect so they start bringing you "hot" deals. In the beginning this will be a learning process for you, later on they will be a good source for properties. A good realtor can be a valuable source of information too. You will discover that there are some people in the real estate industry who will not want to work with you, and the feeling is likely to be mutual. Be selective in picking teammates. Good ones are truly hard to find, and you will know them when you have been

around them for a short time. The best real estate broker or salesman will be the one who wants to help you attain your goals, and they know how to make things happen.

13. **Meet with several real estate lawyers and pick one for your team.** Do not rush this process. One of the best places to find a good real estate lawyer will be at the planning and zoning meetings. There will be a lot of good lawyers making presentations there. They specialize in real estate, and although they may not be your kind of lawyer, they can introduce you to other real top-notch lawyers in their firm or in your part of town. You may also discover a few not-so-good lawyers at these meetings too and, believe me, you will know them when you see them in action. Avoid them.

This list of 13 steps to becoming a real estate insider will start you off and running. Now let me give you one word of warning. Learning to be a real estate insider can be like becoming a first-year student of psychiatry. A little knowledge can be dangerous, and like the fledgling psychiatrist who suddenly discovers that everyone he knows is nuts, the newly initiated real estate insider may believe that being a real estate insider has opened a universal door to riches anywhere you go. This is not so. The knowledge you will learn will work with the greatest effectiveness and success as long as you stay within your investment area and your comfort zone. Do not venture far from that protective area until you spend the same time and effort in other geographic areas as you did in the first zone.

HOW TO RECOGNIZE REAL ESTATE OPPORTUNITIES

There is no computer as effective as the human brain. But like all computers, if you program the darn thing incorrectly, you will produce lousy results. In many ways the ability to see real estate opportunities pop out is like learning a foreign language. After five years of studying Spanish, the best I could do was to read and write a little Spanish, and my spoken communication was dismal. When I went to Spain, I discovered how little I really knew. I realized I was in trouble the night I went to dinner at a modest restaurant. The restaurant offered fixed menus, which seemed to be an easy enough option. I did not understand much of the menu so I pointed to the first group of items that made up the first fixed meal on the menu.

The waiter left and a few minutes later brought me the first of my four dishes. It was a fish soup—not just any fish soup, but the fishiest of all fish soups, and I hated fish soups. I smiled at the waiter when he removed the empty bowl and leaned back to await the next dish knowing that nothing could be worse than that fishy soup. As he slid the next item in front of me, I knew I had made a terrible mistake. It was another kind of smelly fish soup. Instantly I realized that the following dishes would be two more kinds of fish soup.

The next day I buckled down to my studies, and at the suggestion of one of my teachers, I started going to movies every day. I discovered there were many movie theaters in Madrid, where I was living at the time, that showed old American films that had been dubbed into Spanish. I picked movies that I had previously seen so that I could understand what was being said.

I remember the film I was watching when my brain finally figured out the Spanish language. It was a John Wayne war film called *The Sands of Iwo Jima*. As I left the film I suddenly realized I was thinking about the film in Spanish. Ever since then I am able to think in Spanish. The jump from the inability to converse in Spanish to suddenly think in it came in a natural way. By bombarding my mind with the combination of watching something I had seen before and hearing the spoken language, I was continually soaking in the language. Once I could think in Spanish, my ability to converse in the language rapidly advanced. Real estate opportunities will appear to you in much the same way. As you eat, drink, and sleep the real estate market, your mind will be storing the information for later use. The people you meet, the meetings you attend, and the knowledge you build will all pay off. The day will come when you suddenly begin to see the opportunities in your investment area. You will see that old run-down house, check your zoning map, and, joy of joys, it is actually sitting on a commercially zoned lot. After you do a little more checking you may discover that it's worth double what the owner is asking.

Zoning is a powerful tool. It affects the future use of a property. It is a hidden quality because there is nothing on the side of the house that will tell you what the zoning actually is. Property owners may not even know the full story about the existing and current zoning of property they own. They may have been told something at the time they bought the property, but over the years the actual zoning may have changed, been upgraded, or made more restrictive. The current use of the property may no longer be allowed, and its present use may be a conditional one that is "grandfathered" in as a nonconforming legal use. Nonconforming legal use simply means that if the building is substantially damaged (that may have a varying degree of percentage of damage from community to community), the property cannot be repaired back to the old use. This would be a major setback to the new owner of that quaint restaurant that just burned down to now discover that despite his full insurance coverage, the zoning will not let him build anything except a single-family home in replacement of the previously thriving business.

Economic Conversion: The Modern Trend to Wealth in Real Estate

There is a trend taking place in real estate that I call economic conversion. This is one of the best ways to make an instant profit in real estate. It occurs when you discover a new use for an old property that produces greater income and profit than the old use would allow. There are many examples of this trend. Say you find an old motel that is located on a great commercial location but the income appears to be as good as it will get no matter what you do to fix it up. Think of the use for a moment. You check the zoning and find there are several different kinds of commercial uses allowed at that location. You could convert the motel into offices, an antique retail center, or a private school. The idea is to convert it to whatever there is a market for so that the rents you collect less the reduced expenses of operation will give you a greater economic return than the old motel.

There are also instances in which particular older homes are too big for most families but the zoning allows professional offices to locate there. Many of America's older cities have such properties, and if you drive around, you will see examples where the real estate insider has taken advantage of such properties. Lawyers, doctors, insurance companies, and so on occupy beautiful homes that have been turned into more beautiful offices.

But beware—there is an illness that I call the "greener-grass syndrome." It bites almost all real estate investors at one time or another and likely will confront you somewhere along the way. Everyone has a tendency to see something that truly looks like the grass is greener on the other side of the fence. For me it was Hawaii, Bermuda, and even Jamaica—all in the aftermath of a wonderful week's holiday in each of those places. Did I lose a fortune in my real estate investments in those greener-grass syndrome places? No, because I came to my senses just in time. Now do not jump to conclusions that any of those three places, or anyplace that becomes your greener-grass roadblock, are bad places to invest. The key is not to be swayed by the green grass until you have checked out the nematodes that eat at their roots. The farther you get from your investment area and your comfort zone, the more that something different will attract you. This is the time when mistakes are made. Did you know about that volcano about to blow, the 15 hurricanes predicted for next year, or the sugar cane blight that will turn the economy of the area into mush? You might know all these things if you do some preliminary real estate insider due diligence. Invest in those greener-grass places only after you have devoted some time as a real estate insider in that environment.

DISCOVER THE POWER OF USING OTHER PEOPLE'S MONEY

The balance of this book is dedicated to the concept that you use your own money only when it's impossible or when it's impractical to use other people's money (OPM). Right now and for perhaps the next million years, other people's money is the most attractive option to take.

The Power of Using OPM

You might ask yourself, what do you mean use other people's money, and how does that work? First let's take a look at what we already know about purchasing property. Without using OPM you purchase a property that costs $100,000. You pay all cash and say it goes up 15 percent in value in one year. You sell it for $115,000 and pay $5000 in cost of sale (commissions, etc.). You net $10,000 gain, on which you pay tax. To keep it simple, let's say it's 20 percent tax, which is $2000. So your final after-tax return is $8000.

Selling Price	$115,000
Deduct: Cost of Sale	$5,000
Net Receipt from Sale	$110,000
Less Original Investment	$100,000
Gain on the Transaction	$10,000
Less Tax on the Gain	$2,000
Gain After Tax	$8,000

This represents a yield of 8 percent on the original investment of $100,000. That's not too bad. It's better than losing your shirt, and a profit is a profit.

So why then use OPM? Let's take a look at what happens when OPM enters the arena. Using OPM, things start to look more promising. Instead of doing the above, you purchase the same property and invest only $5000 (5 percent down) and have a $95,000 mortgage that costs you $8000 per year in payments. This $8000 is divided into $5500 of interest and $2500 of principal reduction of the mortgage. The interest is a tax deduction (which we will look at in later chapters). The principal reduction of the mortgage is important because when you sell the property you recover those funds. If, as we will see in later examples, your mortgage gets paid by other people (tenants), they are putting future cash into your pocket.

You sell the property for $115,000, as was the case in the first example, and have the same selling expenses. Review this transaction below.

Original Purchase Price	$100,000	
Initial Debt	$ 95,000	
Down Payment	$ 5,000	
Sales Price, One Year Later	$115,000	
Less Cost of Sale	$ 5,000	
Less Balance of Mortgage	$ 92,500	
Net Receipts from the Sale	$ 17,500	
Subtract Your Original Investment	$ 5,000	
Gross Return	$ 12,500	(of which $2,500 is debt reduction)
Less Cash Paid Out During the Year	$ 8,000	(of which $5,500 is interest on debt)
Your "Cash in Your Pocket Profit"	$ 4,500	
Less Tax on the Above Profit	$ 900	
Yield After Tax	$ 3,600	

The return of $3600 on a $5000 investment is a yield of 72 percent. Okay, so you say that is an extreme example and making a profit of only $3600 is not going to make you rich. Well, consider this: If you had taken that $100,000 and made 20 similar investments, your total net profit would have been $72,000 instead of a profit of only $8000.

What if you were to kick it up a notch? Where OPM really gets interesting is when you double dip on OPM. How this happens is when you get money from one source to buy the property and then make the mortgage payments with other people's money you collect as rent. If the investment above were a small apartment building that was throwing gross rents over and above operating costs of $8000, then the first example would have put another $8000 into the pocket of the investor who had paid $100,000 cash to buy the property. This would increase his return to $16,000 ($8000 rent plus $8000 profit on the sale). This would also increase the overall annual return to a whopping 16 percent yield on the invested $100,000.

Double Dipping on OPM

In the second example that $8000 of rental profit would have increased the "Cash in Your Pocket Profit" (cash flow) to a total of $12,500. Why? Because this investor is using OPM to pay off his mortgage. This time the OPM comes from the rent he is collecting.

In this example the $8000 rent collected went to pay the mortgage, so there was no "Cash Out of Pocket." We will use the same 20 percent calculation for taxes owed.

Your "Cash in Your Pocket Profit"	$ 12,500
Less Tax on the Above Profit	$ 2,500
Yield After Tax	$ 10,000

The yield to the investor on his original $5000 investment is now 200 percent. Now this is powerful economics at work.

OPM and Its Partner—Inflation

Accept the fact that inflation is a way of life. Think of it as a fire that will burn your fingers (as well as take the shirt off your back) or, if you know how, will keep you warm and help build your fortune. Your only hope of success is to realize that while everyone else is losing the battle against inflation you will be using inflation to win the war against poverty—your own poverty.

Investing in real estate is the best way to find your fortune using inflation. Inflation is a natural force that, like the tides of the ocean, will either help you or drown you depending on how you use it. Stop drowning. Learn how to invest in real estate and, like thousands of millionaires around the country, use inflation as your private ally.

Let me give you an example of one way I beat inflation. In 1963 I purchased a vacant lot in a nice area of Fort Lauderdale. My plan was to build a place for my bride and me to live. I chose a multifamily lot, in one of those areas I mentioned earlier that was full of single-family homes built on multifamily-zoned property. We constructed a four-unit building, with the fourth unit as a nice two-bedroom apartment for ourselves. I paid the previous lot owner $1000 down with an additional $4000 to be paid over several years at a nominal interest rate. This was not a mortgage on the lot but an unsecured loan cosigned by my parents, which was necessary since my net worth, at that time, was less than zero.

A local savings and loan (S&L) association lent me 100 percent of the funds needed to build the apartment building and also pay off $2000 of the $4000 owed to the former lot owner. When the building was completed, we moved into the two-bedroom apartment and rented out the other three one-bedroom units. The rents from the three one-bedroom apartments more than covered the mortgage and taxes on the property so I was maximizing the use of OPM by double dipping. With the exception of a little cash out of my pocket, I started with OPM from the S&L, which was eventually paid off with OPM from the tenants in the building. At the beginning one of the one-bedroom apartments rented for exactly the amount of the total cost of my electric and water bill as it was allocated to my two-bedroom apartment. I have owned this same building for approximately 40-plus years now, and the OPM the tenants have been giving me completely paid off the mortgage by the end of the first 25 years. My present yield on my original investment is over 200 percent *every month*. Over the years my family and I have owned several different homes; the present one is nearly two times the size of the entire four-unit apartment building. Guess what? The rent from one of those one-bedroom apartments still covers the electric and water bill of where I live. If numbers are what you want, and I caution you on using numbers in this kind of thought process, the original monthly rent was $87.00 per month and the current rent is $675.00 per month.

Why the caution on using numbers? It is easy to forget that what is relative is not the number but rather what the number will get you today. Because of inflation we have seen how one dollar today will purchase less than 50 cents would buy 20 years ago. If you can obtain the same benefit today that you did 20 or even 40 years ago from the income that single element (a one-bedroom apartment) produces, then that is a true inflation fighter. Only real estate can do that. Nothing else will even come close.

Let's look at another OPM example. Charles has $50,000 of cash he can invest. He finds a duplex priced at $50,000. It is completely rented at a net rent (after all expenses) of $6000 per year. This is a yield of 12 percent on his money.

As we have already seen, OPM can come into the transaction and instead of using all his cash, he could use some OPM to help purchase the property. In this case he might put $5000 of his own cash down on the duplex and borrow the balance from the seller (or another lender) at 7 percent interest over a 30-year term. The payment on this $45,000 mortgage would be $3788.88 per year. This means Charlie would take in a net operating income of $6000 and pay out $3788.88 per year. This would leave him with $2211.12. This represents a before-tax yield of 44.22 percent yield on the investment of $5000. If Charles buys 10 properties like this, using all of the $50,000, his benefit will be far greater than buying one for all cash. But even if Charlie purchases only the one duplex, saving the other $45,000 cash for another deal, it is wiser than a cash transaction that uses up all his capital and produces zero leverage.

Now this looks easy, and it is. I know that we think of inflation as an evil thing the young worry about and the old cringe at. It's only evil when you don't know its secret and how to make it work for you. Let's assume that in the next few years the rate of inflation will level off at 4 percent per year. This means that what costs $100 now will cost $104 next year, $108.16 the year after, $112.48 by the end of the third year, and by the end of the tenth year $148.02 (4 percent compounding each year.) This is the effect of inflation alone; it is not a function of the normal supply-and-demand effect in a healthy market where there is no inflation. It is a sure thing.

If properly maintained, the duplex Charles buys will react to this inflation just as almost everything else does. The rents he collects will increase by similar if not higher inflation percentages and the value of the duplex will also increase to reflect the higher cash flow the property generates. By the end of 10 years, a steady 4 percent inflation will increase values by 148 percent. This would mean that the value of the apartment building would be $74,000. This is due to inflation alone. Many other factors could push the value even higher.

Now let's look at what inflation does to Charlie's equity. Remember that Charlie bought the duplex for $50,000 with $5000 down and a $45,000 mortgage at 7 percent interest. If Charlie sells the duplex at the end of the 10-year period, the new value due to inflation alone will be $74,000. He will owe a balance of $35,785.60 on the mortgage. If we deduct the amount owed on the mortgage from the price he receives for the duplex, you can see that Charlie's equity (the value after deducting mortgages owed) is now $38,214.40 as shown below:

New Value	$74,000.00
Less Existing Financing	$35,785.60
Equity at the End of 10 years	$38,214.40

As Charlie invested $5000 at the start of the year, his equity has grown to $38,214.40. If we were to look at what inflation would do to that same original $5000 if it were earning interest at a compounded rate of 4 percent, the same as the inflation rate we used, that $5000 would be worth only $7400.00. To invest $5000 in your local S&L association and have it return $34,214.40 would require the S&L to pay you an annual interest rate of close to 20 percent per year. Try to get that kind of a return from your local S&L.

How does inflation cause this increase? What you are witnessing is the incredible multiple effect inflation has in real estate. As values rise because of inflation, it is the whole value of a property that increases. Cost of operation increases, and rents increase to maintain the status quo. Annual yield may stay the same, but the spread between the value and the original equity (invested capital) is racing forward at an astounding rate. The reason for this is that the cost of the debt has been fixed. It is the only thing that has not increased and is a major part of the original investment. If you have played your investment cards properly, you will have a mortgage at a "fixed" interest rate and it does not increase. Keep in mind this example used a modest 4 percent inflation. There have been times when inflation was much higher. This is why, even in times of high inflation, real estate is an exceptional buy.

The logic is easy to follow, but many people who understand it fail to use it. The key to battling inflation is in using the purchasing technique that meets your specific need. This book provides a number of techniques that turn the secrets of investing into simple, clearly understood axioms. When you finish reading this book you should have gained the confidence to invest in real estate and the edge to success. You will have literally hundreds of different investment strategies at your disposal.

What about deflation? Deflation, as well as inflation, is a fact of life. Take a look at what a computer used to cost compared with present-day values. That might appear to be an effect of deflation, but in reality it is the result of lower manufacturing and distribution costs. During the middle of 2003 many economists feared that the world was slipping into a deflationary cycle. In general economic terms a case could be made that indeed there was that possibility. However, what was happening as it related to real estate was that the cost of OPM was getting cheaper. The interest rates on mortgages were going down to the lowest they've been in the past 40 years. This cheap OPM and the lack of other, more attractive investments fueled the real estate market.

Cheap money, which is one of the major benefits of a deflationary cycle, also benefits real estate. The key again is using OPM to protect your invested capital.

WHAT YOU DO NOT NEED TO USE OPM SUCCESSFULLY

Before we discuss the prerequisites for successful real estate investing and effective use of OPM, let's review what you *don't* need to be a success.

A college degree is absolutely not required. Look at history. Some of the wealthiest and most successful men and women in the world didn't graduate from college; many didn't even finish high school. Some professions, of course, require higher education, and many high-paid professionals are also successful real estate investors. But you can do it with or without college. In fact too much of the wrong kind of education can stand in the way of success here. I've seen CPAs, bankers, and lawyers analyze, plan, and think about doing something so long that some dumb guy with a dream and some guts took the opportunity by the horns and made a bundle of money before the thinkers knew what had happened.

Knowledge of the real estate industry must be a requirement then, right? Wrong. You can be a success in real estate investing without a lot of detailed knowledge of real estate finance, appraisals, management, trends, law, or accounting. Those areas are important elements of the business, but you can hire that expertise when and if you need it. In-depth learning is great if you are in the business. As an investor you should stick to the basics and learn the insider moves of how to make deals work.

There is no magic age for investing in real estate. It is true that age is a product of time, and there is a right time for everyone to buy real estate. That time is always now. Success comes to people of all ages in real estate. I have known young men and women who were just starting out and were achieving major successes. At the same time I have known people who shunned real estate for years while working at nine-to-seven jobs. When they took a little of their cash and finally bought some real estate, what happened? Past their prime of life, they discovered a way to an independent life free of financial worry beyond their wildest dreams through real estate investing.

Your age is not important when it comes to buying real estate. But it is a factor in your real estate investment planning. The young can establish a buying plan whose goals differ from those of their elders. Success and financial independence are achieved when you feel you have attained them in accordance with your established goals.

Money, then, is the one thing you must have in order to invest in real estate, right? At this point the answer is no. Money is not a prerequisite to investing in real estate. Not a lot of money, and often not even any money.

Other books have shown investors how to develop new and creative ways to build their fortunes into larger fortunes. But what about all the people who are still wondering where they are going to find the money to pay the rent at the end of the month? What about the young couple struggling to make it in this world of rising costs? Can you imagine the problems the elderly have in trying to match 1990 or even 2000 retirement incomes with the out-of-proportion costs they are going to be faced with? It is not important what your background has made you think. What is important is that you think you can succeed. I already know you are capable of achieving far greater goals than you have attained thus far. Only you now have to believe in yourself.

Out of every 325 persons living in the United States, as of the writing of this book, about one is a millionaire. That is more than double what it was just a few years back and is an impressive statistic. What about the other 324 people? Are you one of those? If you are, then it is time you started getting smart. Smart, not brilliant. Smart, not a college degree. Smart as in money. You can do this by learning the three secrets you will discover in this chapter about getting money and keeping it.

LEARN BUYING TECHNIQUES THAT WILL REDUCE YOUR RISK AND USE SELLING TECHNIQUES THAT WILL MAXIMIZE BENEFITS

These two topics are best discussed together because you will learn them simultaneously as you progress in this book. Risk and benefits go together like both ends of a teeter-totter. When you are up in the air on one end and at risk of falling off, the other end has safely reached the ground. The middle point of the teeter-totter is the fulcrum balancing both sides so there is little effort for the lightest end to move up and down. Even a child knows this works by where you put this balance point so that each end is at an equal equilibrium to the other.

When risk and benefits are in balance, they offset each other. This is a far better position to be in than where there are so few benefits there is no reasonable way to balance out the situation. As you become more and more in tune with your investment area you will recognize values when you see them. More importantly you will have already made a major leap in your own thought process. By the time you finish this book you will not only begin to see future use, which will equate to enhanced value, you will start to think of one or a combination of the many ways to close that transaction. You will learn to decrease your risk to such a great degree that you will obtain far more benefits than you thought possible.

I had a long phone conversation with one of the real estate licensing officials from California about the techniques of investing in real estate with OPM. We were discussing the certification review of one of my seminars within California as a part of its continuing education courses for the real estate profession. This particular seminar focused on using creative financing and closing techniques. The program was devoted to showing a buyer how to use the different techniques and strategies to buy properties and also how sellers can use the same techniques to sell their properties.

It took a long time to explain how buyers and sellers could use the same techniques. I noted to her that if a seller could "show" a prospective buyer how to purchase the seller's property using an OPM technique, wouldn't that help the seller sell the property? She was in disbelief. Why would a seller be willing to sell and not get anything down? Furthermore why would a real estate salesperson make those kinds of deals—where would he get his commission?

She fell into one of the biggest misconceptions of OPM—that it means no paper money. To clear up this misconception, let's set the record straight. The principal strategy of using OPM is to close deals. With that in mind, here are some key points about OPM.

The seller's primary goal is number one. As you get into the individual chapters dealing with the actual techniques of using OPM, one of the first things you will see is that the primary goals of the seller are critical to every transaction. No buyer is going to make a deal unless the seller agrees to it. No seller is going to accept an offer when there are "better deals on the table." In most OPM transactions the seller gets cash or cash equivalent. Perhaps not all credits to the seller are in actual cash, but more often than not that is the case.

Although many of the OPM techniques involve secondary financing, the mortgages sellers often end up with are first mortgages on other properties. That is often a benefit to the seller who might be ready to hold a second mortgage on the property being sold.

OPM techniques work for both the buyer and seller. There is no doubt that not all techniques will work for all deals. But savvy OPM investors know it is a waste of their time to mess around with concepts that will not work with a specific seller. For this reason real estate insiders who use OPM techniques spend a lot of time getting to know the motivations of the seller.

Savvy sellers use OPM to attract buyers. If I have a property I want to sell and it isn't moving or offers made on it have been way below my selling threshold, I will start to think of how I can bring a ready, willing, and able buyer to the table. My bag of solid OPM techniques can help.

HOW RISKY IS IT?

Anyone who understands—truly understands—real estate and motivations of people will know that money, in particular your money, is not always a necessary commodity in buying or selling real estate. Money only aids in the selection process. What is risky is not to own real estate.

There is nothing sure in life. Not the next real estate deal you might make, not the ground you walk on, and not the food you eat. There has never been a stock sold that could not have gone down as easily as it went up or an ounce of gold traded where someone didn't lose. Even in the most ambitious market for the least risky item of all (whatever that is), there will be risk. Even putting your cash in the bank or tying it up in government bonds is risky because it locks you into something that may itself go down in value.

Real estate has its risk. Because it is connected to people, real estate is affected by the demands of people. If they want it, its value goes up; if they won't sell it, the price offered goes up; and if they still say no and the buyers begin to look elsewhere, the value goes down here and up there. People determine what real estate is worth by being willing and able to buy. People create the value, and they can increase it or decrease it.

Your real estate is a mixture of rights given by people and limited by people. You will never get all the rights to land. Some of these rights have been taken away in the name of "betterment." Or it might be that the previous sellers didn't sell you everything. They kept some mineral rights, an easement across the property to other property, or 50 percent of the water flowing through the river on the land, and so on. Subdivisions, in an attempt to keep values up, require (in the deed) that homes of a certain size be built and that they conform to certain styles. If you want something smaller or bigger than those rules impose, you either fight them (and likely lose) or give in or move on. Cities impose a vast multitude of ordinances restricting your free use of your land. They tell you where to put a building, how much grass to plant, what trees you can cut, and what you have to plant. They tell you if you can build, keep you from building, make you tear down, or close your building because they don't like your attitude about safety. Indeed, if they want, they can make your life miserable to the point where you wonder why you ever bought a piece of land or got involved with that thing called real estate.

Real Estate Is the Bright Light at the End of the Tunnel

If I sound cynical about the state of the real estate market, don't despair. Despite all these headaches, there is a bright light at the end of this tunnel. The rewards of investing in real estate are still there. But don't turn one more page of this book if you expect to find an easy way to build your wealth. The secrets to this success are easily found within this book, but they require tenacity, perseverance, and dedication to a larger plan that can turn your life around. While it is true you can become a millionaire, if that is what you want, it won't be handed to you on a silver tray. You will have to earn it. It will take a lot of hard work and some risk to be sure.

A Bit More About Risk

Investing in real estate through the use of other people's money is not flamboyant, wild, or risky. I say this with clear understanding that this is a bit of a paradox. The word "risk" is relative: What is risky to you might be child's play to another. Working within your comfort level is one of the keys to being a success in anything. What is needed is a method for you to expand your investment techniques so that you will be comfortable with real estate. The level of comfort will vary for different people and will also change as time goes on. As you begin to utilize the techniques I provide here, you will find that your concept of risk will be greatly different from what it is today. This will be relative to the deal and to the person. This book discusses many different techniques of investing to use in hundreds of combinations. They have their application to both the buyer and the seller, and knowledge of them will benefit you no matter on which side of the closing table you will be sitting.

THERE ARE HUNDREDS OF COMBINATIONS OF INVESTMENT STRATEGIES

Each technique will be presented in detail as to what it is and how it is used in each situation. As each technique can be applied to the buyer and the seller, you will want to pay close attention to each side of the transaction to see how you will use the techniques when you buy and when you sell. I will give you details on how to approach the situation from both sides of the transaction and how the different techniques might be used in tandem with the other techniques offered. There will be many examples of actual uses of these techniques. I want you to see the technique in action because most investment books are too theoretical to be applied in real situations. This book is for you to use. I will not bore you with unnecessary technical details, which would be like trying to explain exactly how an electronic calculator works. You don't need to know that in order to make the tool work for you.

Over the past 40 years I have found that my reflections on the training of real estate salespersons and the education of real estate investors have changed. In my younger years I was obsessed with explaining the details and the reasons why this or that worked. I've since come to understand all that information is best left for the purist who won't do anything without understanding why it works. To launch the rocket all you have to do is push the little red button; you do not have to know how to engineer the trajectory. Let's move on to what does work and how you can make it work for you.

THREE SECRETS ABOUT MAKING MONEY

   1. You will never keep anything you didn't attain through a goal.

   2. The best way to obtain wealth you can keep is through real estate.

   3. Anyone can own real estate.

You will never keep anything you didn't attain through a goal. You can luck into anything, but never count on luck. By establishing a sound goal and a well-devised plan, you will get—and keep—the things you want.

People who go about their lives without goals are never truly aware when they have gained something worth keeping (this includes more than just money). They overlook opportunities just as they don't recognize the sound of its knock. They trust in luck and most often end up losers. Only if you have a goal and work for that goal will you have a lasting success at anything.

Therefore your admission into the ranks of successful real estate investors must be preceded by your development of a goal and then a plan by which you will work for that goal. To begin at something as worthy as making a fortune, surely you can start off on the right foot.

Of course there is a missing link to this. It takes more than just a goal or just a plan. It must be a goal that you can attain and measure. A goal that has no specific and well-defined moment of attainment is not a good goal. "I want to be wealthy beyond my wildest expectations" is hardly a correct goal, for you would never truly attain it. Your concept of wealth will constantly rise as your achievements rise. As you attain both successes and failures, you will look ahead and no longer feel the same needs or, for that matter, the same desires. I know that I need specific goals to reach for. When they are in my grasp, I set new goals, higher than the first. This should be your plan. Constantly seek a higher goal as you attain each goal along the path.

The plan you set must be a good plan that is designed to fit your goal. For planning to be effective, you must have clear goals. This will enable you to keep your plans simple and direct. The most worthy goal, the best plan, and the greatest intentions won't make you anything unless you act on them. Action is the key. It is far better to act on a mediocre plan than not to act on the best plan devised.

The best way to obtain wealth you can keep is through real estate. The second secret you should learn is that wealth can be quickly obtained through real estate investments. One of the basic reasons for this is only in real estate can you maximize the use of OPM to build your wealth. Stock market minded investors would be quick to say you can use OPM. All you have to do is buy on the margin. Let the stock brokerage house be your source of OPM. Unfortunately that just does not cut it. Cash on the barrel is what buys the majority of all stock. If you want to play the market on the hard line, then buy on the margin where the brokerage house will sell you out cold if the stock slips a bit and you don't have the cash to make up the difference. Or you can buy a commodity contract where up to 90 percent of the price is held by the brokerage firm. You can profit handsomely if the price of that bushel of winter wheat goes up a few cents, or you can blow your whole wad if it goes the other way. Only in real estate can you acquire an income property with long-term financing that will not sell you out three weeks later. Keep in mind that over 90 percent of all shares of stock sold in the world's stock exchanges produce no income to the investors. The only source of profit or benefit is what comes when and if the stock is sold at a profit.

In real estate you can ultimately sell at a loss and still profit hand over fist. How? Watch this. You acquire a property for $500,000. It is a 20-unit apartment complex that has a Net Operating Income (NOI, which is gross rent less operating expenses) of $50,000. A real estate insider would call this an investment valued at a 10 times its net income. But you don't pay all cash. Instead you acquire the property with a $450,000 mortgage and a $50,000 value down payment. Note I said value and not cash. The down payment might be a vacant lot you purchased some years ago for $5000 or it could be a second mortgage on another property you own. It does not have to be cash. But for this example assume it is cash.

You collect enough net rents to pay all your expenses and still put $5000 in your pocket at the end of the year. Your debt represents OPM that allowed you to purchase this property. The OPM, for the next 20 years, is paid off by OPM that comes to you in the form of rents on the apartments. Now assume nothing happens to the value of this property. It stays static and never appreciates. In fact for the sake of this example, assume it goes down in value to $400,000. At the end of 20 years you have pocketed a total of $100,000 in rents. Your OPM in the form of rents has paid off your mortgage so you now own this property "free and clear," meaning without debt. A buyer offers you $400,000 and because you are about to retire and move to Paris, you take the cash even though it is $100,000 less than you paid for the property 20 years earlier.

Did you lose money? Look at the history of this deal. You gave a value of $50,000 for the property. Got a 10 percent return each year for 20 years. Then walked away with the original $50,000 you paid plus $350,000 additional cash. Not bad, but imagine what the deal would look like if, in a more realistic scenario, your total rental earnings amounted to $250,000 and your final sale was $1,000,000.

Anyone can buy real estate. There are countless reasons why real estate is the number one wealth builder if you know how to use it and to invest in it. Yet all the reasons I could give you would only add embellishment to one basic fact: Real estate is an immovable necessity. Food, clothing, and shelter are the three basic things people must have in both quantity and quality to live in comfort. And each of the three—food, clothing, and shelter—comes from real estate. Real estate is the foundation for all the food we eat, the clothing we wear, and the shelter in which we live. Because real estate is immobile, we live where the real estate is that provides these necessities.

It is our need for real estate, its limited quantity, and its immobility that cause wide differences in value and make real estate investing a science of variables. Understand the relationship between these three factors and you will succeed.

REAL ESTATE INVESTING: WHAT YOU NEED TO SUCCEED

All of this sounds basic, but that's how simple it is to become a successful real estate insider. All you need is that basic understanding, a goal, a plan, and then action. It requires guts and that inside feeling that comes as you make a decision that might shape your life, your future, and your financial independence.

Some of you will move cautiously into the realm of real estate ownership. Many of you will never buy. The nonowners will rationalize their inability to buy real estate, but the real reason likely is their failure to develop goals or plans. Millions and millions of people will never own real estate because they either don't know how simple it is or they fear the consequences of their own actions. You, on the other hand, are ahead of that game. You can buy. You can own.

2 CHAPTER

Set Higher Goals— Get Rich Quicker

Winning the real estate game is a multifaceted event. There is no exact point when you can say you won or the other person lost. In real estate investing winning is not really defined as a position of the victor. After all the goals of both the buyer and the seller can be attained in every transaction. So if both parties can win, does there need to be a loser? There is no point in saying, "I won, the seller (or buyer) lost." The reason for this must be carefully understood if you plan on playing the game of real estate because it is possible for both the buyer and seller to lose. It is a matter of knowing who is the enemy. Trust me, it will rarely be the seller.

Of all the enemies that will confront you, there are two that are the most dangerous to your success. The first is not a single predator but the mass of other investors who are out there looking for the same thing you crave: good real estate investments. Some of them will usurp you and gobble up the very investment you have been analyzing for months, simply because you have been dragging your feet. Others will scoop up the property around the corner two days before you got a chance to see it. It will be these people who will keep you on your toes. Fortunately the vast majority of these investors will not have the street smarts you are about to discover. They will not know the best plan to follow, and their luck will not hold up against your growing knowledge of your investment area and your comfort zone. But there is the second predator even more voracious—your own indecision and lack of confidence in the knowledge you are about to learn. This will be a natural tendency, and you have to let a few deals slip past you to realize that your initial intuition was sound. Let some other guy beat you out once or twice. But that's enough. There are still other enemies out there so read on. Your first line of defense is a strong and believable goal—and it is you who must believe in it.

THE REAL ESTATE GAME

Know the Players of the Game

Let's choose up sides. Team A consists of you and whomever you can get to aid you in your fight to win. Believe it or not, both the buyer and the seller are on Team A. Who then is on Team B? It consists of all the players against both buyer and seller. Here's Team B's roster:

1. Income taxes
2. Sales taxes
3. Social security contributions
4. Real estate taxes
5. Devalued currency
6. Inflation (unless you get it over on your side)
7. Higher cost of living
8. Lower purchasing power of the dollar
9. Supply-and-demand cycles
10. Rising medical costs
11. Rising insurance costs
12. Rising fuel costs
13. Rising unemployment
14. Tougher job competition
15. The multitude of new taxes yet to be devised
16. Growing government power
17. Reduced personal powers and freedoms
18. Those who do not follow the golden rule
19. Governmental giveaways that sap you to death
20. Your own indecision

21. All the other investors out there looking for the same thing
you are

And so on and so on . . .

You can see that it's an unequal match unless you know the weaknesses of Team B's players. Many players on Team A find that it's easier to submit early. The towel can be thrown in at any time, the game comes to a halt, and Team A simply shines the boots of Team B's players until the game is played again or until Team A wins. Against seemingly impossible odds, Team A can win and without having to resort to intimidation. Be positive and attract positive people. Avoid everything negative.

Know the Rules of the Game

If you are going to win, you have to know the rules. Once you know who the players are and how to distinguish them from the good guys out there trying to help you, the next thing you must keep in mind is exactly what game you are playing.

Does that sound like a stupid statement? Well, hold on. If you play basketball, the higher the score, the better, right? On the other hand, golf is just the other way—a lower score is great. The problem is that in real estate you have more choices than just a higher or lower score.

Select the Goals You Want to Reach, Then Play the Correct Game to Reach Those Goals

In the next chapters you are going to feast on specific techniques and strategies for buying real estate by maximizing the use of other people's money and minimizing your own cash at risk. These techniques are the building blocks to all creative real estate dealmaking. Most of them can be used together or in combinations. They will create hundreds of different ways to structure a real estate transaction. Most of these techniques will be adaptable to any kind of real estate while some are specifically oriented to certain kinds of real estate. There are, however, six elements that you must recognize as goals to attain. They are your key to the weakness of those players on Team B.

Use these six benefits of real estate when setting your goals:

- Equity Buildup
- Appreciation

- Tax Shelter
- Cash Flow
- Inflation Fighter
- Personal Satisfaction

Equity Buildup

Every dollar that is paid against the principal owed on a mortgage goes to build up your equity in that property. When a part of the purchase price is covered by a mortgage, you will have a predictable equity buildup as you pay down the mortgage balance. When investing in real estate, the idea is to let other people pay off your debt.

If you bought a $500,000 apartment house and put $100,000 down, you would have a mortgage of $400,000 to pay off. As you reduced the amount you owed, the value of the property to you would grow. This occurs even if the value of the property itself doesn't increase at all. If you have reduced the mortgage to $300,000 10 years from now, your equity is now at least $200,000, which is double the original equity. This increase in your invested capital comes from the mortgage payoff. Take note that in this example I actually use the term "put $100,000 down." Later on you will discover that this down payment may or may not be your cash. It might not be cash at all. But for the moment, review the example as presented.

In the following example a $500,000 apartment house is purchased with a first mortgage of $400,000 at 6 percent for 30 years with a monthly payment (principal and interest) of $2398.20. As you can see in Table 2-1, the amount of principal reduction of a mortgage increases as the mortgage

TABLE 2–1

End of Year/ Payments Remaining	Principal Owed on Existing Mortgage	New Equity Added Original Down Payment
0/360	$400,000.00	0
1/348	$395,087.95	$ 4,912.05
10/240	$344,742.90	$ 65,257.10
15/180	$284,195.38	$115,804.62
20/120	$216,014.34	$183,985.66
30/0	0	$400,000.00

matures. While the monthly payment itself doesn't change over the 30 years, the amount applied to interest is greater in the first years. By the end of the first 15 years, the mortgage had dropped from $400,000 to $284,195.38. This is a reduction in the amount owed of $115,804.62. Note that in the next 15 years the mortgage will be entirely paid off. If you were able to have someone else pay off that mortgage, you can quickly see that in a 30-year period you will have socked away a minimum of $400,000.

The key to equity buildup is to get some one else to pay off your debt for you. Remember the mortgage is OPM in the first place. You used OPM to help you buy this property when you took out a new first mortgage from a local savings and loan (S & L) association or other lender. Now you use OPM to pay off that mortgage.

Appreciation

Appreciation is a highly sought-after element of investing in anything. You don't buy diamonds, gold, or real estate hoping it will go down in value. You want it to appreciate, often because you have made improvements or sometimes due to improvements made by others in the neighborhood. For example, a great new school can create overnight appreciation of the entire neighborhood. Appreciation, however, is not automatic. It is possible for values to go down no matter what you do. A nearby landfill project can turn a nice neighborhood into a dump, literally.

Table 2-2 shows the result of an investment of $100,000 on a $500,000 purchase, as was illustrated in Table 2-1. This table shows the effect of a 3-percent-per-year compounding appreciation as well as the eq-

TABLE 2–2

End of Year	Equity Due to Appreciation	Balance Owed on the Mortgage	Total Investment Equity
0	$ 0	$400,000.00	$ 100,000.00
1	$ 515,000.00	$395,287.95	$ 119,712.05
10	$ 671,958.19	$334,742.90	$ 337,215.29
15	$ 778,983.20	$284,195.38	$ 494,788.32
20	$ 903,055.62	$216,014.34	$ 687,041.28
30	$1,213,631.00	0	$1,213,613.20

uity buildup from the payoff of the mortgage. By this you must consider that each year the value of the property has increased by 3 percent over the previous year. This is due solely to appreciation. The balance on the mortgage will decrease as in Table 2-1 because that is a set function of the mortgage. Your investment equity will increase much faster in Table 2-2 than in Table 2-1 because of appreciation of the asset.

Some land goes up in value very rapidly, creating very large gains, yet what some investors never seem to grasp is that the value of the property doesn't have to double for you to double your investment. In fact, small gains in the appreciation can double or even quadruple your equity.

Again the price of the home is $500,000, with a 30-year mortgage of $400,000 at 10 percent. The second column is based on a simple 3-percent-per-year increase in value. Table 2-2 shows how this works. If this property was an apartment house and if the rent only covered expenses and mortgage payments, you could still profit handsomely. Considering that was the case, you could retire $1,113,631.23 richer than when you started. This is a benefit you get when you use OPM.

It is possible, of course, for the market value of a property to decline, and then reduction of the mortgage may not increase equity. However, reduction in value rarely occurs if you have followed the simplest investment techniques. In a depression, of course, real estate holds on better than most investments because it is a necessity, and I have already shown you how you can still profit handsomely even selling at less than you paid for the property.

Tax Shelter

Tax shelter is a technique as well as a strategy where you use the tax laws to maximize your yield. This is one of the best OPM techniques when it is available to you because you are using Uncle Sam's money. Instead of paying extra tax on the revenue you make, you put those funds into your pocket. You may have heard of people—often doctors and other professionals—buying into tax shelters. You may have bought into one yourself. There used to be lots of different kinds: movies, books, cattle, oil, art expeditions, charities, and, of course, real estate, to name just a few. One by one the IRS has been knocking them off, until the only one left that makes any sense is real estate.

Tax codes go through a constant fine-tuning. Congress, the IRS, and the courts all have their hands in these changes. Most of the tax shelter methods involve the conversion of immediately taxable revenue to revenue on which the tax has either been eliminated or is deferred to another time. Depreciation of the principal asset (everything except the land) for any investment real estate is the fundamental basis for tax shelter. The IRS allows an investor to deduct a portion of the value of the improvements on the land from the revenue collected from that real estate or to offset revenue from other investments just as if the deduction was an expense that was paid for by cash. This deduction is a paper entry in the accounting of the revenue and expenses because there was no actual outlay. Over the years the IRS has modified and will likely continue to modify the method in which this deduction is allowed. At present the IRS gives you the deduction and even allows you to accelerate the deduction faster than a "real-life" deduction would occur. In typical IRS logic the taxpayer will recover excessive depreciation that is more than the allowed straight-line depreciation if the property is sold and produces a taxable gain. By "recovered" the IRS means that if you take an unauthorized fast write-down of the book value when you sell with a profit, then you will have to pay earned income tax on this excess deduction. This "recovered" depreciation will be taxed at the taxpayer's earned income rate rather than a capital gain rate.

Tax shelter is a trade-off and conversion of ordinary income to income taxed at lower, long-term capital gains rates or income that escapes tax altogether. Over the years as you depreciate a property, you reduce your book value in it. This book value is called your basis. This is important to know when you refer to tax shelter deals because if there is no ultimate conversion of ordinary income into capital gains, the tax shelter may not produce any benefits. Remember, book value is the depreciated value of your business equipment, your car (used for business), and your real estate. In real estate the exclusive term is tax basis, or basis.

When you sell a property, the gain is the amount of money you get above your basis. Remember, basis is not the price you paid for a property. Take a good look at how basis is determined:

1. Start with the price you paid.
2. Add any closing costs that are part of the acquisition of the property.
3. Add any capital improvements while you own the property (buildings, repairs of a capital nature that you do not take as expenses for the year).
4. Add expenses such as taxes and interest you have not taken as a deduction from earned income.
5. Subtotal the amount at this point.

6. Subtract from the subtotal all depreciation you have taken while you have owned the property.

7. What's left is your basis.

You can see the only deduction in arriving at basis is depreciation. Because depreciation is your tax shelter and what you are sheltering is ordinary income, when you sell, the amount of the capital gain (assuming the income qualified as a long-term capital gain, which is 12 months from ownership to sale) is the value that exceeds your adjusted basis. Because you can pick your own time to sell, you can convert and move the income from one year to another. Sometimes you postpone the conversion until well down the road to when your ordinary income tax rates will be much lower (in retirement, for example).

Keep in mind the best tax shelter is one that shelters most of its own income. Several years ago syndicates were putting together deals that gave investors a lot of instant shelter but no long-range conversion. Properties were being burdened with high loan-to-value ratios on terms that often never amortized any principal. Some actually led to the principal balance being built up. The pro forma (a projected analysis) of the income properties was often overstated, and deal after deal got into trouble. Many tax shelter deals failed because the property was so heavily mortgaged that the income could not support the expenses and there was no other benefit to balance the loss of income. When it comes to income-producing property, take advantage of the kind of tax shelter that most benefits you. The fast tax shelter through fast depreciation may not be the answer to your problem. You might do better to remember that for most people the best shelter is a new source of income with which to pay the tax. In selecting a property you have to look at all of the magic factors of real estate. Remember also that whenever you can get Uncle Sam to kick in and pay part of your investment, take advantage of this.

Cash Flow

If someone pays you for the use of some of your real estate, you may have cash flow. Cash flow is the money you have in your hand at the end of each month (or year) as a direct result of your real estate investment. In essence cash flow is the bottom line. It's what is left when you begin with gross income and deduct actual expenses and mortgage payments.

For example assume you own a duplex and you rent out one side for $800 per month. You live in the other side with a friend, who pays you $250 per month for rent. Your gross income would be $1050 per month, or $12,600 per year. Your upkeep, mortgage payment, and other costs to carry the property might cost you $9600 per year. With this information look at the cash flow calculations below:

Cash Flow Calculation

Gross Income collected	$12,600.00
Less Expenses and debt payments	$ 9,600.00
Cash Flow	$ 3,000.00

While $250 per month may not seem like an enormous amount of money, keep in mind that you are getting other benefits as well. You are (1) living free, (2) building equity, (3) seeing your investment appreciate, (4) sheltering not only income from the investment but perhaps other income as well, and you are (5) taking control over your financial future. When you progress in your investment capability, you will see that there are many properties that will score highly on the four magic factors of real estate discussed thus far.

Inflation Fighter

Take another look at the three basic necessities of life: food, clothing, and shelter. These three items have many similarities. Each is subject to the supply-and-demand rules regulating their values. Each involves the input of raw materials and the manipulation of people to create the finished product. Each item can be bought, held, used, traded, and, to some degree, used up.

The first two, food and clothing, are needed in a steady flow. Who would say, "I've bought all the food I'll ever need" or "I don't have to buy any more clothes"? Because it's impractical to stockpile a lifetime supply of food and clothing, you will constantly be at the mercy of inflation when you go out to buy these two necessities. The food or clothes you buy today will certainly cost more five years from now to replace. Yet a five-year-old loaf of bread is worthless, and a five-year-old suit of clothes is next to worthless. If you don't consume these two necessities, you may not have any value at all. There are exceptions, of course. It is possible to store some food stocks that will reach maturity at an increased price over a period of years, such as wine and fine brandy.

Real estate is an absolute item. It simply exists, and it exists in a certain location. If this sounds like double-talk, don't be misled. Real estate is valuable not because of the space it occupies on this earth but because of its location in relation to other locations and the ultimate use in which it can be applied to that location.

Any given duplex of the exact design and condition will vary in value depending entirely on which of a thousand different places it happens to occupy in the United States. It is possible to set this duplex on land that costs the same in different locations and still end up with different values, simply because its location may be the single element that has attracted a buyer willing to pay more than someone else. Because all real estate does begin with land and because land is valued first for what you can do with it then for its location, real estate is not only unique but is also the only true inflation fighter.

This fifth magic factor of real estate is a combination of all, or most, of the first four. It is important for you to recognize that all of the first four factors will not always occur in all real estate transactions. Investment in vacant land, for example, will not necessarily produce cash flow. By itself, this is no reason to avoid purchasing vacant land. What is needed is some counterbalance. There must be the promise, at least, of a greater benefit from one or more of the other factors.

Personal Satisfaction

There's a modern approach to investing in real estate, or at least in some kinds of real estate: If you like it and you can afford it, then buy it. The concept is that there will be times when you just want to own whatever it is. There may be no logical economic reason: The cash flow may be nonexistent, there may be no hope of appreciation, and the only tax shelter might be the loss you take when you have to give it away.

People react emotionally when buying other commodities, don't they? How about those fancy cars, exclusive designer clothes, or expensive dinners at the hottest spots in town? Emotion is a real factor when you buy something you can use.

Don't let your analytic mind get you so bogged down with the economics of an investment that you overlook this most important aspect of all. Do you like what you are proposing to buy? If not, then you should ask yourself the next question, "Am I forced to buy something I don't like because there is nothing around I can afford that I do like?" If the answer to this last question is yes, then you simply need to work hard to expand your investment area.

You will find that no single real estate investment will accomplish all six of these elements. There is a trade-off between them and your goals. Some properties appreciate more than they develop cash flow, or tax shelter. Some properties don't appreciate but are magnificent moneymakers. Your winning in this game means playing toward the correct factor. If you need a tax shelter, buying property for appreciation is not getting you closer to winning the game. It might even cause you to lose.

Warren G. Harding, one of the nation's foremost real estate exchangers, once noted, "I never saw a piece of real estate I didn't like." He went on to say in his famous "Acres of Diamonds" seminar that all real estate is good; it has a use, a purpose that is determined not just by the real estate but by the person using it.

When Is It Time to Buy or Time to Sell?

I've been asked this question a thousand times: When do you sell real estate? The best answer is to sell or exchange the moment the property no longer satisfies a need or helps you attain a desired goal. If there is another property or investment that will do that, then it is time for a change. As you will learn when I discuss tax-free exchanges, your best strategy may not be to sell but to exchange.

For example I own a tract of land I feel is worth at this moment around $850,000. I have leased part of it to cover my annual expenses and pay a few dollars into the till. I bought the property for its potential appreciation, paying only $42,000 in total about six years ago. Appreciate it did. Now I need cash flow and some tax shelter to offset that.

However, I don't want to sell for two reasons. First the capital gains taxes would take away a great portion of my reinvestment capital. Second the city is about to build a major highway that will join with the road this property fronts on not more than 200 yards away. The impact of this new road could cause the property to double or triple in value in two or three years and also provide a potential tenant for a building or buildings I could construct to generate both cash flow and tax shelter. My goals are clearly in my sights. But sometimes the solutions are not so obvious.

Remember that whatever you buy will reach a point where it is no longer as economically desirable to you as another investment will be. This is the relative point of real estate. From your point of view, everything will reach an economic disposition time. Now that doesn't mean you *have* to sell or exchange that property for something else. The sixth factor, the emotion factor, might cause you to say, "To hell with economics. I can afford this, so I'll keep it." There is nothing wrong with this line of thinking as long as you are rational about it—and as long as you recognize the reason you are making that statement.

DO YOUR OWN THING

This is essential. Buy only if you are satisfied you got the deal you can live with. Remember, you are the buyer. Don't ever feel that offering 5 percent interest on a seller-held second mortgage is an insult. Sellers may surprise you and accept deals that solve their problems. Make offers you like as a buyer, not how you'd want it as a seller. Here is when the golden rule does not exist. Fairness is not a double-edged sword. Remember that interest alone is not the most important factor; give-and-take can make the deal fly just as easily if you know how. This book will help you discover those techniques.

As you move on now into the world of doing, keep this in mind. The techniques you are learning work two ways: They are buyer's and seller's methods. You can use them wisely to buy, and you can use them to sell. It will all begin to unfurl on the next page in Chapter Three.

3
CHAPTER

Value: Where It Comes From and How to Make It

Successful investing in real estate is tied to your ability to recognize opportunities and to have an investment plan that will enable you to take advantage of those opportunities. To accomplish this it is important that you have a sound understanding of real estate values and what the factors are that can cause the value to go up or down. This chapter approaches this topic. While entire books are written on this subject, this single chapter will wipe away all the smoke and mirrors that often accompanies the creation of real estate values.

This chapter also provides you with specific examples of how these factors work and a list of steps you can take to quickly and inexpensively increase the value of property you acquire—without the smoke and mirrors.

ALL REAL ESTATE VALUES ARE LOCALIZED

If you remember little else from this book, remember this as an absolute concept: Real estate value is completely and irrevocably tied to the local market. It is one of the most misunderstood elements of all real estate investing. What this means is that when you assess the value you should pay, as well as the value you hope to get, you need to know the local market. It will not do you much good to try to assess the value of an apartment building in Spartanburg, South Carolina, using the standards for New York City when your investment area is actually Sedona, Arizona. Nor will you make meaningful decisions on values using London, England, as a benchmark for property in Fort Lauderdale, Florida. Naturally you can gain some insight into trends looking at similar cities, but be sure to tie those trends to the values of the local market, where the property you want to invest in or sell is located.

Wall Street Gets It Wrong Every Time

I feel compelled to bring this point out into the open. The localized nature of real estate is very important, but Wall Street seems to fail to grasp that aspect. There is a trend for Wall Street to generalize real estate by trying to make direct comparisons between real estate investments and stocks sold on the market. Wall Street's version of real estate is the Real Estate Investment Trust (REIT), which has become a very large segment of a fund-type of investment sold through Wall Street. A REIT is a special kind of trust allowed under unique IRS rules. REITs fall into three categories: equity, mortgage, and hybrid. An equity REIT owns real estate and generally specializes in a specific kind of real estate. Some equity REITs own shopping centers, others industrial buildings, and so on. Mortgage REITs lend money and buy and sell mortgage and debt instruments. A hybrid REIT does a little of what both the equity and the mortgage REITs do. Although an equity REIT functions much like a corporation that owns real estate, it is governed by separate rules that allow the income to "flow" through to the investors, somewhat like an "S" Corporation. They can be good investments if you are careful, and they are popular because they often pay a good dividend to the investors. I have personally interviewed many of the REIT CEOs and other REIT insiders and am convinced many of them have been brainwashed into thinking REITs are exactly like any other major stock market company. I have read articles written by officials of the National Association of Real Estate Investment Trusts (NAREIT) where equity REITs have been touted as a stock investment not much different than buying stock in any major listed stock, such as IBM, Ford, or General Electric.

This is wrong. IBM, Ford, and General Electric, and just about any other company that is not in real estate, are able to adjust quickly to market changes. Ford can and does follow this rule, just as thousands of product-making companies do. If one product brand is selling faster with a higher profit than other items they make, then they turn those items out by the millions (if possible) while at the same time they stop making the poor-selling models. They can shut down, crank up, fire, and hire as the need fits. When it comes to real estate, REITs are tied to what they own. A hotel REIT can close and buy new ones, but it is limited to what it can do to maintain its overall value.

Avoid National Trends

News about trends and patterns that happen in one place in the United States does not mean the entire market is following those trends or patterns. This is another side effect stemming from Wall Street in its attempt to make real estate as universal a commodity as IBM stock. When you see that housing starts are down in Ohio, for example, consider first why. Is it the middle of winter? Have there been some major cutbacks in industry unique to Ohio? If you see the same thing happening across the board, then there is some fundamental economic reason for this. Only then might there be a trend affecting housing starts across the country.

Real estate values will go up and down all the time but generally not universally. In any town there will be some real estate declining in value while others are going up. The same reason for that specific event is likely to have the same results elsewhere, which gives you the advantage of knowing what you can do to properly assess a market condition.

For Wall Street to attempt to turn real estate into a global commodity or for the National Association of Real Estate Investment Trusts to say a REIT is like any corporation is simply stock market smoke and mirrors. Your best bet is to pay little attention to this kind of comparison. Real estate is unique, local, and tied to use.

REAL ESTATE VALUE IS AFFECTED BY NINE ELEMENTS

In my book *The Real Estate Investor's Answer Book* I delve into this subject in detail. I want to touch on that same topic here because value and how to create value are very important to profiting in real estate. After all you want to purchase something going up in value. So let me restate that same premise in a slightly different perspective. You want to purchase something not yet at its highest value and something to which you can increase the value. This is the proper point of view that an individual real estate investor has. It differs, by the way, from an institutional (Wall Street) point of view. REITs, for example, generally buy brand-new properties (when they are available in areas and types of property they buy) that are likely to be at or very near the maximum revenue generated without taking into account cost-of-living increases.

Nine Elements That Cause Values to Go Up or Down

1. Inflation

2. Changes in Infrastructure

3. Increased Bottom Line

4. Level of Capital Expenditure

5. Market Supply and Demand

6. Neighborhood Sizzle

7. Governmental Controls and Regulatory Changes

8. Economic Viability

9. Motivation of Buyer and Seller

Each of these nine elements can affect real estate value in both directions. I will give you brief examples of how this occurs. Take a moment to review each.

Inflation together with its sister, deflation, affect values by causing them to reflect the general movement of the economy. Because there are many different elements causing inflation, it can be considered a mixture of all remaining eight elements. There is little you can do to change the effect of inflation except to try to avoid investment areas likely to be greatly impacted by a combination of the other eight elements. Inflation as it pertains to the United States tends to be lumped together as another universal statistic, but the reality is it is a blended number that takes into account many different elements. Real estate is just one of those elements and is treated more as a "cost-to-rent" than actual value. The Cost-of-Living Indexes, which are the benchmarks to establish inflation or deflation, are published by the United States Department of Labor. You can surf the web and find many different sources for inflation but most are based on the source data that comes from the Department of Labor. As I have mentioned before, inflation increases the overall value of all items and commodities and services. Real estate is the only commodity that is a true "inflation fighter" when you maximize OPM forms of investment.

Changes in Infrastructure have a dual-edge effect on the value of real estate. Any change can, although not especially, increase the value of a real property while at the same time decreasing the value of another real property. Let's say the city decides to build a new highway to ring the city. The idea is to allow traffic to flow around the city rather than through it, which would exasperate an already congested situation. The benefit and increases of value come to those farmlands that are now prime new subdivision areas. The decline can occur to the inner core of the city as people and businesses move to the new, more economically viable areas. Naturally in the long term, that hastened decline can have a rebound as the circle becomes just as congested as was the downtown traffic, decayed city areas are bulldozed down, and new development growth occurs.

Sometimes the simple opening of a new entrance/exit on a highway can have profound effect. It dumps the wrong kind of traffic into a residential area, and property along the route goes down in value. A revamping of an old main artery with the idea of beautification and expansion can have an ultimate benefit to everyone, but the three years of construction, detours, and added congestion kills the businesses on that old road. The old businesses move out, the old owners can't meet their mortgage payments, the old lenders foreclose on the old properties, eventually new owners come in as the road is nearing completion, and they buy at prices where their future profit is ensured. It is important to know what infrastructure changes are going to take place and to understand how those changes will affect the community, both during the change and after.

Increased Bottom Line is a function of management and market acceptance to what you have to offer. If you purchase an income rental property you want to know that you will be able to take all or most of all the following actions.

- **Increase Rent** by improving the property to the point where it can successfully compete with properties able to demand greater rent than at the present time.
- **Decrease Cost** is a sign of good management since they will find ways to decrease the cost of operation. This is a percentage figure of the total gross revenue and is tied to the first item. If you purchase a property that has an annual gross income of $100,000 and $35,000 in annual operating expenses, your ratio is 35 percent, which means that 35 percent of your gross income is operating expenses. The remaining 65 percent, or $65,000 in this case, is your Net Operating Income (NOI). To increase your NOI (gross revenue less operating expenses), you need to either increase rent while holding operating expenses at the same or

lower level or increase revenue at a greater rate than the increase of operating expenses. So if you can increase your gross income to $120,000, that is a 20 percent increase from the previous gross income. If your operating expenses increase to $40,000, then that is an increase of only 14 percent. Your NOI will have increased from the previous $65,000 to $80,000. Of course, if you had been able to hold your operating expenses at the old level, your NOI will be $85,000, demonstrating even better management. This is critical because if you have purchased this property with a 10-Cap in mind, that means the added $15,000 (from $65,000 to $80,000) of NOI will flow directly to the bottom line. At a 10-Cap this will generate an added value of $150,000 to this property.

Review this scenario in detail. You purchased a $600,000 apartment building using $120,000 cash or OPM as your down-payment and assumed an existing debt of $480,000. At the time you purchased the property it was producing $100,000 in gross revenue and had Operating expenses of $35,000, leaving a net operating income of $65,000. The mortgage principal and interest was a total of $53,000 per year. This leaves you with $12,000 as your bottom line, or cash flow. You now increase the revenue to $120,000, and your expenses go up as well to $40,000. Your NOI is now $80,000, and your cash flow ($80,000 less $53,000) has gone up from $12,000 to $27,000.

Your investment was $120,000 based on a 10 percent return to $12,000. Now your investment would be valued at $270,000, which is an increase of $150,000. This is a total investment increase of 225 percent. All this with a simple sound management strategy that increased revenue by 20 percent, while increasing expenses by only 14 percent. Do this once a year and you are off and running toward financial freedom you never dreamed was possible. Remember you purchased this property because you already knew the opportunity was there to do this.

- **Decrease Fixed Expenses.** Your fixed expenses is your debt service. Mind you this accounting form is not universal and some investors will include other elements into the fixed-cost part of the Income and Expense calculation. Sometimes land rent, depreciation, taxes, and other items show up as fixed cost and not Operating Expenses. You will have to make adjustments in this accounting to remove all cash expenses from the fixed-cost line except debt. You must then remove depreciation from the

Operating Expenses since that is not an actual cash outlay. It is used to either offset a need for "reserve for replacements" or calculate the income tax consequences. I like to have a separate "reserve for replacements" as I know I will eventually need to replace items in the property.

If you can refinance the debt so your overall cost is less than the existing debt, you will also increase the bottom line. Let's say your mortgage payment of principal and interest can be reduced to $50,000 per year. Your NOI is still $70,000 but your bottom line is now $20,000. Your original investment is still $120,000 so your new value (at the same 10-Cap) is $200,000, or an increase of 166.7 percent.

Level of Capital Expenditure is the upkeep factor. If you don't properly maintain a property it will begin to slip into economic obsolescence and that is the first step to a major drop in value. Many property owners milk their properties and do little or no overall maintenance. If they have milked it dry and can unload the property without having to pour money back into it, they might profit. But in the long run this is not a good strategy. Maintenance is far less expensive if taken care of little by little before the breakdown occurs. When you see a property that shows its wear and tear, you need to look closely at every aspect of the property. A coat of paint might hide some major problems. However when you see that diamond in the rough, it may not matter how rough it is if you are planning an economic conversion to some other use. For example it is better to buy a motel ready for rehab than one where the owner spent money to keep it alive as a motel, if you are going to turn it into something else. Otherwise the owner will want to recoup that wasted effort and capital she put into the upkeep of the motel and demand a higher price.

Market Supply and Demand is what distinguishes hot areas from stagnate ones. What and where do people want to be? This is up to you to determine by getting to know your market and your investment area like the back of your hand. Remember not to be persuaded by what is going on somewhere else, unless you are ready to move there.

Neighborhood Sizzle is what to look for in the community. Almost every community has a neighborhood that is hot. It may not be too late to get in on this area as an investment potential, as long as you are careful and purchase only what you know you can improve so that you generate greater revenue than the former property owner was able to do. If you don't feel that is possible, then back off a little. Look into the history of what made that neighborhood take off. Then look around for a similar situation about to hatch in your own community. I'll bet you will find one or two on the verge of being the new hot spots.

Governmental Controls and Regulatory Changes are factors you need to find out about. You will never see or hear about them unless you have begun to be proactive in your investment arena. One little change in setback or height restriction can have large impacts on the area. Can you now build eight units to the acre instead of five? What a difference that can make to the land available. Add to that a strong demand for multifamily properties and the combination can produce a real winner. On the other hand a reduction of density or a building moratorium while the city devotes the next five or more years to study the impact of the environment on the lives of green-spotted snails, and you can see your dreams slipping.

Economic Viability is another important factor. It is not realistic to build a shipyard 50 miles from the nearest waterway. So even if the zoning was right, would you build an apartment building next to a train track or a steel factory in a residential part of town? Surely you would not, but what if one of those was suddenly proposed to be built next to your property? You would know this well in advance. You could fight it, and with time and neighbors on your side you might win. Or you might have time to sell before the world knows what is going on.

Some local governments and community leaders are pro development. They espouse the ideals that the way to improve a community is to expand its tax base and to generate sound employment for its citizens. This kind of local leadership is good for real estate development but not always for real estate values. The ultimate benefit to the community as a whole may not be good for all real estate in the city. It is important to know what is going to happen before it happens. On the other side of this coin, some of the fastest value growth areas occur in limited access communities. Gated residential areas or office parks dedicated to one type of business or that restrict the park from certain "dirty" industrial or commercial uses can be hot for development. It is a good idea, however, to avoid communities where there is no easy way to do anything. Some cities impact you to death with building permits and special assessments for just about everything. But even here there are opportunities, if you are ready to dig for them.

Motivation of Buyer and Seller is what you need to look for. There is a saying that when you are desperate to sell the only buyer that shows up is the wolf at the front door. Improved properties are generally easier to sell than vacant land, but as with every rule there are exceptions to this.

Right now, as I write this, vacant residential land is the hottest item in South Florida. The housing boom continues, even when you can read in the papers that there is an impending real estate bust. It is almost 2004 now, and while there are some areas of the country that have felt the pinch of overbuilding, the country is growing and real estate is still strong.

As an investor you will seek to find motivated sellers. There will always be another property to buy, always another buyer or seller to deal with, so do not fret if the buyer or seller you are dealing with does not warm up to your deal.

TIPS ON HOW TO IMPROVE PROPERTY VALUES QUICKLY AND INEXPENSIVELY

In general there are some universal things you can do to improve any real estate. Cosmetics are very important, as well as aspects that date the property. A well-maintained property can quickly obtain that look, even if it has gone through a decade of poor maintenance as long as there is nothing major to be done. Investors are always looking for a good "fixer-upper"— and the key word here is good. In giving these and the following tips, I will assume you are familiar with your investment zone and know what the market will support. Look for properties that can make a quick turn around in value with a little tender loving care and attention to these tips.

- **Paint.** Any property that has not been painted in the past four years or longer may be due for an upgrade. By upgrade I mean a change of some kind. If a change in color scheme will update and improve the properties look, then make the change. A good paint store will be able to advise you in this direction. One thing you can do is arm yourself with a quality paint chart, the kind that has hundreds of colors and shades of those colors, and drive around in some of the better parts of town. Look for colors that make a property stand out as a valuable asset. Match those colors to your chart, purchase small samples of those colors, and put them on the walls you want to change. Be sure to look at the finished product after the paint has dried and during different times of the day to see how the shifting sun makes a difference.

- **Repairs.** Look first for the important and noticeable elements of the property that need to be repaired. If the property needs a new roof, you better find this out prior to buying the property and try to get the seller to give you a discount or to cover the total cost of the repair. It is likely the seller knew all about those needed repairs and was just hoping to be able to sell prior to having to do that work.

- **Front Door.** The front door and entranceway is one of the most important elements for any property but especially a single-family home or apartment building. It might take a new door or a combination of new door, exterior lights, and a new mailbox. Whatever you do when adding or replacing elements of the house, think beyond that single factor. What else can you do? Would some decorative pots with plants add to the effect? What about a brick or slate walkway to the front door? All of these are important to the initial impact of the property to the would-be buyer.

- **Landscaping.** There is a lot you can do quickly, as well as over the long haul. One of the first members of your investment team should be your landscaper. This might be a designer you pay for design tips and plans or just a great plant guy from a local nursery. If you want a quick impact then look at the existing landscaping. It might be all it needs is a good trimming, thinning, and tender loving care. A month of such effort can green up the grass, show off the house hidden behind full bushes, and add to the other cosmetic things you do to the property.

  For a long-haul approach, the planting of shade trees and other slower growing plants might require a five- or seven-year plan. The time to do this work is as soon as possible because waiting will just postpone the effort. Be sure you plan new plants when it is the right time of the year to do so.

- **Flooring.** If the property has a hidden gem, such as real hardwood flooring under the old carpet then consider having that restored. Other hidden gems can be tile or slate that has been covered with carpet or vinyl as well. Check those things out.

- **New Kitchens and/or Bathrooms.** These are two items that seem to give the best return when trying to upgrade a property for ultimate resale. However these can be very expensive, and expensive may not be the way to go. Consider changing the cabinet doors or hardware. Perhaps just the countertops with some other color changes on painted walls.

- **Smells.** If you own a dog, and have lived around that dog for awhile, you probably do not notice the smell of that dog. But others do. Animal smells sink into the furniture they lounge on, the carpet they roll on, and almost any other fabric that is within their touch. You should ask someone, a local realtor, a painter, or neighbor, if your home or apartment is suffering from "old animal smell." I am sorry to say that sometimes the "old animal smell" can be coming from a closet of clothes that have not been cleaned in several years. If you have teenagers in the home there can be a "locker room" odor that seems to have gone away but is really still there—only you no longer notice it. Great thing, the human nose. If you have such a property and cannot seem to get rid of the smells, then at least create other more pleasant smells, especially when having an open house for prospective buyers. Baking creates an appealing smell. Make an apple or cherry pie, pop popcorn, make chocolate cookies, or just pray a buyer who owns an animal hospital stops in.

- **Upgrade tenants.** One of the first things to do is to improve the tenant list. It doesn't matter what kind of property you have, apartments, office buildings, or mall stores, if it is a rental you will find that there is a top price any given demographic will pay. If your tenants are in a lower demographic, then you need to wean some of them out and replace them with starting-out lawyers and doctors. This process generally is preceded by improvements to the property. Once you are able to upgrade the tenants, you will find it much easier to upscale the annual gross revenue.

TOOLS AND TECHNIQUES

The chapters that follow describe several techniques you can use in various real estate deals. It is simply a matter of choosing the right technique for the right deal. Think of each technique as a tool you can use. Like picking up the right wrench for that stubborn nut and bolt, the right technique to select will be the one that will do your bidding and clear the smoothest passage toward your goals. Some of these techniques might be great from your point of view but not acceptable to the other side of the transaction. If the other side of the transaction balks at your offer and won't sell (or buy, if roles are reversed) on the terms you have offered, you must find a technique that will work for you both.

The key to using these methods is to be flexible. Above all understand that some people will be governed by inertia; they won't want to do anything that isn't exactly as their advisers have told them it should be or as it presently is. If you don't present them with a simple contract with easy-to-understand, conventional terms of cash to the existing mortgage, many people won't understand it. It is possible to be so creative that you frighten the pants off your sellers or buyers, so remember to keep it simple.

When you come across one of these "set in their ways" types, or a seller or buyer who relies on the counsel of the greatest advisers of them all: the bartenders and hairdressers of America, you can understand how being creative can confuse them. You might suggest they read this book to understand that creative financing and creative concepts can be beneficial to all parties as long as individual goals are attained or placed in closer proximity.

4

CHAPTER

The Split-Fund Transaction

A common technique is to split-fund the real estate deal. This is a way to divide up the funds so you pull together a major part of the cash down from income of the property. The split-fund technique is a simple use of mathematics in creating an illusion that often works to put deals together with little actual upfront cash. The illusion occurs when the buyer offers to meet the seller's down payment amount but spreads the total down payment over more than one installment. The illusion is that the payment is being agreed to but in reality it isn't. Sellers can use this technique equally well to create an illusion that the down payment is much less than it will be in reality.

ONE AMOUNT BUT TWO OR MORE PAYMENTS

What creates these two different points of view with the split-fund method is simply the splitting of what would be the total down payment into more than one amount and then requiring these separate amounts to be paid over a short time. If the buyer had only $10,000 in cash at the moment but the seller wanted $20,000 cash down, the buyer, in using this technique, would agree to pay the $20,000 but on the basis of $10,000 now and the balance of $10,000 at another time. This second payment might be very close in time, say a few months, or over a longer period of time.

This second payment is not a mortgage, however, and will differ from other techniques where the seller holds financing in the amount of the balance. In fact there could be mortgages held by the seller in this transaction that would not be a part of this split-funding.

This sounds like a good deal for the buyer, right? So why would the seller go along with this deal? Sellers might offer the property for sale on the basis of $10,000 down and the other $10,000 six months later for tax reasons (such as moving payments into two different years) or just to help sell the property.

Brian's Deal

Let's take a closer look at how this technique might work. Brian was interested in buying a small, seasonal apartment building in Vero Beach, Florida. He found a nice five-unit property that the owner was willing to sell at a bargain price (for the area) of $250,000. There was an existing mortgage of $185,000 on the property. This left an equity (total value less mortgages) of $65,000. The seller was willing to hold $30,000 in paper, which would be a second mortgage if it was secured by the apartment building, and he wanted $35,000 cash down. Brian had $15,000 cash that he was willing to invest at this moment without taking a risk of reducing his operating capital and reserve for opportunities.

However, Brian knew that as the tourist season was just a month away, he could count on some of the needed down payment from the revenue that would come in at that time. Because of this he felt he could absorb a second payment to the down payment in a few months, with a third payment a few months after that. Here's what Brian offered:

To assume the existing mortgage of	$185,000
To give the seller a second mortgage of	$ 30,000
To pay the down payment wanted of	$ 35,000
Total purchase price	$250,000

Brian showed the seller the offer, which, on the face of the agreement, was what the seller wanted. On the second page of the agreement, in the details of the terms, Brian spelled out the format of the down payment. Brian said he would pay:

- $15,000 cash at the closing
- $10,000 cash at the end of 6 months
- $10,000 cash at the end of 18 months

These payments had nothing to do with the second mortgage and did not provide for interest on the two $10,000 payments. The seller examined the offer and, after some deliberation, made this counteroffer:

- $15,000 cash at closing, just as offered
- $15,000 cash at the end of 6 months
- $5000 cash at the end of 12 months.

Brian accepted this counteroffer since it gave him the time he needed to get the total cash required.

THE FINE POINTS OF THE DEAL

The fine points of using the split-fund deal will depend on the situation, of course. Knowing as much as you can about the income potential and the timing of that potential will be crucial in using the revenue from the property to cover some or all of the delayed down-payment portion. If the property has a seasonal income that is very high during parts of the year, then this can be put to use.

You should be aware of your own tax liability during the year of the purchase. This can aid you, as you might get sufficient shelter in the year of the purchase to warrant buying now when you might have been inclined to wait until you had more cash to invest. At the same time, as a seller, you might want to spread the cash over two years to lessen a tax liability, while avoiding including this delayed portion in a long-term mortgage.

NEGOTIATION STRATEGY: NARROW THE CONFLICT

This is a good time to point out a strategy that is used in all kinds of negotiations—from trying to get the North Koreans to adhere to the United Nations demands on nuclear arms manufacture to narrowing down which pair of shoes a woman buys for an upcoming ball. The method works well and is based on getting the "other side" to focus on the single item where you may have some flexibility. When using creative financing, especially when it involves OPM transactions, this can be one of the more critical aspects of the transaction. In the example just given, Brian wanted to get past some of the fundamental items that the seller had already indicated were acceptable to him. The price was okay, and at the first glance the down payment was right on target. All Brian had to do now was fine-tune that down payment to the point it worked for him and was acceptable to the seller. As you go through this book, watch for other examples where this negotiation strategy could play an important role in making the deal work.

THE SELLER'S VIEWPOINT

While the split-fund transaction is usually thought of as a buyer's tool, the seller can very effectively use the technique to entice buyers into the marketplace where a more conventional kind of transaction frightens them away. Naturally the primary goal of the seller must be met by the use of this tool, and if that goal is the "move" of the property, then the sale generated by its use is the proper result.

Motivation Plays a Major Roll in Any OPM Transaction

Sellers who are highly motivated to sell will find the split-fund transaction an ideal way to get a reasonable upfront cash payment and still not have to wait out a long-term mortgage for the rest of their equity. Also an important point for both sides to consider is that many sellers will take a drop in price anyway. By using the split-fund technique the seller might be able to stand pat on his price, since the sacrifice of the interest he does not get on the second and/or third payments of the split fund would have been a taxable event. This softens the impact of losing a little interest by not having to pay tax on the amount of the interest.

In Brian's deal the seller might have decided the best way to move the property was to offer it at only $15,000 cash down. An advertisement at this cash down might have attracted someone who, once hooked on the deal, wouldn't mind the two additional payments of $10,000 each to meet the total $35,000 entrance money.

Think of the Split-Fund as Key Money

This entrance money, or, as it is often termed abroad, "key money," is treated separately from the mortgages, when in reality it might be secured by a mortgage to give the seller protection and assurance of its eventual payment. We will see other techniques that look similar to this one where the amount of the second or third split-funded payment is actually secured by a mortgage, one on the property being purchased, or perhaps on some other property.

THE BUYER'S VIEWPOINT

If you are a buyer attempting to get the most leverage and benefit out of your cash, then the split-fund is just another tool you can use to that end. Builders and developers who know they will be going through a refinance in a year or so can use this technique to great advantage (and so can you) since they know that when the second or third split-funded payment is due they will be refinancing the total transaction anyway. A condo-conversion of a rental apartment building also works nicely with this kind of financing since the second payment can often be met from the sales of the condos, or at least out of the new financing placed on the property.

This OPM technique can be used in every kind of transaction where there is a down payment to reduce the upfront cash. If you use it with no interest on the split-funded payment, then you can reduce your overall carrying cost. Keep in mind that the government may impute interest at a nominal rate (the rate changes, so see a current bulletin or check with your accountant for the current imputed IRS interest rate). This means the IRS will assume the increased price and will recompute the transaction in that light. If the amounts are small and the time short, the interest imputed may have little effect on the transaction from your point of view. However large amounts for long durations can have a major effect on the seller. His accountant will tell him all about that. Buyers who know they have a lump of cash coming from another transaction where they are the sellers, or from the refinancing of another property, will find this technique particularly of interest. If, for example, Brian had a contract on his own home and knew that when it closed in four months that he would have more cash available than allocated to a new home, then the split-fund works nicely.

PITFALLS FROM THE SELLER'S SIDE OF THE DEAL

I just mentioned one pitfall—the imputed interest in a noninterest-bearing transaction on the split-funded part of the deal. As long as you are aware of this, it won't make any difference. In fact sellers often take that into account and let the split-fund run without interest. After all it might not be more than a few hundred dollars, and even if it is more it will be before-tax money. Remember even 9 percent interest on $10,000 is only $900 at the end of a year, and if you are in a 30 percent tax bracket that cost is now down to $720. In a large transaction that shouldn't break the deal for the seller, but it might be enough of an incentive for the buyer to come and look at your property.

The biggest pitfall, though, is the seller not getting sufficient cash to secure the deal. This will depend on a multitude of circumstances, for example, the condition of the market, how badly the seller needs to sell, how tight are conventional loans, the competition, and the will and nature of the buyers. Are there any? Do they have cash? If there are buyers who do have cash and who want to purchase, perhaps you should exhaust every possibility to make a deal with them.

PITFALLS FROM THE BUYER'S SIDE OF THE DEAL

Can you as the buyer meet the obligation of the split-funded payment? And even if you can if you are enticed into the deal because you can afford the low down payment but nothing more, then you may have a short-lived ownership unless the values go up and you make a killing in a resale. Mind you a lot of buyers do exactly that, with the luck of the Irish or whatever on their side. I have seen many not so lucky, however, so plan your finances so you don't get caught with the Irish on the other side of the deal.

5 CHAPTER

The Caveman Down Payment

Bartering is one of the oldest methods of exchange. I can just imagine the cavemen offering each other a bit of this and that: a fish for some bananas; a hunk of lizard for some bird eggs; and a pretty rock for starting a fire. Each item given was taken by the other and something of equal value or interest passed back to the first party. They were bartering. It was and still is an interesting way to make transactions work—all kinds of transactions, by the way, and not just real estate.

Let's look at how bartering, or what I call the caveman down payment, might work now. Isabel runs a small backyard business, more a hobby than a vocation. She has a green thumb, so she grows exotic and rare tropical fruit trees and shrubs. Her product, then, is plants. In a barter situation she can offer these plants as a down payment on something. Perhaps the developer of a condominium, contacted well before any other arrangements are made, might be delighted to let Isabel use $30,000 or more of her plants as a down payment on one of his condominiums. The developer would use the plants within the project (or another project) as landscaping or decoration.

Bartering of a product is slightly different from the other forms of barter I will illustrate. In this situation we are dealing with the actual plants—not a craft or trade such as doing landscaping or planning the landscaping, which are services and not products.

THE PLANT BARTER: MAKING A DIRECT TRADE

Josh grows palm trees as a hobby. He purchased a vacant lot 10 years ago that was alongside a fresh water canal, and he had no immediate plans for the property so he started collecting Royal Palm seeds. This was easy to do as Josh lives in Fort Lauderdale, Florida, where many of these trees grow along public roads and sidewalks. When the seeds are ripe, they just fall to the ground. Josh found that his portable "dirt buster," which hooked to his car cigarette lighter, could pick up several hundred seeds in just a few minutes. Josh then started the seeds in small containers made for exactly that purpose. Once the seeds sprouted and the plants grew a few inches long, he would plant them in predetermined and prepared rows on the vacant lot. Royal Palms grow like weeds—as fast as lightening—and in 10 years time Josh had hundreds of these beautiful trees in a wide range of sizes.

Josh wanted to purchase a condo in Palm Beach as both an investment and a getaway place. He took photos of several of the trees, standing next to each of them to add perspective and size to the tree. He then sent the photos, along with offers to purchase, to a dozen different builders who were in the process of developing residential product for sale in Palm Beach.

It did not take Josh long before several of these builders contacted him, and in a month or so Josh had cut a deal with a developer who was in the process of finishing up a club house at a new golf course. Josh was able to barter around $25,000 worth of trees at just under retail value as a down payment on a nice oceanfront condo.

THE WINE BARTER: NETWORKING THE TRADE

In another example let's assume that Phil is a winemaker. His product is wine—all kinds of wine. Now while this might seem like a difficult product to barter for real estate, the trick is to find a user for the wine. The owner of a wine shop or restaurant would be good a choice. However can Phil find someone who would take the wine and who also has real estate that Phil would want to buy?

If that person does have real estate for sale and takes the wine, the story is over and the deal is made. However it usually doesn't work that way in real life. The wine shop owner or restaurant owner may not have what Phil wants. As is often the case with bartering, you must become creative. This means you must keep the user of your barter item in the back of your mind while you go out to find what you want. The key to bringing one of the possible "buyers" into the picture is to ask them the following question: "Under what circumstances would you take this wine off my hands?" You might be surprised at the answer. In one similar transaction involving wine, I was going to receive 50 cases of fine California wine. I checked with a few restaurants and a couple of wine shops and found one shop owner who would take the wine on consignment and pay me a bit more than I wanted or take the whole inventory off my hands and give me a discounted payout of less than I wanted. I made a note of this offer and proceeded to find what I wanted to take in trade.

In Phil's example he found a nice vacant lot he wanted to buy for an investment. It was offered at a fair price of $50,000. Phil had $14,000 worth of wine (at retail value) he wanted to unload. He was willing to take $7000 for the whole inventory as a bulk sale, so he offered the wine to the owner of the lot at that price for the down payment. He would then owe the lot owner the balance of $43,000 on terms satisfactory to the seller.

The lot owner balked at the offer of the product, but Phil then pointed out (through his broker) that there was a restaurant owner who would take the wine off the lot owner's hands, either on consignment for resale or in cash upfront of $5000. The owner now has a choice: He could take a chance of picking up $3000 by letting the restaurant owner stock the wine at the restaurant (if they sell, he gets paid; if not, the wine is his), or he can take the instant cash of $5000. If you were the owner of a lot interested in converting your equity into some cash and a mortgage at good terms, what choice would you make?

On the other hand Phil could just as easily have been a jeweler, able to pick up gemstones at a bargain rate and, with a few hours in his well-equipped workshop, turn out magnificent and expensive jewelry. This kind of product would easily be passed off in a transaction, assuming it is genuine and priced competitively. I've never seen a million-dollar transaction where the seller wouldn't have been able to absorb a $30,000 piece of jewelry if there was motivation to make it work out that way. (The broker who might lose out on a nice commission could be just the guy to end up with the $30,000 ring.)

It is not difficult to get builders to take building materials or to get land developers to take machines used in land development. The true test of your creative ability to use this caveman down-payment technique will be in finding the user for your product, and then making that person an instrumental part of the deal, as either the main principal or a third-party taker to make the transaction work.

TEN QUESTIONS EVERY SELLER SHOULD ASK

So you're thinking that this caveman down-payment method might just work. You may already have some ideas of what you could barter for your real estate investment. Before you make the leap into bartering, here are 10 key questions to ask yourself.

1. Is the value of the product being offered fairly assessed?
2. If it isn't, then can one be set, or is the buyer way out of line?
3. Do you have a use for the product?
4. Can the product be easily sold to a user?
5. Must you take a discount to sell it, and how much?
6. Do the rest of the terms meet with your approval?
7. Will the broker take all or part of the product?
8. Will the broker hold off his or her commission until all or part of the product is sold or further exchanged?
9. Can you exchange the product with someone else for something you would like or would take?
10. Is this the only way you can see a deal being made?

The answers to these questions don't require any discussion other than to say you will have a good understanding of the pros and cons of the deal once you have gone into each of them. Even if the first nine answers are unsatisfactory, the deal might still be good if the answer to the last question is that bartering is in fact the only way you can make the deal. Need is the strongest motivator of all.

Some sellers actually seek bartering as a way of moving their real estate. Some property-rich (also called property-poor when the cost to keep the real estate becomes a burden) people find themselves with a lot of real estate, little cash, and in need of material items. I've seen such people barter for boats, airplanes, machinery, and almost any other product you can think of to get out from under real estate they were unable to sell for cash at a reasonable value. They decide on a product, then find an owner of that product or a manufacturer of the product, and then make a deal.

Some landowners use vacant land as money. They buy large tracts of land at a low price, subdivide them into lots now worth 10 times the original price, and use these inexpensive lots in nearly every transaction they make. Buy a $20,000 car, and give the car dealer one lot worth $5000 along with $15,000 in cash to pay for the car. Buy a $450,000 home and give the seller $50,000 worth of lots and some more cash down. That's the idea. Can you see other applications?

Buyers will best use this tool if they do some homework on their sellers. In essence find sellers who are inclined to use your product.

PITFALLS FROM THE SELLER'S SIDE OF THE DEAL

While bartering can be exciting and open more markets for you, there is a lot of junk out there ready to fall into your lap if you aren't careful. Always have the offered product appraised if you are not sure of its real value; never take the word of the other party or the appraisals he offers you. He may be honest, but there is a natural tendency to bolster one's own product and to overlook the fact that values don't always remain the same. Get an opinion you feel comfortable with, and try to get it from the most qualified person available for the product at hand. You might be offered a real bargain, and you don't want to miss the opportunity.

PITFALLS FROM THE BUYER'S SIDE OF THE DEAL

As an investor giving up a product, are you getting full value for your product? Or has the seller simply absorbed your product into the overinflated price he was asking for his real estate? This is a real hazard, so you must know values. One of the best ways to ensure you aren't being underpaid for your product is to negotiate without the product first, if you can. This is difficult in many situations, so you may have to offer to barter with the idea of starting low and working up the ladder to make the best deal possible.

WHAT DRIVES ALL CREATIVE OPM TRANSACTIONS?

Bartering is a great way to go, and if your "sales" market is off, it might be the only way to go. But that's not the only driver for OPM transactions. Here are three key motivators for creative OPM transactions:

- No-cash buyers
- Massive debt
- Goal attainment

No-cash buying does not mean that the property offered for sale has no value, it means only that there are no immediate users or speculators for that specific real estate. There are many reasons this occurs. There might be a building moratorium imposed by the city and no set date when the property can be used. It could be that there is a lot of construction going on along the roadway and it might be years before things will be restored to normality. Or the bridge over the river is under repair for the next two years, and so on. All of these examples, by the way, might ultimately cause the value of this real estate to go up, but if you are the owner and need to get off that $5000 a month mortgage payment, then you might truly be motivated to take almost anything of value that costs nothing to carry. When you make an offer to a seller for any kind of OPM transaction, keep in mind that sellers will attempt to make a comparison between your offer and what they are asking. This is a tragic error in how to do business. The only realistic comparison is between your offer and another offer that is still on the table. Sellers that take the attitude (and most do) that they are insulted by your offer to barter $20,000 of palm trees for their property have it all wrong. You at least see value in their property. You would like to own that property and do exactly what they have been hoping for: Be the person who buys the property they are trying to sell. If they want to be insulted, let them be insulted by all their friends and advisors who have not bothered to even make them an offer at all.

When it comes to debt, massive is a relative word. An extra $500 a month would seem massive to some people, where $5000 is just a pittance to someone else. When debt gets out of hand, there is a day when the handwriting is on the wall; actually it's nailed to your front door and it begins with the words "eviction notice." I am always surprised why someone lets things go so long that they get into this situation. Once this happens you can kiss a reasonable offer goodbye. By this time the wolves are already at your door. The idea is to plan far enough ahead so you can negotiate without the already posted notices or advertisement of eviction in the local paper. So take those cases of wine if you must—and throw a party.

Any transaction that will help you move closer to your goal is a good deal. Keep an open mind, of course, but be darn sure you have some goals in the first place. People who do not see an opportunity to take an OPM deal usually do not have any specified goals.

6

The Pivotal Person

A "Pivotal Person" is more than a transaction. It is a situation where the buyer's status is the main ingredient of the transaction. In this kind of deal the position, reputation, or influence of the buyer is generally more important than cash. There are many reasons why the buyer is in such a position, and it is important not to jump to the conclusion that only the famous or the most respected in their professions fall into this category. In real estate the localized situation might create an environment where simply owning the adjoining property puts the would-be buyer into a pivotal position. Sellers of certain kinds of property would be well advised to seek out these pivotal people in hopes of making a deal with them to quickly dispose of their property, thereby solving their problems or meeting their goals. Real estate brokers and salespersons are well advised to know the names, addresses, and phone numbers of these people within their community because they are the creators of big deals.

Remember when I discussed the importance of being recognized as a true real estate insider? Well, here is the proof of the pudding. All pivotal people in the real estate field have already attained that insider status. Many real estate investors seek to become pivotal people but never attain that stature. It's not absolutely necessary if your goals are modest, but should you select some specialty in real estate that would make you worth more than cash, you will find that deals will seek you out. You will then discover the real power of OPM transactions in which you can buy without using cash, using only your good name.

THE SUCCESS OF GOOD OLD TOM

The pivotal person strategy is not as difficult as it may seem. Your skills and talents build the foundation for becoming a pivotal person. For example Tom used his talent in making himself a pivotal person. Tom had been in real estate for many years, and over that time had put together about a dozen highly successful real estate syndicates. These group purchases of investments were the product of several elements. First was Tom's interest in finding good investment properties that he and his father could jointly invest in. Second was the realization that if he found many good investments and spread his capital around, he could take advantage of a reduced risk by having more baskets in which to place his eggs. The third element was the fact that, by having some co-investors, he was able to buy larger properties than he and his father might have considered for themselves alone.

As word got around that Tom was successful at this kind of real estate transaction, sellers began to seek Tom out to "market" their property for them. They were in essence giving Tom free options on their property so he could form a syndicate, which would then buy their property. For Tom this was an ideal situation since he could now spend the time necessary to check out the real estate properly and then form the syndicate, knowing that he wasn't risking the usual upfront money to tie up the property. Later on these same "sellers" would come to Tom asking if he would let them invest in his next deal.

This is the easiest form of specialization for a new or expanding investor to develop. When you have completed several group deals like Tom's, you will be on your way to becoming both wealthy and well known.

THE SHOPPING CENTER KING

Another way to become a pivotal person is to be an "expert" in a specific area. Louis is the shopping center king in his area, and it pays off. His specialty is developing shopping centers, and there are many people like him around the country. Some are more nationally known, like Farber, Debartolo, or Simons. Others are local people who have a good reputation for building strip malls or local centers. If you were a seller of a good site for one of these centers, you might find that offering your site to one of the local pivotal people would entice her into an ultimate buyout of your site.

You will get a higher price, by the way, if you offer a buyer good terms. And when it comes to developmental property, "good terms" does not necessarily mean long-term mortgages at low interest. A developer wants to know the site she is buying is ready to go and there aren't any hidden charges in the deal. Taking a tract of raw land and turning it into a shopping center or condominium apartment building is a hard task filled with countless nickel-and-dime costs that occur as the land is brought to the point where buildings are ready to break ground. The best terms you could offer a builder might simply be some time—time for the builder to examine what these costs might actually be or to even begin the process prior to his having to give you some upfront cash.

THE IMPORTANCE OF TIME

Time is the sugar pill of all real estate projects. Given enough time, a developer can win most battles with even the most adversary planning and zoning board or city commission, or whatever other enemy that confronts them. Be certain, there are many: local civic associations, homeowners associations, neighbors, fellow developers seeking to keep you out of their hair, and so on. But give that developer time and she will spend the money and devote her hard-earned time to win. Short change them by saying, "I can't give you that much time," and you will often see a seller who sits on her property for years, unable to sell it because she does not understand the nature of real estate development.

Time can be the single element that burns you too. I have seen property owners attempt to wait out the local environment in hopes of better times that never come. There used to be a time when if you held on long enough, time would heal any wound. In real estate there is a trend to remove rights, not to grant them. Many local governments are out to "get" the local speculator. The guy who has held onto those few acres of land in hopes a condo developer will make him rich is a dangerous way to invest today. Buy vacant land and hold it long enough and you might be lucky to be able to grow tomatoes on it, not build a high-rise condo.

THE SELLER'S VIEWPOINT

Unless you are already a pivotal person, this type of technique is better as a seller's tool. To use it to your best advantage, you should first attempt to ascertain what kind of use the property should be put to. Naturally the existing or potential zoning will play an important role with this decision. It is possible the city would allow a different use than the current zoning would allow. This factor would open different directions for a developer to go and might require a different pivotal person for you. If the property is already developed, you might need to find a ready user or an investor to simply replace you as holder of the property. The right person might be the user or a known investor who has a lot of cash or property.

The other side of this is the buyer coming into a deal and telling you, "Hey, look, I'm a real top banana and I'm the best person to make this deal. I'm your pivotal person." Personally I've heard this line so much that I discount it about 90 percent of the time. Indeed so skeptical are many sellers that it may be hard for a buyer to convince the seller that she is a pivotal person unless a savvy broker can tactfully convey this fact.

THE BUYER'S VIEWPOINT

The buyer's viewpoint is one of mixed emotions. This form of the transaction is excellent if you can develop the situation with property you want to acquire. On the other hand if you have gained some specialty, then you will have opportunities knocking at your door. When you have a motivated seller who has sought you out to participate in the deal, don't assume this is out of desperation. Instead be flattered. Real opportunities can come out of this kind of situation, and you should be willing to look into the deal to see whether it fits your goals and whether you can take advantage of that opportunity.

PITFALLS FROM THE SELLER'S SIDE OF THE DEAL

Sellers, beware of false profits. "Not all is as it seems" is not just a saying, it is a fact. Remember the pivotal person technique is a better seller's tool than a buyer's tool, but that doesn't mean sellers aren't at risk. Any transaction that allows a buyer to get in without much, or any, upfront cash and risk adds to the risk of the seller. It doesn't matter how big of a name the person has, prudence dictates that all sellers protect themselves to the utmost in all transactions; and when there is little or no cash in the deal, protect yourself to the maximum in as many areas as possible.

Nothing beats cash as a form of protection when it comes to making deals. But not all buyers have cash, and some who do may not want what you are trying to sell (or won't pay your price and you won't drop down to theirs). Of course before you can weigh the risk against the gains, you must understand exactly what it is you are risking. If you are risking time by holding your property off the market while the buyer goes through a series of determined, or yet to be determined, steps to ascertain the value or the development potential of your property, that is one thing. However if you are passing title to a corporation about to go into bankruptcy, then you are risking more than time.

Sellers can protect themselves relatively securely by retaining title to their property until they get that ultimate cash upfront. This means giving options rather than closing on the no-cash or little-cash deal. Time then becomes the major element of risk, and if there are no other ready buyers, that risk may be acceptable.

Check out your buyers in every deal. Never rely on what they say about themselves. I believe this is one of those instances where what others say about the person is more important. Get references, ask the industry people they deal with questions, and look primarily for their record of performance. Do they pay on time? Are they successful in all their projects?

PITFALLS FROM THE BUYER'S SIDE OF THE DEAL

If you already are one of those pivotal people, then my most sincere congratulations. But watch out for all those deals you have thrown at you. Devote some time to examining each deal. This might be done by one of your staff members if you have capable people who can spend a few minutes on each deal offered to you. Short of that you will have to do your own due diligence. Remember to beware of gifts sellers offer.

One way to make that task easier is to make a checklist of all the specific things you want to know about each deal. When you get a call or inquiry, send the person this checklist. This compels them to give you the kind of data you want in the form you are comfortable with. It can take hours just looking at a presentation to find the simplest data because you aren't sure where it is. I've examined countless presentations that no doubt had taken a lot of time to prepare but were thoroughly confusing to me. Not because the presentation lacked data, but because it contained too much data. I had to wade through too much unimportant data to get the meat of the deal. Too much information looks too complex, and many developers and investors have learned from experience that sellers and some brokers often try to make a weak deal look strong by the weight of the presentation. Don't let that kind of presentation distract you from getting down to the nitty gritty quickly and decisively.

7

CHAPTER

The Future OPM
Paper Transaction

The future OPM paper transaction is the technique of using OPM that you do not yet have but is owed to you. This involves using notes or mortgages you hold as collateral for a loan. The loan might have resulted when you sold property and took back secondary paper or it might be a loan on a car, boat, or diamond ring you sold. Whatever it is, it represents OPM that has not yet come to you. The idea is to put this future OPM to work. This kind of transaction can generate ready cash in situations where, for one reason or another, you need additional value to close the deal. While you could go into the secondary market and sell the note or second mortgage, lenders who buy that kind of paper expect a substantial discount from the face of the note or mortgage. It is highly likely that you will not want to sell the notes or mortgages you are holding at a discount because you believe the security you are holding is worth keeping the note or mortgage; you would like to get the cash though to use in another deal. In essence you take a note (which may be secured by real estate or some other collateral or may be unsecured and backed by someone's signature alone) and borrow the money you need using this note as collateral for your loan.

THE NOTABLE DEAL: USING OPM FROM MORTGAGES

Charles was a buyer and seller of real estate and frequently took back mortgages and notes when he sold his properties. These notes and mortgages varied in interest rates and term of years, depending on their maturity. The amounts of these notes and mortgages also varied depending on Charles's motivation when he sold properties and took back secondary financing to facilitate the closing of the transaction.

An interesting situation developed for Charles on a property he had been looking at for some time. The seller of the property suddenly became more motivated to sell, and Charles wanted to take advantage of that opportunity knocking at his door. Charles and the owner went through a series of offers and counteroffers to the point that Charles believed the deal was as sweet as it was going to get. He was able to get most of the down-payment money he needed by cashing in some certificates of deposits that were due. Yet he was still short about $10,000 to make the deal, and nothing he attempted in the way of creative dealmaking seemed to work. The seller wouldn't back down on his demand for that extra $10,000 in cash.

None of the notes and mortgages Charles had were small enough to sell, even at a discount to generate the needed $10,000. And anyway the interest rate was greater than he could get from a bank. Charles didn't want to sell the notes at the discount the current market would demand if there was an alternative.

Charles knew all the makers of the notes well (after all, he had sold them real estate), and he knew that in each case there was a chance the note would be paid off prior to the due date. This prepayment of notes is not uncommon. As a matter of fact it is typical of real estate loans. The average loan lasts around seven to nine years, no matter how long the term of the mortgage. However when you discount a note that has 15 years remaining on its term, the buyer of the note won't take into account the potential early payment. The early payment thus becomes a great bonus in discounted mortgages. (I'll describe this in more detail later in the book.)

Not wanting to take a discount when the notes stood a great chance of being prepaid, Charlie hit upon another idea. What he did was select one note that had about a $25,000 balance. He took this note to the maker's bank, introduced himself to the commercial loan officer, and proposed the bank lend him $10,000, which Charles would sign personally for and, in addition, place as collateral for the loan the note in the amount of $25,000. The bank knew the maker of the loan, of course, and knew that in the event Charles defaulted on the loan of $10,000, they would have the entire $25,000 note in their hands as security.

Charles received his cash without having to sell any of the notes. Now mind you Charles could have offered the note to the seller but he had already negotiated the price to as low as he felt it would go, and he was anxious that if he continued to try to cut the price, then the seller would slam the door in his face. This can happen, so it is important to watch for signs that you have reached the bottom before it actually happens.

THE FINE POINTS WHEN BORROWING AGAINST NOTES

There are several things that are useful to know about this tool. First and foremost, do your homework when you borrow against notes. Whenever you attempt to borrow on notes, or when you plan to attempt to sell them, make sure you approach the maker's banks first. Note that I said *banks*. It's possible the maker of the note has more than one bank. You would know of at least one simply from the checks you have been receiving on the mortgage payments. Another source of information on other banks is the maker himself at the time you consider taking them in the first place.

When you sell real estate and hold mortgages, it's a good idea to have a financial statement from the buyer. If you are holding a large sum of paper in the deal, you might even require annual updates of the financial statement. This statement should be simple to fill out and can follow the kinds most savings and loans associations use. What you are looking for are bank references and businesses the buyer deals with. There are other things that might be helpful, of course, but with banks and other businesses to deal with, you have two potential lenders against this note. By doing your homework early, prior to a sale, you will have the data you might need at your fingertips when you need it.

The second point is that you do not need to pledge the entire note and mortgage. It is possible, for example, to pledge only the first $25,000 of a $100,000 note. This way if you default for some unforeseen reason, you won't lose the entire note.

Third you should develop a position of strength when you negotiate any loan. If you are offering to pay a reasonable interest rate, and the note you are willing to pledge as collateral has some seasoning (a history of prompt payments), your deal should be attractive to the lender or the seller of the property you are attempting to buy. Loan officers, however, do have a way of making borrowers feel uncomfortable. Don't be arrogant, but don't be intimidated either.

The last point to borrowing against notes is to do it when the situation warrants it. I've seen many prospective buyers sit on their assets and let good opportunities slip past them because they didn't want to borrow money. If you are collecting on money you loaned out (via a note and mortgage you are holding), why not get some cash out of the note through a loan and let the note pay off your loan? You are using advance OPM in this kind of transaction.

Let's say Nancy owes me $30,000 on a mortgage and pays me $500 each month. I want $10,000 to buy something, so I borrow the $10,000 from the bank and give the lender the note from Nancy as collateral. I pay the lender $250 per month until it's paid up, but who makes the payment? Me or Nancy? All I do is take $250 out of the $500 and I am still ahead $250 while I am paying off the $10,000 I needed.

THE SELLER'S VIEWPOINT

The seller is getting cash, so he looks on this transaction as a simple matter of holding firm and getting his cash. The wise seller will help buyers think of this possibility. After all you will find buyers who aren't aware they can borrow on notes they are holding. A smart seller won't let a qualified buyer get out of his grip. If the seller were motivated, as it seemed this one might have been in Charles's case, Charles would normally have offered a note to the seller as a part of the down payment. If he did, the seller would want to know as much about the property that secured the note or mortgage as possible, as well as the history of payments.

In any event anytime a seller takes a secondary note or mortgage secured by something other than the property he or she is selling, it is critical to make sure there is some cross-collateralization back to the property being sold. This means the buyer (Charles in this case) would stand behind the note or mortgage and pledge the property he was buying as additional collateral to the deal. Charles may be reluctant to do that because his plans are to make some improvements to the property, and then refinance it for more than he is currently paying. If he was tied into a cross-collateralization of paper he used to purchase the property, he would have to remove the connection and that might require him to pay off the seller, defeating the purpose of keeping the debt off the purchased property.

THE BUYER'S VIEWPOINT

Once the buyer understands the concept of making the best use of the money he has as well as the money owed to him, he is on his way to making more deals through creative efforts. Generating cash or a cash equivalent when you need it is an important aspect of dealing in real estate or any other investment. Holding notes and mortgages in the sale of real estate is a matter of it eventually happening. If you buy and sell enough, you will, sometime along the way, hold a mortgage. Using this future cash as collateral for cash you need now is not only okay but also prudent if the deal you have coming up is indeed a good deal. Clearly getting the seller to shortcut the deal by taking the whole or part of the note or mortgage is a far quicker way of doing the deal. But that will not always happen, and you need to know how to produce a new approach to the problem.

THE LENDER'S VIEWPOINT

The lender might be a bank, of course, but don't overlook private sources. Lenders are businesspeople looking for the most secure deal or the greatest yield at the lowest risk. You are offering them a business transaction, and the note is their security.

PITFALLS FROM THE SELLER'S SIDE OF THE DEAL

With the future OPM paper transaction, there really are no pitfalls for the seller since the seller gets cash in the deal. So it is a strategy that benefits the seller. If he ends up with the note or mortgage as collateral for a loan as a part of the down payment, then he needs to pay close attention to the data mentioned earlier in the chapter.

PITFALLS FROM THE BUYER'S SIDE OF THE DEAL

Buyers will find any source of borrowed cash an additional risk. When you borrow, you risk. This risk might be acceptable, but the loan becomes another obligation you will have to pay back or accept the consequences. If the maker of the note or mortgage defaults, then you may be required to step up and cover the lender's loss, plus legal fees.

Buyers who approach any transaction with an early refinance in mind need to be careful with cross-collateralization of any note or secondary position. There are two primary reasons for this. First buyers generally use an early refinance of the deal to pull out cash or to maximize the amount available when financing the property after they have improved it through a short-term ownership. It would be likely that any cross-collateralized notes or mortgages would have a provision that would require them to be paid off at the time of refinance. Remember when you cross-collateralize a loan you are giving the lender more than one item or property as security to the loan. Sometimes this is one loan document (a blanket loan), or it can be several different loan documents all tied together so that a default would become a default on them all. Try to avoid offering sellers cross-collateralization if there is a future plan to refinance or sell any of the properties prior to the pay off of the cross-collateralized loan, unless you had a provision in the documentation that would allow you to a release of the property to be sold or refinanced.

Going into a deal with more debt than you can handle can be the straw that breaks the back of this deal. The heavy leveraging and overextending of debt in some real estate purchases can spell disaster. If there is reversal in your economic well being, you could be courting bankruptcy. The investor who never accepts risk, however, rarely profits as he should. The key here is to know the real value of the note or mortgage. If the underlying security is sound, the payment history good, and the strength of the maker is solid, then take the risk.

8

CHAPTER

Scrip: The Legal Money You Print

There are three basic forms of scrip that you can use to buy real estate. Because each of the three forms utilizes the same type of negotiable instrument, I will treat the three in detail in this chapter and then describe the finer points of two of them in later chapters.

Scrip is a form of money. Short of real currency, diamonds, or gold, when properly done, it is the best cash equivalent I have ever seen. It has a long history of use and is frequently found within large companies as a type of negotiable instrument that employees can use to redeem merchandise or services at the company store. Scrip, in the context in which I use it, is a promise in written form that clearly binds the "banker" to honor the value of the paper against claims against those specific promises. These claims may have some restrictions on them, and the obligation may have a beginning date as well as a termination date. This written form can be anything from a gift certificate to a formalized legal document spelling out the complete terms of the obligation. Most of us have used different forms of scrip many times. You may not have realized it but traveler's checks are a form of scrip, so chances are you have used scrip before.

Scrip is either written against something the "banker" has, such as a service or tangible items, or it can be used to acquire service or merchandise from other vendors or persons. Like a traveler's check, scrip is backed by a promise to convert to U.S. dollars, or some other currency. The latter form has two variations: If you don't have a service or item to use, you can buy those services from someone else, using your "soft paper," or you can sell those services or items at a discount (commission).

THE SPAGHETTI TRADE: SETTING UP THE PAPER

Louie runs a fast-food spaghetti house named Louie and Rose. It is doing very well, and Louie wants to open up several more outlets, maybe even start a franchise. However, like a lot of restaurateurs, Louie has most of his money tied up in his one restaurant.

So Louie decides to do the next best thing. He will start buying sites so that when he does have enough capital, he will be ready to go with the right locations. Instead of paying top dollar for locations that are presently the hottest, he will buy locations he believes will be hot a few years from now.

Louie locates a site that he loves because he knows the area will be ideal for a restaurant in a few years. New roads are being built, and the single-family and multifamily homes in construction are naturals for a good fast-food spaghetti joint. The site belongs to the owner of the local car dealership (a fact that will work out nicely for Louie, as you will see) and is most reasonably priced at $55,000. The seller is willing to take back some paper, but she wants at least $15,000 cash upfront. And because she is highly motivated to sell, the $40,000 balance can be paid off over 10 years at 7 percent interest.

LOUIE'S DEAL

Louie wants to take advantage of this opportunity since it will help him attain his ultimate goal of opening more restaurants. Louie has only $5000 in cash, but he knows the seller is willing to take paper as part of the down payment. Now he just needs to come up with what that is. He has his broker draw up the following offer:

Cash at closing:	$ 5,000.00
Interest only at 7 percent per year	
Outstanding balance of mortgage	$35,000.00
Total offer	$55,000.00

Louie has also worked out the paper. The scrip is redeemable at Louie and Rose's restaurant in meals, wine, and spirits (not to include tip or tax). There is no termination date on the redemption of this scrip, but it is limited to $1000 per night and a 15 percent tip will be due on all service payable in cash.

Louie's offer differs in several respects from the terms the seller is requesting. First of all he is offering only $5000 in cash but $15,000 in scrip increases his cash and cash equivalent to $20,000 down. He has lowered the mortgage term to seven years, but he is asking for interest-only payments. These elements of the offer are to catch the attention of the seller, and at the same time to give Louie some negotiating room.

The seller, as I have already mentioned, owns a sizable company with many employees, and therefore will have ample opportunity to use up the scrip. She can offer top salespeople, executives, buyers, and so on free dinners and drinks as a premium—and it solves her problem of unloading the site.

Louie is willing and able to cut the amount of scrip by any amount the seller wishes and to add that sum to the mortgage. Of course, to balance this, Louie would ask for longer terms or even a reduced interest rate.

THE FINE POINTS OF THE SCRIP DEAL

The key to using scrip is to use it whenever you can. If you are a businessperson with service or inventory usable by the owner of a property you are buying, you should attempt to use some scrip as a part of the deal. For example, if Louie had been the owner of a hardware store, he would have made his offer to buy giving scrip against his merchandise.

Of course these aren't the only options. You don't have to own a fast-food joint or hardware store to use scrip. The next two chapters will show you how to make exciting scrip deals without owning a shop yourself.

Another fine point to discuss is the presentation of the offer. It is often the most crucial part of a scrip deal. If your broker or salesperson making the offer is skittish about the method of purchase, you will be doomed from the start. A short pep talk with the salesperson on the advantages of the scrip to the seller might be in order. The most important thing, however, for the broker, salesperson, or lawyer who is the intermediary in the deal is to let the seller make up her own mind. Here are a few tips to those presenting the offer:

- Have some details on the "banker" of the service or merchandise handy when the offer is presented. Make sure you have the appropriate information ready—what the paper offer is, what it includes, and any additional material that might help "sell" it. For example, you might say, "Here is a brochure on Louie's resort in Martinique, at which he is offering you three weeks, including meals and beverages, as a part of the down payment." That way the seller knows exactly what the deal is. Be sure to leave room to negotiate to more than three weeks.

- Show or indicate how the seller can "unload" the scrip if she should choose not to use it up herself. She can use it as cash the next time she buys or give it as premiums. A good broker will already have some ideas in this direction. There are several sellers who would love to have a vacation or even a year's worth of Sunday dinners at Louie and Rose's fine restaurant.

- Point out the benefits to the seller of achieving her goal to get rid of the property. Sellers sometimes need to be reminded that the offer on the table is the only offer they should consider. Old offers turned down by the seller may have gone away by now. The key to any kind of offer is to negotiate. It is a big mistake to simply turn down an offer because you do not see the benefits. If there are no benefits, then tweak the deal until some appear.

THE SELLER'S VIEWPOINT

The seller gets scrip in all three of the scrip transactions covered in this chapter. She needs to closely examine the nature of the promise to be sure the future draw against services will, in fact, be honored. Once the quality of the promise is assured, the seller needs to review the factors of use. Can the seller use the merchandise or service offered? If not, or only partially, then can the seller spin off the balance of the offered item? If the seller can get rid of the scrip, the scrip then was the same as if the buyer had paid cash.

The most dangerous aspect of scrip from a seller's point of view is disuse. If there are great delays in using the scrip, the end product can disappear: Restaurants go out of business, hotels are converted to apartments, etc. Also, as the paper has no interest accruing to it, the longer the seller holds on to the promise, the less valuable it becomes. Therefore if the paper promise is good and the service or merchandise valuable, the seller should make every attempt to either use it or spin it off quickly.

THE BUYER'S VIEWPOINT

When you offer someone your merchandise or service at face value as a part of your offer to buy their property, but they only have a future delivery of the service or merchandise, you have a double profit in the transaction.

First of all you have gotten an interest-free loan from the seller: She gave you cash (which you used in the purchase of her property) and you told her to come in and eat it up in spaghetti. Each time she comes in, however, you not only reduce what you owe her, you also profit from the fact that she spends the paper money you gave her at your place of business.

You have a built-in profit in your goods or services. Every time you sell your goods or service at face value, you make a profit. If that profit is 20 percent, for example, and you are able to use $10,000 worth of scrip, which is redeemable against your own product, then it really costs you $8000, and then only if it is redeemed on the day you make the deal. The longer the delay, the more you gain from the interest buildup you earn on the money, as well as the likelihood that a healthy percentage of that scrip will never find its way back to your place of business.

There may also be another benefit to you: In many businesses the very act of doing business is beneficial. When the seller balks at this kind of a deal it might be because she got burned in a similar transaction or knows someone who did. Getting burned occurs because the buyer often goes out of business long before the value of the scrip is used up. One way to counter, or partially counter that problem, is to let the seller get his value in advance. Say you start with $15,000 of scrip; every time the seller uses up $1000 in value, the $15,000 you owe her is reduced by that $1000. If you go out of business and can no longer deliver the goods you promised, you still owe the balance. Sellers would want this documented with a secure cross-collateralization to tie the amount you owe to the outstanding debt. I did this with a dentist not long ago. I suggested that I give him some holiday time at one or more timeshare apartments I own or would be able to exchange into. They would all be two-bedroom units, I told him, and he could pick from the RCI catalogue. Naturally this was subject to space being available. I told him to go ahead and take one of the holidays upfront. If he did not like the resort, then he could let me know; otherwise he would give me a credit of $1000 against my future dental bills for each week's holiday. This worked well—until I moved to another part of town and changed dentists.

PITFALLS FROM THE SELLER'S SIDE OF THE DEAL

There are several pitfalls sellers should watch out for when taking scrip as a part of any real estate transaction. I've already discussed the obvious necessity of being sure the document (the scrip itself) is properly executed and that it covers, for example, the potential sale of the business from which the promised merchandise or service is to be drawn. A new owner of Louie's spaghetti restaurant may not take kindly to a party of 500 people who, having eaten and drunk their fill, smile and hand over a letter signed by Louie giving $15,000 of scrip against the bill.

The scrip itself should be freely transferable to have maximum value to the seller receiving it. You don't want to sell your property to someone and take $50,000 of nontransferable scrip from a car dealership unless you plan on owning several cars yourself. Instead you would take the scrip in smaller denominations and use them to trade into other items or property.

Be very careful of the time limitation on scrip. I once took some scrip for accommodations at a hotel owned by one of my clients for a fee he owed me. The "due bill," as this kind of scrip is frequently called, had a five-year duration. I still find it amazing how fast the years went by. At the end of the fourth year, over half of the due bill was unused. Bad planning on my part, but I kept putting off full use of the scrip thinking of that big party we would soon have. Then guess what, my client went belly up, and I lost all the remaining value of the "due bill." Don't let this happen to you.

Scrip, by the way, is the same as cash when it comes to the IRS and taxes, except that you cannot pay your tax with spaghetti dinners. Do not be tempted to "forget" the amount of paper money you receive in a transaction. Keep in mind the buyer is reporting having paid you that amount. Remember when you spend scrip on expenses that would normally be tax deductible (like advertising for your business or business cards or any other normal business expense), the cost is the same as if you used cash and will be deductible at the end of the year.

PITFALLS FROM THE BUYER'S SIDE OF THE DEAL

There are some special pitfalls for buyers who give scrip on their own goods or services. Let's say you have just given Barbara $15,000 of scrip that she can use anytime in the future to buy anything in your inventory. So far you have made a good deal. However before you can turn around, there is an increase in the wholesale price of your merchandise and your cost almost doubles. The result: You have promised to give up $15,000 of merchandise that now costs you $18,600. Further cost increases can eat up your investment in a hurry.

Investors using scrip must take into account the potential increase in their cost of goods. If the profit margin is good and the benefits of paying no interest on scrip cover the potential price increase, then you will come out fine. If the cost of your merchandise is very volatile, then be careful.

It is a good idea to try to put some restrictions on the use of scrip by the seller. Setting a maximum on the return of scrip during a week or month can help stop a heavy run against the business during a peak time of normal business. A restriction on transferability is not good for the seller, but she might accept exempting your steady clients, at least, from the transfer.

The toughest pitfall of them all, however, is the inability to cover the drawdown of the scrip. Some buyers give scrip with all good intentions of being able to cover the value when the time comes. Plan for the eventual draw on the scrip, and don't get caught short.

The next two chapters will cover two additional forms of scrip: scrip you buy from someone else (soft paper) and scrip you "buy" on a commission and trade at full value. Since I have covered many of the viewpoints and pitfalls of scrip transactions mostly from the seller's side, these two subsequent chapters will look only at the two variations of scrip transactions and the view from the buyer's side.

9

Watered Scrip

Watered scrip is scrip you buy from someone else on soft terms. Before diving into this chapter, make sure you have reviewed Chapter 8, which discusses the basic concepts of scrip transactions. In Chapter 8 you saw that the use of scrip (papers as a cash equivalent, which you use against your own merchandise or service) is an exciting way of generating more business. Scrip provides an alternative to cash when you are buying property. However not every buyer has a business or service against which he can create scrip. In fact most buyers find themselves without either a service or merchandise of interest to sellers of available real estate.

Fortunately the concept of scrip is so flexible that it is not necessary for you to use your own scrip. Indeed, as I will show you in this chapter and in Chapter 10, you can get scrip from other people and use that as your form of money. Moreover you can "buy" this scrip from other people without spending cash of your own.

Because scrip is essentially manufactured "money" that anyone who has a service or merchandise can create, these same people can "sell" their scrip to you. This sale will need to be initiated by you since most people don't know of this form of transaction. Even if they do know about it, they fail to see how it can benefit them (which gives you another edge).

The purchase of scrip can take several forms. This chapter deals with one way of buying scrip while Chapter 10 deals with a separate method of dealing in the scrip of others. Let's take a look at how the watered scrip works.

THE TIME-SHARE DEAL: BUYING SCRIP ON SOFT TERMS

Assume you approach a shopowner, restauranteur, or other vendor of goods or services with this kind offer: "Give me scrip in the amount of $10,000, which can be spent in your furniture store, and I'll give you a first mortgage on my snake farm with a principal value owed of $7000. The mortgage balloons in three years together with 5 percent interest for the term of the mortgage." (Note that this is a zero coupon type of mortgage. There is no payment at all until the balloon, and when that comes, the total payment will include the principal plus interest for the three years.) Or you might say: "Give me $5000 of scrip good at your spaghetti house, and I'll give you a second mortgage on my home with a principal value of $3000 and will pay you interest and principal of a total of $3500 in 18 months." These are just some examples of offers you can make.

In each case I've given you something for your scrip. You might get a mortgage, a vacant lot, the use of a time-share week, or something else I own. You give up, at some future date, furniture, spaghetti, a car, or whatever the product or service is that you have to offer. Each of these items is a profit item to you, and trading them for scrip is additional business that you might not have had otherwise. The cost to the "banker" is zero. No risk at all if you are willing to take a small discount in the deal. Keep in mind that many businesses discount their merchandise all the time. Shops have mega sales, so it's okay to restrict the scrip to "non-sale" items. Restaurants are notorious for offering two-for-one on meals, without getting anything from that except business that might not have come into the establishment otherwise.

Many businesses buy scrip in the form of plastic credit cards at a big discount. These businesses then use this scrip as a bonus or perk items in other transactions they do. One great example of this came my way several months ago while checking out of a resort that was also a time-share facility. "Mr. Cummings," the checkout person began, "if you fill out this questionnaire you will receive a nice gift." I looked at the two pages of questions and said okay. It took me about five minutes to fill out while he processed my checkout. When I was finished, he handed me two plastic cards each in the amount of $25.00 of food and beverage service at a national restaurant chain—one that I happen to eat at all the time. Now was he giving me $50.00 that someone he works for had shelled out $50.00 hard cash for? Absolutely not. They had boxes of these plastic cards, and the deal is they pay the restaurant only on redemption of the cards and then only at the discounted price they have previously negotiated. Can you guess what the fall-through-the-cracks percentage of lost, unused, or expired cards is? The percentage is very high. In my experience, and depending on the business and location where the scrip can be redeemed, the percentage that falls-through-the-cracks can be as high as 50 percent.

So why not learn from these time-share promotions? You can create the same type of deal with watered scrip. If the vendor or person who supplies the service you want to offer will not sell you his scrip at a discount, then agree to pay the actual amount on the face of the scrip at a discount but only on redemption back to you.

THE FINE POINTS OF THE DEAL

So what do you do with the scrip once you have it? This is a question you have the answer to before you go through the trouble of getting the scrip. The scenario is like this: You are looking for some real estate to buy. You find what you want and make an offer on it. But the seller won't take your snake farm, swamp lot, or whatever other item you are offering as a down payment or part of the transaction. So you ask him, what would you take? Ask him questions. Do you eat out? Where? Do you travel? Where? Pretty soon you have a short list of something this person is interested in.

Now let your fingers do the walking, line up a couple of suppliers for what you think the seller will go for, and then make a cold call. By the way, furniture storeowners are used to selling their goods to decorators at a mega discount. Do not be afraid of offering them a deal where you take their future merchandise off their hands at some immediate benefit to them now.

How this works, for example, is I might take the $10,000 dollars of scrip from the furniture storeowner because I believe the developer of a condo down the street (the very one I would like to live in) has use for fine furniture. As long as I don't overburden the deal with furniture, I have a good shot of removing my hard cash from the down payment and passing on, at a bonus to me, something I didn't own in the first place. The condo developer can use the scrip at the furniture store as he buys furniture for his apartments, so it is cash to him.

Another example is that I might take the $5000 of scrip from the spaghetti house and offer it along with the $5000 in printed money from the car dealer to another seller as all or part of my down payment on a villa in Spain. The rest of the purchase price I finance in some other way through banks, credit unions, or even the seller.

In each instance I am giving the seller of the real estate something more tangible than the concept of additional debt. Obviously if I had been able to give the mortgages or lot east of Naples directly to the sellers of the real estate I wanted to buy, I might have done that. But if I was able to get $10,000 worth of restaurant scrip at a real cost to me of only $5000, I would rather do that than give up a $7000 lot.

You will find that the same seller who took the $10,000 in scrip at the furniture store might have balked at the $10,000 mortgage on the snake farm. The seller of the condo didn't want to hold a mortgage; he would, however, take the furniture. It is all a matter of need. He didn't need the mortgage. He could use the furniture. What he wanted to do was sell the condo. The seller of the furniture, on the other hand, has a nice profit with the furniture and can use the extra business the scrip brings in. Taking the mortgage isn't a problem for a merchant who is making a profit on the sale. Furniture is a high mark-up item. Restaurants throw away food every night. It's snake farms and swamp lots that just sit there.

Some sellers simply don't like the thought of a buyer getting in for "no cash down." This fact works against the buyer trying to pyramid or exchange mortgages on a direct one-on-one basis. But by doing some homework, the buyer can find the kind of scrip the seller would be able to use, and then "buy" the scrip on terms favorable to the investor. Once you are in possession of the right kind of scrip, the real estate transaction can be made. Obviously you don't want to go out and "buy" $10,000 worth of scrip in a fast-food item or some other merchandise or service you have no need for yourself unless you are sure the seller of the real estate you want is going to take it. Therefore you must set up the scrip deal but not close on it until your real estate transaction is finalized.

THE BANKER'S VIEWPOINT

Dealing with the merchants and professionals, who are, in reality *bankers* of their own scrip, can be difficult if you don't come right to the point with the person capable of making the decisions you want. It will do you no good to spend hours trying to convince a clerk at the furniture store of your plan. You must talk with the owner or the decision maker. Go right to the top and spell it out very clearly. Let them read the three chapters on scrip in this book; you might open their eyes to a mountain of new business they can generate for themselves. Explain some of the details, but keep your intended investment secret. You don't want to be too generous with your plan, since you are using their scrip to make your deal.

Bankers of scrip who read this chapter should note that you must exercise every effort to secure your scrip. If you know the person with whom you are dealing, then you can rely on your past history of business dealings to a great degree. However, always insist that the notes, mortgages, or whatever you receive for your scrip are well documented and bona fide. If the deal is that you get paid when you redeem the scrip make sure you still have something as security that you will get paid.

Real estate investors seeking to buy scrip should be prepared to follow the above requirements. The concept of dealing with scrip is more than buying with little or less of your own cash; it is a matter of moving the transaction to a close the best way possible. There will be times when the introduction of scrip to the deal will require proper backup material. For example you might say: ". . . and in addition to all the other aspects of this offer, I'll give you $5000 of scrip good at Magic Carpet Travel Agency for any cruise or package trip to any place in the world you'd like to go (from these following tour operators) . . ." If you already know that you are dealing with someone who travels a lot, this offer just might be the bit of magic that can make the hardest seller melt a little. Of course the better you have done your homework, the better you can select that item to do the trick you want.

VIEWPOINTS AND PITFALLS

The viewpoints and pitfalls for both the buyer and seller are much the same as those discussed in the preceding chapter. The added dimension of a third party banking the scrip can in some instances increase the security to the seller of the real estate, but this factor will depend on the actual case in hand. The general warning to all sellers of real estate is to make sure the scrip you are taking is valid at the establishment on which it is drawn.

One pitfall for the investor using third-party scrip: You give the spaghetti house owner your mortgage for his scrip, which you then use to buy some real estate, only to find later that the spaghetti house owner refuses to honor the scrip. Because of this all investors buying scrip on any terms must assure themselves that the scrip is indeed good and that there are some teeth in the contract to back up the other person's promise.

Sellers can use this technique in reverse. Let's make this a simple example that could happen to you at any time. You want to sell your house because you want to move to another home or town. Think of what you will be spending money on in the relatively near future: moving expenses, new furniture, remodeling costs, and so on. Make up a list and then send a flyer advertising your home to suppliers and vendors of those goods and services. Send the flyer to local bartering organizations (try the phone book), and you might hit it big quickly and save a real estate commission to boot.

10 CHAPTER

Commissioned Scrip

Commissioned scrip is the third method of using scrip. It is a third-party scrip that you redeem at a discount but trade at full value much as you have done with the other two methods. How it differs from the first two, which were discussed in the previous two chapters, is in the way the scrip is obtained.

As I mentioned in the previous two chapters, unless you have very desirable service or merchandise, most of the scrip transactions you make will be with scrip from third parties. Sellers will naturally be more willing to take scrip that can be used to purchase items or services they can use. This fact reduces the amount of scrip you can use from your own business, but it does not reduce the availability of scrip transactions. Some simple homework can give you clues to open up even the toughest deal and offer that hard-nosed seller the right terms.

THE TRAVELING DEAL: BUYING SCRIP ON THE DELAY AT A DISCOUNT

Assume for a moment that you own a travel agency. Your commissions vary according to the kind of trip sold and the carrier used. One of the top commissions paid to travel agencies comes from wholesale ground operators. These companies package tours, which agencies then sell. The agency's pay rate increases as the volume of business increases. It rises to the point where the total commission might be double the beginning rate, and, best of all, the rate at the high end is sometimes retroactive to the first sale.

Selling travel requires no inventory stocking for the travel agent. Unlike a shopkeeper the travel agency does not normally pre-purchase the travel. With this in mind I enter the picture. I want to buy a property owned by a Ms. Reynolds, and I discover that Ms. Reynolds enjoys traveling. (I learn this by asking her administrative assistant if she likes to travel.)

As part of my offer to buy her property, I might include $20,000 of scrip for any travel presented by "the following tour companies." I would then attach to the offer several brochures featuring the travel offerings of those specific tour companies, such as Gateway and American Express. The fact that my offer includes, in addition to all its other aspects, a carte blanche selection for any travel offered in these brochures will naturally get the seller's attention.

Now what I have left out here is the fact that I went to you first (remember you own the travel agency). I offered to become your outside agent for the year, or longer, during which time I am going to sell a package of $20,000 worth of one or more trips from the selected tour companies. For doing this, I want from you a "commission" of 10 percent of the sale. Keep in mind that if I have guessed right about Ms. Reynolds, she may surprise her family with a $60,000 jaunt around the world, even though my offer is just a $20,000 value.

DISCOUNTED SCRIP IS LIKE A ZERO INTEREST LOAN WITH A KICK

After making this deal with you, I now "sell" the scrip to Ms. Reynolds. I give her the other parts of my deal, of course, but until she picks out her travel program, I haven't paid any of the $20,000 needed to redeem the scrip. In fact when she comes into the travel agency, I only have to pay the net of whatever tour she picks. If it is a $20,000 tour, then I pay $18,000 when it is due. But if she picks a $60,000 round-the-world tour, I only pay $14,000 since my commission is $6000, which is deducted from the $20,000 credit to Ms. Reynolds.

In some situations I might cut a deal for an even greater commission, such as 15 percent. After all the travel agency doesn't pay the commission, the tour operator does. Some travel agencies like to increase their gross revenue because it increases there overall commission with most tour operators and cruise lines so the travel agency will benefit because you build up their gross revenue with those tour operators.

Look around your neighborhood and talk to some of the merchants to find some you can work with. Sit down over a cup of coffee and tell them of your plan to help build their business by increasing their volume of sales. If you can't get past this first step with the merchants, then let them read this book—or at least the three chapters on scrip. It could change their lives.

PITFALLS IN COMMISSIONED SCRIP

Remember that with commissioned, or third-party, scrip you don't actually pay for the scrip until it is redeemed. This can cause some problems—for you and for the "banker."

From your point of view the most important thing about having scrip like this is that you can pay for it at a discount. Keep in mind, though, that you must get your deal with the "banker" in writing. You don't want to find yourself charged with a penalty on the scrip because of a misunderstanding about the commission you were to earn. Have it clear that until the scrip is turned in you don't have to pay anything. Make sure that the contract is good for the specific items covered and that the merchant once cleared by you will redeem it.

The "banker," who in the earlier example is the owner of the travel agency, must be sure that you will pay once the scrip is redeemed. The best way to assure this is for the scrip to state that the redemption is to be covered by you when turned in to the store or merchant. Just add a simple clause on the scrip such as: Any merchandise [or service] against which this scrip is to be used for payment will be delivered to the bearer of the scrip within five days of presentation at the merchant's store, and upon monetary redemption by [your name].

A QUICK REVIEW OF THE THREE SCRIP TRANSACTIONS

In these last three chapters I have presented three types of scrip transactions.

1. **Scrip:** This is the paper deal you write against your own services or merchandise. Scrip is your first choice if you have

the service or merchandise to offer and if the seller will take it. It gives you the advantage of making a profit from the sale of your own service or merchandise, as well as giving you an interest-free loan. Don't hesitate to use this technique anytime you can. All the seller will do if she doesn't like the idea is eliminate it from the offer. Then again she might take some of the service and offer the broker the balance as part of the commission.

2. **Watered Scrip:** This scrip deal is when you buy from someone else at soft paper. This type can sometimes be bought at a big discount. In fact you might buy scrip from one person at a big discount using scrip you get from a third person at a discount. For example Matt owns a restaurant. I offer him $10,000 worth of scrip he can redeem at Magic Carpet Travel Agency for cruises or other trips. I have a commission due me on the $10,000 of 10 percent, so it will only cost me $9000 when Matt turns in the scrip. But because he gets the travel money now, he sells me scrip at his restaurant at a big discount. He gives me $20,000 worth of spaghetti dinners in scrip in exchange for the travel benefit. I have made a great deal if I can get someone to take the spaghetti off of my hands.

3. **Commissioned Scrip:** This technique is a third-party scrip you redeem at a discount but trade at full value. Because of adding a third party, it opens a vast world of potential scrip deals. The options are limitless. So it is up to you to do your homework: "Seek and ye shall find."

11

CHAPTER

The Commission Down Payment

For some investors, the real estate agent's commission is a compelling reason to have an active real estate license. Real estate commissions, after all, can add up. If you are pinching every penny, then the salesperson's split, which might be yours if you are legally entitled to it, can aid in making the transaction work for you.

When a buyer of real estate is a broker or salesperson, he can, under the right procedure, participate in the real estate commission that would be due if the property were listed to include such a commission. The proper procedure might depend on the state, but, speaking from an ethics point of view, all real estate salespeople participating in the sale and commission should make sure they have carefully and duly notified the seller that they are licensed real estate salespeople or brokers. Some states allow a party to the transaction—the buyer and/or the seller—actually to participate in the fee as well. The quickest way to check this out would be to call the office for business and professional regulations in your state and ask for the real estate section. Once connected with that department, ask if it is legal for a nonlicensed real estate person, acting as a buyer or seller in a specific transaction, to participate in part of a commission in a transaction. Be sure to find out what, when, and to whom the notice should be given of that fact.

An example of such an event would be one where I, as a broker, entered into a purchase of a property listed with another office. It would be natural for me to be interested in buying a prime property that was on the market. First I would draw up an offer spelling out my intent to buy the property and indicating the terms of the offer. I would include a paragraph that said something like this:

> "It is herein noted that Jack Cummings, principal broker with Cummings Realty, Inc., is a licensed real estate broker within the state of Florida and is buying this property for his own account, and that other licensed brokers or salesmen within the state of Florida, or outside the state, may participate in the purchase either now or in the future. This fact does not waive any rights that Cummings Realty, Inc., has in participating in the realty fee or commission due as per the MLS (or other listing form) with Try County Realty, Inc."

As a buyer I would have another option, which I frequently use, and that is to make offers without commission to anyone. I make my offers net to the seller, leaving out my participation in the fee. But at the same time, I would deduct it from the amount of my offer. The end result is basically the same. I get the benefit of what commission I would have obtained but do not let the commission issue enter the picture. Generally I use this technique when the seller is another real estate broker or salesperson. Usually the seller recognizes that I would have been able to claim half the fee, so he adjusts the co-broker's fee accordingly at the final accounting.

If the commission was 6 percent of the total price (the average percentage across the country for single-family homes), the salesperson in the deal, after splits with his office and the co-broker office, could expect to receive anywhere from 50 percent to 80 percent of the office portion of the deal. So if I were buying a $180,000 property at 6 percent, the total commission would be $10,800. If there were another broker (the listing office) involved, then my office would get $5400, or half of the split. As a salesperson with my own firm, I would then be entitled to at least half of that (depending on my performance plateau), or $2700. If I were paying 10 percent down, or $18,000, I would have reduced my cash down to only $15,300. And you can see that if I received 100 percent of the commission, I would have reduced the cash down to only $7200.

THE FINE POINTS OF THE DEAL

Not all deals are made through outright purchases. Indeed it is not unusual for a deal to be made using the Internal Revenue Code (IRC) 1031 or other form of real estate exchange. The IRC 1031 is, in my opinion, the "last loophole to maximize reinvestment in real estate." When brokers deal together in exchanges, there is a fee due from both parties of the deal. In these events sometimes the custom is to "pool and split" the commissions between brokers. In essence all the sellers in the deal will owe a commission on the property they are contributing to the exchange. If I were exchanging one of my properties for something else, I would potentially owe a commission myself into this pool. If the commission from my side of the exchange is larger than that from the other side, then there is no benefit to me in "pooling and splitting." In these situations I will do a YKYIKM. This is called a "Yook-kem" and means simply, You Keep Yours—I Keep Mine. In short, if there is a fee from each side of the deal, one broker is telling the other that each will keep the fee from his listing and not pool and split the fees. Obviously if the commission I am liable for is $70,000 and the other side is liable for only $30,000, I'm far better off letting the other broker keep his while I keep mine.

The amount of commission in larger deals frequently depends on the value the broker places on himself at the time he lists the property. I have a high regard for my abilities, thus I feel I earn the substantial fees I ask for my services as a marketer of property. Other brokers, however, sometimes take high-priced listings at low percentages with the hope that a more qualified broker will sell the property for them. I run into these brokers from time to time and don't feel bad at all in using a YKYIKM deal.

THE SELLER'S VIEWPOINT

When you are the seller and you are dealing with a real estate broker or salesperson who represents that they are the buyer (such notice is required in most states), you should review the situation before getting into serious negotiations with that person. The key is to ascertain what that person's relationship is to your property. If you had the property listed with a real estate firm, does this broker or salesperson work for that firm? If they do, then they may have some inside information about your motivation that the general buying public does not have. This may or may not affect the transaction from your point of view, but you should be careful of a situation where your listing salesperson may have divulged critical information that another buyer uses to get a steal before other buyers see the property. If you are satisfied that there is no such connection and the notice of their agency relationship is okay with you, then proceed in a normal offer and counteroffer scenario.

Take note, however that there are several kinds of brokers and sales-people. Here are just a few to keep in mind:

Type A: The broker or salesperson who is in the business to sell real estate but will from time to time buy what he is sold on himself after making a diligent effort to find another buyer.

Type B: The broker or salesperson who is in the business of buying real estate and utilizes his inside knowledge to make the best deals for himself.

Type C: Brokers or salespeople who act as "buyer's brokers," representing the buyer and not the seller. Most states require the agent to include a statement in the contract or in a listing form whom they represent, either the buyer or seller, or if they represent only the transaction. If the agent represents the buyer, and the seller is aware of this, the agent can use every bit of knowledge he can obtain to aid the buyer in acquiring the property at the most favorable price and terms possible. When the agent represents the seller, the agent is bound by most state laws governing real estate transactions to do everything legally possible to help the seller maximize the return from the sale. A transaction agent is one who represents neither party and is paid as shown in the offer (generally by the seller). Buyer brokers, even though they have given notice that they represent the buyer, will be paid as the contract illustrates, which can be by the buyer or by the seller.

Type D: Brokers or salesmen who didn't know there was a difference between Type A and Type B.

Naturally the first three types described above are the clearest of all possibilities. In reality there are various shades of the four. It makes little difference which category you deal with as long as you know which one you are dealing with.

THE BUYER'S OR BROKER'S VIEWPOINT

The buyer (or the broker) must be sure he has done everything he can to keep himself clear of any unethical dealings. The opportunity to take advantage of an unknowing seller is a constant reality.

Most buyers, however, view the taking of a commission rightfully earned in the sale or disposition of a property as both legal and ethical. Informing the seller of your intent and position and giving him ample time to seek out other advice is only logical; using your in-depth knowledge of your profession is prudent.

PITFALLS FROM THE SELLER'S SIDE OF THE DEAL

Sellers should be careful of brokers who list their property for sale and then, after a short period of time, offer to buy the property themselves. Mind you, I said to be careful, not to avoid the situation. It's not unheard of for a broker to deliberately undervalue a property so that he can take advantage of a quick profit. One way to avoid this problem is to have more than one brokerage firm present you with a proposed marketing plan for your property. This program should include:

1. A list of all comparable properties in the area that have sold within the last six months
2. A list of all similar properties for sale at the moment
3. The suggested offering price for you to list the property

It is a good idea for you to have some idea of the market yourself, and a good way to start is to take a look at several of the properties on the "for sale" list mentioned above. Keep in mind, however, that as a property owner you will tend to overestimate the value of your own home.

PITFALLS FROM THE BUYER'S OR BROKER'S SIDE OF THE DEAL

People who become real estate salespeople for the purpose of investing in real estate must bend over backward to be open and aboveboard, lest their ethics be called into question. Buyers also face some interesting pitfalls when they attempt to get a full return of their commission in the deal. The usual problem in this kind of deal is the broker who forgets the real advantage of using a broker in the first place, and thus finds himself isolated in the deal.

As a seller I rarely negotiate my own deal. I may not even want to meet the buyer, except on the most social of occasions or for introductions. As a buyer I never want to be in the same room with the seller when my offer is presented, and I don't want to do any face-to-face negotiating as a buyer.

Why? Because most buyers and sellers put themselves at a disadvantage when they negotiate face-to-face with the other side. In my opinion there should always be an intermediary to allow the buyer or seller to discuss the offer without having to give away any weakness. What kind of weakness? Nonverbal cues and body language can speak more than words. As a broker myself presenting a client's offer, I have seen everything from throwing the offer on the floor and stomping on it to tearing the offer up into a thousand pieces. This intermediary is one of the important roles a broker can play, and both parties need a strong and competent person to negotiate the deal for them. The ability of the broker to take the heat of the transaction is important. A good broker will absorb the anger and the frustrations of the buyer and seller, rather than let them direct those feelings at each other.

I maintain this position when I make deals for others. I want the buyer and seller to blow up at me and not at the other party. I also want the buyer and seller to have time to think over their answers, not to have to come up with a fast answer while the other party is sitting across the table. Because this is real life, when I am a buyer I look for a good salesperson to stand between the seller and me. That salesperson earns his percentage of the deal, and all parties end up happy.

12 CHAPTER

Turn Land into Cash

The concept of selling the land under a building and then leasing it back isn't new. In some societies leasehold ownership of land by its users and occupants is commonplace. Two good examples of this are found in England and Hawaii. A real estate investor may better her cash position and reduce her investment capital through the landlease technique.

THE TIE-UP DEAL: MAKING A LANDLEASE ATTRACTIVE

Due to the lack of tax shelter inherent in land, there is no economic benefit of ownership of the land itself as long as the cost to lease it is less than the cost to own it. In essence if you can lease land for $10,000 per year and in doing so free up $100,000 of cash that would have gone to buy the land (or can be generated by the sale of the land), then the economic questions to ask are: "Can I make more from the $100,000 than the annual cost of $10,000?"; "Will I have to forgo the purchase of the property because I can't come up with the extra $100,000 cash down?"; and "Can I lease the property on terms that will enable me to get full use of the improvements and to benefit from appreciation at the same time?"

Keep in mind that leasing land does have some disadvantages to both the buyer and seller. And I will cover those disadvantages and advantages, from each of these points of view, later in this chapter. As a buying technique selling land and then leasing it back is a very refreshing way to structure your transaction. It can enable you to break down some real barriers with stubborn sellers who have some specific problems. In short this technique can frequently get you a property that has eluded more astute buyers.

Let's say you are interested in buying a motel, but you don't have the $500,000 cash required by the seller. The simplest use of the landlease technique would be to tie up the property for sufficient time to enable you to find a buyer for the land under the motel. This buyer will agree to pay you in cash for the land, which you in turn lease back.

For example, Jon was negotiating on a 100-unit hotel in Myrtle Beach, South Carolina. The deal was all set at $5,000,000 for the whole package of land, buildings, and furniture, fixtures, and equipment (FF&E). The seller was motivated because she needed cash and was going to hold $500,000 in secondary financing secured by another hotel that Jon owned. Jon was able to get a commitment from a local savings and loan for $3,500,000. So far, so good, except that Jon knew he was going to be short $400,000 in closing the deal because all he wanted to put into the transaction was $600,000. He had more cash available but wanted to use it to upgrade the hotel, since it badly needed some tender loving care.

Jon had time, however, to find an investor who would be interested in a management-free income and who would buy the land and allow Jon to lease it back. Jon went to some of the investors he had done business with before and made the deal. The closings took place at the same time: Jon got the motel, the owner of the motel made her deal, and everyone was happy. (Jon, by the way, had an option to buy the land back a few years later. The intention was to eventually refinance the property and pick up the land at the same time.)

In another transaction Brad was trying to get a seller to hold a large second mortgage on a small strip store he was trying to buy. The owner of the strip store was reluctant to hold a second mortgage, so Brad shifted techniques: He suggested the owner keep the land, sell Brad the improvements only, and Brad would lease the land.

The economics of the landlease, which is much like an interest-only mortgage, were in fact more favorable to Brad as long as he was able to buy the land in the future. The owner of the strip store took the landlease deal because there was always the chance that Brad wouldn't be able to pick up the option, and then ownership of the land subject to the lease would be better than the mortgage.

THE FINE POINTS OF THE DEAL: EXAMINING TRADE-OFFS

While the landlease technique has its benefits and works well if used appropriately, as in any deal, there is give and take in using this technique. The finesse of the deal depends on these five elements:

1. **The terms of the leaseback.** If the payments on the lease are much the same or less than mortgage payments would be, then the first part of the comparison of ownership versus leasehold is solved. On the other hand if the lease would be more costly than a mortgage, there is no economic benefit in the lease if a mortgage to cover the cost of the land was available. When the cost to lease the land is greater than a mortgage, the only reason to trade a mortgage for a landlease is because the seller will only do the deal if the land is leased. Why? It might be because the seller has such a low basis in the land that the tax on a sale would substantially reduce the reinvestment of the capital.

2. **The conditions of the lease.** The lease must be realistic for the technique to work well. A three-year lease with an option to buy at the end of that time would be ridiculous, and would obviously force the buyer to pick up the option to purchase. Also, the IRS will look at the terms of the lease as well as the conditions to the deal if there were any question as to the establishment of a lease or a mortgage. This difference could have tax consequences for the seller who didn't want to have a sale (even an installment sale) in that year. A mortgage denotes a sale, while a lease means the owner still owns the land. A short lease with option to buy might have merit if the buyer knew that the property could be refinanced at favorable terms once the property had been improved and upgraded. If that were the plan, it would still be a better idea to allow some extra time on the lease to cover the eventuality of an economic downturn in the business. As long as the lease provides for a span of time in which the option to purchase can be exercised, then the added time on the lease does not hurt the buyer. The buyer of the land wants to set up the best terms, of course, but the investor using the technique does

control the deal to the extent that she can insist on certain
requirements to make the whole deal work.

3. **The terms of the buyback.** In this technique the investor will
want to have an option to buy back the land she is leasing. This,
in my opinion, is very important, because even if the economics
of leasing are favorable throughout the life of the investor,
another investor looking to buy the property might think
differently. Landlease transactions without an option to buy them
out are not as attractive as a similar deal with a buyout option. If
you are the investor using this technique, make sure this option is
not too restrictive or you may get caught in a tough money
market and lose the opportunity to buy out your landlease. You
would not want to enter into a 99-year landlease with a purchase
option that read: ". . . can be exercised in the month of November
2068, and at no other time." Why would a seller want to have a
very tough or specific option date? It could be connected to some
other event and could have a major impact on estate planning if
the option was exercised at some other time. I have seen
landleases that had one specific deadline date with notice of
exercising the option given each year for a period of several
years; if not given on or before that specific date, the option could
not be exercised that year and then after a set period of years the
option expired. Make sure you have a reasonable length of time
in which to exercise your option. The optimum for the would-be
buyer would be, "can be exercised at any time."

4. **The escalators.** If you can obtain agreement on a fixed price to
buy out the land and have a lease price that never goes up, then
you don't have any escalators in the deal. But usually there are
some, somewhere. Buyers of the land want a cost-of-living
clause to enable the rent to keep pace with the rise of inflation.
They also want to get a higher price for the land if and when the
option is exercised.

Investors must take these escalators into consideration. If
you anticipate exercising the option on or before the tenth year,
however, you don't give up anything if your escalators begin at
the tenth year. Unless, of course, your timing puts you right in
the middle of a "sorry, but we don't have any money to refinance
your deal" epic.

There was a hotel in Fort Lauderdale sitting directly on the beachfront. It was built 40 years ago on leased land. The land had an original value of $300,000 based on what similar land was selling for in the same area. The owner of the land wanted to keep the land, so she leased it to the investor who wanted to build the hotel. The landlease payment was $30,000 per year. It was a fixed landlease with no increases in the rate of the lease. Over the years, as a broker in various transactions I sold the hotel four times. Each time the price went up from $1,000,000 subject to the landlease, to a final sale of $6,000,000 subject to the landlease. The final buyer had to negotiate with the executor of the estate of the original landowner to buy out the lease. Mind you, even though the lease payment was only $30,000 a year, the executor knew there was more value than 10 times that amount. The investor who later tore down the hotel to build a condominium paid well over $2,000,000 (in the form of cash and some condos) to get ownership of the land.

5. **Getting a lock on the deal in the first place.** You sure as hell don't want to go out and knock down the forest finding a buyer for the land in your up-and-coming deal, only to find that, by the time you get back, the owner of the property has sold it to someone else. Always make sure you have the deal locked in. If you are the buyer of the land, make sure the entrepreneur has a firm lock on the deal.

THE SELLER'S VIEWPOINT

If you are the seller and the investor is giving you 100 percent of your equity in cash, then the methods she uses to finance the deal are not important to you, provided they are legal. However if you are holding some paper on the deal, say a third mortgage, and you find that 100 percent of the cash the investor uses to close comes from a separate buyer of part (or all) of the land, then there may be a reason for you to be concerned. It's true that the ownership of the land would be subordinate to your mortgage (unless your closing agent slipped up or you had agreed otherwise). In this kind of deal, the buyer has presold a part of the real estate she is buying from you. In this instance it is the land under the buildings she is acquiring from you. Her intention is to sell the land to generate the cash needed to close with you. She then leases back the land. So far, while rare, this is not that uncommon a transaction. The person who has purchased the land now is holding a landlease which, from his point of view, is a stronger position to be in than holding a fourth mortgage. However as long as you (as the original seller and holder of the third mortgage) have not subordinated (given up) your rights as a superior lien holder ahead of the new landowner, holding the landlease will be secondary to your mortgage. In the event of a foreclosure your rights are behind the first and second mortgage but ahead of the landowner's rights.

However, whenever a buyer gets in without any equity or risked capital, it is possible that if the going gets tough the investor will step aside and let it go. In a scramble to protect your own rights in the foreclosure, you might find yourself spending more time and money than you want to (or have).

THE INVESTOR'S VIEWPOINT

As an investor, you will find that the landlease technique works nicely to help leverage your deal. If there is existing financing at low rates, then instead of asking a seller to hold a second mortgage, give her the landlease approach. Remember, your terms on the lease and the ultimate buyback will determine whether you have made a good deal.

PITFALLS FROM BOTH SIDES OF THE DEAL

The biggest pitfall in this technique is excessive leverage where the buyer comes into the deal with too little real equity. This affects both parties because it increases risk for the seller who is holding some paper, and it can add excessive burden to the carrier of the property.

There are trade-offs that occur in the terms of the leaseback that should be taken very seriously. The party who will end up leasing the land will want the ultimate owner of the land to subordinate to financing. It might be an existing or a new mortgage the buyer will want to use to finance the balance of the transaction, or it could be a future mortgage that would occur when the property is sold or remodeled or just to pull cash out of the deal. Subordination can be risky. What happens is the owner of the land subordinates his or her rights to another party who then either lends money or acquires the land under the property. If there were to be a default on the mortgage, the mortgage holder (or land owner) would have the right to foreclose on the building and the land. Whenever there is subordination involved, it is critical to assume the worst might occur.

The following are some specific elements the new owner of the land would want to have in the purchase and leaseback situation:

- Either no additional subordination or at best a single, one time subordination with a limit to the amount of the loan and interest rate charged.
- Very tight guidelines as to how much and what the proceeds could be used for.
- Absolute notice from both the mortgagee and the mortgagor as to prompt payment of mortgage payments.
- A provision allowing the landowner to call the lease in default should the lessee become in default on any of the other debt on the property or fail to make all property tax and assessments in a timely manner.
- A provision allowing the landowner the right to pay any delinquent mortgages or taxes to keep those items from causing liens or clouds on the title.

The majority of pitfalls, however, can be overcome or reduced through the use of sound economics in the deal. Does the buyer have the financial ability to support the added payments? Can the property support itself?

The use of a good real estate lawyer in the drafting of the lease is essential. There are all kinds of leases, and unfortunately some lawyers use boilerplate leases that don't fit anything but boilers. Each deal is different in this kind of transaction, and each lease would be tailored to fit the exact needs and intentions of the parties. The lease has to have certain provisions to protect the investor's option to buy out, or the technique will be far too risky for him to proceed.

13 CHAPTER

The Little Old Lady Technique

In the previous chapter I illustrated a technique in which you sold land to generate cash and, in the final result, you end up with the improvements. With this creative technique, the objective is to establish an income-producing landlease owned by you.

Owning land under improvement and having a long-term lease on that land, though, is not usually the optimum investment. The reasons for this are simple economics. If someone else has the use of your land for a long term (say beyond your anticipated life span), that investor—not you—is the one to benefit from appreciation of the land. Even if you have rent escalations, such as periodic increases tied to the cost-of-living index, the appreciation of the combined land and improvements may likely exceed inflation. So the benefits to the landowner, who continues to have essentially the same income benefits, are minimal. Landleases often end up in estate planning, and many of them are owned by wives who, now widowed, have a steady income without management problems. This is why I call the technique covered in this chapter the little old lady technique. So this fixed, or quasifixed, income isn't suitable for every investor unless you have used this technique as a wealth builder.

Let's look at the situation involving a 10 percent landlease. This term reflects the rent paid by the lessee in relation to land value. If the value of the land (as part of the total) were $100,000 then a 10 percent lease would have an annual rental of $10,000. Tie a cost-of-living increase to this on an annual adjustment basis and you would have the rent going up by the same percentage as the cost of living. If the cost of living increased 3 percent over the first year, then the rent would go from $10,000 to $10,360. Value, however, often goes up faster than the cost of living. Keep in mind that actual benefits of ownership are many, and the totality of these benefits can mean more to the owner than the income generated. Do not forget equity buildup and other personal benefits such as use and job security that can come from ownership of income-producing properties.

Real estate investors looking to build wealth in a hurry often scoff at this kind of investment as a slow way to build a fortune. But if the total investment you made to get this $10,000-per-year rental income was only $1000, then you have hit on a potential gold mine. The idea is to use this little old lady technique to build your bank account.

THE A & B DEAL: KEEPING THE LAND (A) AND SELLING THE BUILDING (B)

Cory found a nice but vacant industrial building of 30,000 square feet. The price for the building was $900,000. The property had an existing mortgage of $300,000 at 9½ percent interest with 15 years to go. The seller indicated he would take back some secondary financing but needed at least $200,000 down. The rest of the price to the seller would be at 12 percent interest-only, with a balloon payment in 15 years.

Cory tied up the property with a contract subject to his finding a tenant for the building within 60 days. If he didn't find one to his satisfaction, the deal was off and the $1000 deposit he had put up on good faith would be returned. (Yes, $1000 is often all you need to put up on even a million-dollar deal.) Cory then turned around and restructured the deal, offering the building for sale. His ad looked like this:

OWN YOUR OWN
30,000 sq. foot industrial building.
It can be yours for less than you'd
pay for rent. $200,000 down. Annual
pmt to own $3.25 per sq. ft per year.

This deal is targeted to a user who either had some cash or could use another one of the creative techniques presented in this book to get the cash from another person. In Cory's situation here is how the deal played out:

- Cory tied up the property.
- There was an existing mortgage of $300,000 with an annual payment of $37,590 in principal and interest. This mortgage would be paid off in 15 years.
- The seller was going to hold a $400,000 mortgage at 12 percent interest-only with a payment of $48,000 per year.
- $200,000 cash had to be generated by Cory to close.
- Cory formulated a landlease (subordinate to the existing and new financing). This landlease had an annual payment of $12,000 per year. The other terms were up to negotiation with the user.
- The buyer of the leasehold had to pay all those amounts shown above. He got the property and the ultimate appreciation. He even was able to extract an option to buy the land from Cory in the future.
- Cory ended up with the landlease and the income.

You will note that the user might have circumvented Cory and dealt directly with the original seller. This could have happened, of course, and might happen to you if you don't make absolutely sure you have the property legally tied up. Cory used the option technique to accomplish this. You should never tell the buyer of the building that you are under contract on the property unless asked.

The Power of the A & B Transaction

Any time you split a property deal into its two elements—the land and the improvements—you are dealing with the A & B transaction. Buying this way can have great impact on your future, and save you taxes when you sell.

In the case of keeping the land in the kind of deal Cory just completed, there were several interesting benefits that accrued. The most interesting and profitable was the ability to turn over a property with little involvement and low monetary risk. Cory had to spend some time finding the ultimate buyer, of course; but aside from his time, his total investment was the $1000 deposit on the contract and a few dollars in sales ads.

Had Cory turned over the entire property for an instant profit he would now be dealing with earned income—and higher taxes. There are a lot of get-rich-fast schemes that will work for some of you in good times, and some of these schemes tell you to buy low and turn over fast at any profit. It is a great idea, except that it creates something called non-capital-gain taxed income, as well as potentially classifying the investor as a real estate dealer. When you are a dealer in real estate, you are no longer able to freely take capital gains tax treatment. You want to avoid the "dealer" classification. In the A & B transaction just shown, Cory didn't actually sell the property; in reality he leased the property with an option to buy. He did this by selling a leasehold interest to the user of the improvements, subject to the landlease. Since the title to the land is still in Cory's hands, there has been no actual sale of the real estate. If Cory kept the property he could always sell the landlease once he has established it as a long-term investment subject to capital-gains tax. Or he could use the 1031 exchange technique and avoid paying any tax on the subsequent transaction.

Tax considerations are important both now and in the future. Since the land generally appreciates faster than the improvements and since the IRS permits the improvements to be depreciated but not the land, the retention of both (A and B) in separate ownership each controlled by the same investor can have favorable results in future sales. The potential benefits will depend on your tax bracket and circumstances as well as the kind of property with which you deal. Generally any property that is underimproved in relation to the zoning or is outdated according to current growth trends will reach a point where the value of the land surpasses the value of the improvements; thus the value of the land is now the value of the total property. This type of property is ideal for an A & B deal. If the investor anticipates a fast turnover, the A & B deal can prevent (or help, at least) his being classified as a dealer and can be a good financing tool for the transaction.

THE FINE POINTS OF THE DEAL

As with any transaction, there are advantages and disadvantages. Let's take a closer look at Cory's deal and examine both of these. In terms of the advantages, this technique can maintain Cory's capital-gains position since he did not sell the land, he only leased it with an option to buy in the future. If the rest of the deal was a washout, that is, if the buyer of the lease paid the same for those improvements as Cory did in the beginning, there would be no tax.

Since the purchase made by Cory would show an allocation between land and building, some of the cash paid to Cory should be allocated as *option money against the purchase of the land.* If the ultimate purchase of the land from Cory was a part of the transaction in the form of an option (lease with option), then part of the down payment for the leasehold should apply as option money, which would be credited to an ultimate purchase of the land.

So why should anyone do this? Let's see what happens when we look at Cory's purchase and allocate $50,000 of the deal to land value.

Purchased the total package:	$900,000
Value of A (Land)	$ 50,000
Value of B (Improvements)	$850,000

Any price over $850,000 for the leasehold (B) will create a profit. So Cory does the deal described in this chapter as follows:

- Cory sells the leasehold.

Buyer assumes the existing mortgage	$300,000
then assumes the second mortgage	$400,000
pays cash for the balance	$150,000
	$850,000

- Cory leases the land at an annual rent of $12,000 plus escalators on a cost-of-living basis.
- The purchase of an *option to buy the land* sometime in the future. This money must be creditable to that ultimate price. The buyer pays $50,000 cash upfront.

Because the $50,000 needed by Cory to close the deal was paid to him as option money, he will not declare it as income until the year the option is exercised. Since the money isn't known to be interest or part of a capital-gain transaction, it will not be taxed (according to current law) until the actual date on which the option is exercised.

Now let's take a look at the disadvantages of this type of transaction. One disadvantage is that many buyers are reluctant to lock themselves into a landlease situation. Most of the time this is due to a lack of understanding of how this technique works. Investors using the A & B transaction will need to spend time seeing to it that the ultimate user understands the advantages to him.

The other disadvantage is the risk to the investment, which is subordinated to the existing financing. As the land has usually been subordinated to the existing financing, a forfeiture on the mortgages by the owner of the improvements will cause the landowner to step in and protect his interest or lose the land. This can be very dangerous if the investor is not careful. Cory was careful to make sure he checked the credit of the user. Of course his risk was only $1000. Yours might be much more.

From the other side of the transaction—the ultimate user of the improvements—there are no real problems other than the normal business decision of selecting this property over others that might be available. There should be no reluctance to make this deal, because the land is not being purchased. And if the values represented by Cory are sound, then the user benefits by having a landlease at 12 percent, which may be below the current interest rate for mortgages. The overall benefits to the user are excellent and make the format acceptable in a wide range of transactions.

THE PITFALLS OF THE DEAL

As in any turnover the key is control of the package. Cory would have a very difficult time making this deal work if there were a wide selection of other properties below his total price, no matter what control he had over the seller. So he must control the deal in other ways—by being within the right price range and by using the landlease as a cheap form of "third mortgage" to make the package more attractive.

Never attempt to put this kind of deal into its user stage until you have a bona fide and signed contract from the owner. A handshake or verbal deal here, or anywhere in the world of real estate, is a mistake.

14

The 110 Percent Financing Trick

Despite the ups and downs of the stock market, it is possible, in nearly any real estate market, to get all the cash needed to close a real estate transaction from one lender and still have cash left over. What I mean is that you can buy a $200,000 property and walk away from the closing with $20,000 or more cash in your pocket. Or you buy a $500,000 property and pocket $100,000 plus are the owner of some more income-producing real estate. It is a matter of proper planning to ensure that you get all the cash you need, plus ending up with some extra cash, which you could use for fixing up money or for a down payment on another property.

There are several different circumstances that offer the opportunity to obtain this kind of financing. Often you can do this with only one lender and other times a motivated seller helps out, as you will see in this technique.

THE NEW CONSTRUCTION 110 PERCENT DEAL

Lenders, such as savings and loans, commercial banks, insurance companies, and pension funds, like to become involved with new construction loans. Although this money is usually loaned through local lenders, the funds may actually come from insurance companies that purchase packages of loans for their investment portfolio. Competition for good loans can be fierce, and money is often offered with very reasonable rates and low closing costs. All lenders, however, look to establish a fair and equitable loan-to-value ratio. That ratio will vary between lenders and the type of real estate being financed. Loans for single-family homes or small apartment properties for example, often range from 75 percent loan-to-value to as high as 95 percent loan-to-value. These higher percentages are attainable with added help from FHA lending or VA (also called GI Loans), which insure the top 15 percent of the loan amount in order to give the lender a spread of risk. In every loan presentation there is the opportunity to make your case that the property is really more valuable than what you are paying for it. In essence, while you have an option to buy a property for $500,000, the real value is actually $650,000. If you are successful in making this case, then there will be a lender who will loan to you on that value and not your purchase price.

There are many ways to establish a higher value on a property, and I will show you several such scenarios that work to that end. Most situations will all have a similar circumstance. The property you will ultimately buy will have the promise of greater value. By this I mean you will look for property to purchase at one value but if you do something to either the property or the circumstance surrounding the property, it will be worth more. If you have done your due diligence correctly, the increase in value can come almost overnight. If there is nothing you can do to change the value of a property then you should not buy it in the first place.

Optioned Property with New Improvements

You look for and find a property that fits the "promise of value" just mentioned. You enter into a purchase deal with the owner of the property as follows. You settle on a fair price, and then show a list of some things you want to do to improve the property. You will want to do cosmetic changes such as painting, landscaping, and adding a new front door. The owner gives you an option to purchase the property within six months (obviously this is a negotiating item), based on accomplishing the work or improvements you have indicated to him you will do, even though he still owns the property. If it is his home, he can continue to live there; if it is a rental property, he can keep collecting the rent.

You invest some time and a little money in doing the improvements to this property. Once you have some results to show, you go to a local savings and loan and make your loan presentation. You ask for 125 percent of the option price, and you back up your presentation on comparable sales of properties that are similar, not to what you contracted to buy, but the value the property now represents. This method works best when the seller is motivated to sell, and can give you access to the property so that you can accomplish the desired improvements. But if this technique doesn't work for you, there are other variations that may help you achieve the desired end results.

Slide Equity from the Seller

All that the lender needs to know is that you have equity in the deal. This means that you are putting cash or some other equity in as a part of the purchase price. Examine this for a moment. If you can get the seller to take something as a part of the purchase price, for example your Lexus, as part of the down payment, then that counts as part of the equity side of your purchase price. Say you are trying to purchase a $200,000 duplex and you offer the seller the Lexus, which is worth $20,000, as a part of the deal. Already you have generated 10 percent of the value of the property. Suddenly you only need $180,000 to make the deal fly based on the purchase price of the contract you have already negotiated.

But what if you could increase the value of the property by showing the lender that you intend to or already have made certain improvements that will allow you to increase the rent by $4000 or more a year? That increase in revenue can increase the value by another $50,000. Wow, you might think, how can I do that? Remember that any increase in the bottom line will increase value by the increased net operating income divided by the investor's anticipated yield. Here is why that happens. Assume the investor has acquired a property on the basis that the property will give that investor a cash return of 8 percent of the cash that investor has put down on the property. If the cash down was $100,000, that investor would expect a cash return of $8000 per year. Keep in mind that this investment is just the down payment, and the property might be a $500,000 apartment building. If you were the owner of this building having made that same investment, and were able to increase the cash return to $12,000 per year, you will have increased the value of the property to any other investor who would be satisfied with an 8 percent return by $50,000. What you did was improve the overall operation of the property, and by a combination of rent increases and cost savings generate an additional $4000 a year. Divide that amount by .08, which represents 8 percent, and you come up with a $50,000 value increase. To accomplish this, a simple increase of the gross rent by $333.00 per month will do that. This increase slides directly to the bottom line, and the value is increased accordingly. Since this property is a 10-unit apartment complex, that means you have to show the lender you can reasonably increase the rent per unit by an average of $33.30 per unit per month. This is not too difficult if you have done your homework.

Add a Landlease to the Deal

Recall the landlease technique? This can move you into a better than 110 percent deal. Let's look at how this can work.

You want to purchase a 21-unit apartment complex. It is priced at $1,000,000. You know if you do some management and maintenance that you can increase the bottom line revenue by $23,000. This will increase the value of the property by slightly more or less than $225,000. You offer the seller $800,000 with a subordinated landlease that costs you $15,000 a year in lease payments, with an option to purchase the land back any time within the first 10 years of your ownership for $200,000. At the end of that period your purchase option jumps to $250,000 (but you are not so stupid to let that happen, so you will buy the land back long before that). You show the lender, vis-à-vis your loan application, that the real value of the property is $1,225,000. The landlease is subordinated to their first lien, so if they were to loan $900,000 on the deal, their loan to value ratio would be $900,000 to $1,225,000, or a loan-to-value ratio of 73 percent to 27 percent. This is an acceptable ratio for the lender and would cash you back $100,000, which you could use to make this deal really fly.

THE KEY TO THE 110 PERCENT DEAL

Appreciation of some kind is the crucial factor in obtaining 110 percent financing. During the period between obtaining control over the property and the moment you must close on it, there must be appreciation in the value. If, for example, you are able to tie up an office building with a five-month option to buy at $150,000, and during the five months you can increase its value to $225,000, the lender appraising the new value will find a $170,000 loan to be well within the parameters of "good business."

This appreciation can occur literally overnight, as illustrated by a situation involving one of my clients. Let's take a closer look at how this works.

The Harrison Deal

I helped Harrison negotiate a fine purchase price with the owners of a vacant industrial building in Fort Lauderdale. The price was $400,000. I examined the building and the property and instantly knew this would be a fantastic investment if he could solve the problem of the vacancy and lack of income. Harrison was an insider to this transaction. He had been an executive of the company that had previously leased the building and had watched as that company decided to close their operations in Fort Lauderdale. But he knew there was still business to be had, and he left that former company and made a deal with them to represent their remainder interest in the area. Now as president of a new company that had just landed a sweetheart contract to represent an international company in Fort Lauderdale, with a dozen years of solid business history in the area, here is what we did next.

Harrison provided data showing that his newly formed company was ready to lease this building at an annual lease of $60,000 triple net (the tenant pays tax, upkeep, and utilities). I prepared the loan application and showed that this rent was reasonable, in fact, lower than what it could be on the open market. I pointed out to the lender that the property was well suited for Harrison and that he would continue operating the building nearly exactly as did the former tenant. This triple-net rent suggested a value of this property somewhere in between $600,000 to $700,000. I asked for a loan that would cover my client's cost and put a few dollars in his pocket. We got a loan of $450,000.

THE FINE POINTS OF THE DEAL

Seeking transactions with the hope of getting 110 percent or more of the needed capital to buy may not be the best thing to do, but I present these options for you to consider. It is possible that all you need is 100 percent of the deal or even less. The key is to understand your goals and to anticipate how much income you need to generate from the investment. As I have discussed earlier, even if you break even in your cash flow, you can still be making out like a bandit. If you look to the long run, all you ever have to do with real estate is to let it pay off a mega mortgage, and with some good management, you will have your retirement well cared for.

So now let's take a look at the advantages and disadvantages of this technique. The ease of obtaining the one-lender loan to generate your 110 percent cash out is its big advantage. In the right circumstance, such as the development of a property or the sudden appreciation of a property tied up with a long-term option, the increased equity above the loan makes it a sound business deal for the lender. When the overleverage problem doesn't exist, then the second problem, the need to worry about manipulating the lenders for extra grace periods, disappears. In a sound deal where the rent will cover the debt and still show a cash flow, this type of transaction is suitable for even the most cautious buyer.

There are also disadvantages of 100 percent or more financing. The potential of overleverage is a big negative, and it occurs no matter how many lenders you have. It is possible to overburden yourself with debt so that, if there is a sudden downturn of the economic circumstances of the area, you slip into a negative cash flow situation. This alligator will eat you out of house and home faster than you realize. The ability to obtain 100 percent or more financing can be tempting and you might think about going full speed ahead and forget the risk. Later you will know better. Prudent investors will examine the total obligation and will do sufficient due diligence to know if the risk is warranted. It is best to side with the potential risk and if there is any doubt about the future income from the property.

Another disadvantage to keep in mind is that a sole lender can present problems that multiple lenders do not. First of all if there is just one loan then that lender has a clear and easy decision as to whether or not to foreclose when you are in default. One lender also means one mortgage payment to cover the total debt. This can be a benefit, but it also has a drawback: Multiple lenders mean several loans and several loan payments. With several loans in a tough market, it is possible to keep current with one or more while letting others slide behind the payment schedule if you get caught behind the economic eight ball and don't have enough ready cash to meet your current obligations. You can pick on one or two weak mortgagees and let them wait for their payment for a while, then later bring them up to date while letting others wait their turn.

When finessing the deal and looking for a lender, stress the new value of the property and your good fortune at having an option to purchase at a lower amount. Be sure to have documented what was done to the property during the option period. Be sure to let your realtor friends help you compile information on resales in the area that support your claim of added value. Your ability to demonstrate an appreciated value will depend on the thoroughness of your homework.

Six Things You Can Do to Show Appreciated Value

Earlier in this section I discussed the importance of showing appreciated value. There are several ways to do this when you are covering the fine points of the deal. Here are six things you can do to show appreciated value:

1. List improvements made to the property. Don't show amounts paid, show only the improvements you have caused to be made after your contract and prior to the closing, such as revamping the front yard landscaping, cleaning entryway, resurfacing driveway, painting the exterior of the building, and painting the interior of the building.

2. Point out the time you will have in between your contract to purchase and the closing time. Stress that this time will give you the opportunity to make certain improvements to the property and that the area is a hot place in the market right now. If your contract was made yesterday and you close in 90 days and you are showing an anticipated 20 percent appreciation, you will have to have good reasons for this appreciation.

3. List recent sales prices of properties in the same price range as the property you are attempting to acquire. Your local realtor can be helpful with this and other tasks by finding as many properties as possible that have sold in the last few weeks. Cull these properties until you have several similar to the property you want to buy. It doesn't matter where these selected properties are; if you have fairly placed a value on the property, then the market conditions will automatically match similar areas. (This is a shortcut method; the usual way of finding comparables is to scour the area for similar properties and then find those that have sold recently.)

4. Have a well-documented list of similar properties available for purchase. If your list demonstrates that your selected property is above the average opportunity or that there is a very small selection of properties on the market, then that should help your new purchase quickly increase in value.

5. Have a plan to create even greater appreciation. If you have some good ideas on how you can generate even better appreciation by making improvements or by some change of use

or whatever, make sure this is known. Lenders will sleep easier if they feel you have a good plan and they can clearly see the future increase in value.

6. Don't do any of the above five if the end result would not clearly demonstrate appreciated value. If you are unable to get the desired financing from one sole lender, don't worry—there are still avenues for you to explore. In fact a prudent investor doesn't wait for all negative votes to come in before he begins to develop alternative sources. You should have some other irons in the fire just in case the sole lender is not available at terms satisfactory to your needs.

CHAPTER

The Double Second

The double second is a second mortgage you create on a second property. In essence, you borrow against one property to purchase another. Borrowing money on real estate is like supermarket advertising. Look in your local newspaper and you will see what I mean. The advertised specials are designed to attract the buyers: "Special this week on five pounds of ham." Meanwhile the prime buying items are not marked down, and the unaware buyers end up paying top prices for the majority of their supplies.

The parallel here is that you should borrow against that supermarket item. If you own a property that is a better buy in the borrowing market than one you are proposing to purchase, then don't be reluctant to use it as security when you borrow the funds to buy the other property. Using a second property as the foundation for new purchases has the added advantage of giving you time to increase the value of the new property. When you are able to present the case of increased value, you can refinance the new property and buy something else with the new capital.

THE DOUBLE DEAL: BORROWING AGAINST PROPERTY

It's easy to see how this type of transaction works. Here are some examples of the steps it takes to generate the double second deal. With a little thought, this method can work for you.

Julie wants to buy a four-unit apartment building and can do so with a $35,000 down payment and assumption of the existing financing. However she can't get the $35,000 by borrowing on the apartment building. Lenders generally shy away from loans with this high of a loan-to-value ratio, and Julie cannot show added value at this time. However Julie owns a home that has a low percentage loan-to-value first mortgage. When she talks to the savings and loan holding that mortgage, she finds that she can refinance the mortgage and generate the needed $35,000. Because lenders like single-family loans they will offer great deals at a much lower interest rate than would be available for commercial loans. Julie's total debt service (payments on the mortgage) will be less if she obtained the needed funds by borrowing on her home than if she borrowed on the apartment building.

In another scenario Jake needs $50,000 to make the purchase he has been working for, and he finds that refinancing the property he wants to buy will be very difficult and costly. He owns some free-and-clear vacant land and decides to mortgage it. A few conversations with the local commercial banks produce a lender willing to provide a first mortgage on the vacant land at a cost far below the expenses of either refinancing the property to be purchased or obtaining a second mortgage on that same property.

THE FINE POINTS OF THE DEAL

A good guideline to follow for this type of deal is to pick the most lendable property. All lenders like certain kinds of properties as security on their loans. A free-and-clear single-family home in which the borrower lives would probably be the first choice, but it most certainly is not limited to that.

Make a list of what you own and your existing debt on that property. This is your supermarket of items on which you can borrow. If you have established some rapport with a mortgage broker (and you should now if you haven't already), discuss the situation with him. Go down to your local savings and loan associations and commercial banks. Meet the lending officers there and discuss your problem. Your problem, by the way, is obtaining the maximum money to meet your needs at the lowest overall debt service.

Avoid undermortgaging your property for the sake of a limited amount of cash you might need to add for the one deal. If, for example, you own a free-and-clear home worth $200,000 and you need $40,000 to make a transaction work, there is no question that you can borrow those funds. The problem is a $40,000 loan against the property is less than the maximum that can be borrowed. You might find that pushing the loan up to

$70,000 would be more practical even if you didn't need the extra cash at the moment. This cash can come in handy when you purchase something else. But keep in mind that you do not want to pay for cash that is not working for you over a long period of time. Get it to work for your investment portfolio as soon as possible.

One really sound approach to the question of what to do with this extra cash is to raise your goals on what you want to buy. If you can purchase a larger apartment complex or office building that would offer greater potential than the original investment and you have the equity available to do so, then go for it.

The ideal situation, then, would be to have a property that will support the amount of money you need in a maximized lending situation. If you need $40,000 and have a property valued at $50,000 and can borrow the required amount against it, then that is as close to perfect as possible (unless you can borrow $40,000 against a property worth $40,000 or less).

It is possible that refinancing might be the way to achieve two benefits at the same time. Let's say you need $30,000 in cash to make a transaction work. You make a list of the property you own and it looks like this:

Property You Own	Estimated Value	Existing Financing	Your Equity
Home	$200,000	0	$200,000
Duplex	$ 90,000	$42,000	$ 48,000
Lot	$ 50,000	0	$ 50,000

It might appear that the best property to use would be the lot valued at $50,000. However when you examine the debt service on the duplex, you find that the $42,000 balance is to be paid over seven remaining years at 10 percent interest. Payments on this mortgage are $697.27 per month. If you refinance to 8 percent at a 30-year term to a maximum mortgage amount of $72,000, your monthly payments would be $528.30. Not only is this a decrease of $168.97 per month but you also generate the needed capital to boot.

Being creative in finding the right property to refinance or use as security in a loan is an important part of this technique. Using the blanket type of loan, wherein you would present the lender with several properties as security instead of one property, might do the trick when all else fails. Remember the greater the security on the loan, the less the lender is risking. Anytime you can present a reduced risk loan to a lender, you will gain his attention.

Does this all sound too good to be true? It might, but as an informed real estate investor you know that there are advantages and disadvantages to borrowing against one property to buy another. Let's look at what you need to consider. The main advantage in using this technique is you present the lender with the best property to be security for the debt, and you buy time to get the new property fixed up so that you can maximize its refinance ability. The overall benefit is to get the money you need at the lowest cost. Some investors have the idea that they must let each property stand on its own; they never look to one property for financing another. In my opinion this is a shortsighted approach that often prevents their getting the edge in the financing arena.

The total payment to your lenders each month is what you should consider. Anytime you can borrow against one or more combined properties more cheaply than you can against the property you want to buy, you should consider doing so.

In techniques involving high leverage and potential overextension of debt, it is possible to get in over your head. What you want to avoid whenever possible is the borrowing of money simply for the expediency of having the cash. If the new property won't support the total added debt plus the existing debt on that property, then you are flirting with disaster.

Mike, for example, needed $25,000 to put down on a small four-unit apartment building he had tied up on a 90-day option. He scraped up the money by obtaining a second mortgage on a property he already owned. The problem was that, after the smoke had cleared, Mike found himself the owner of a property with a heavy four-year payment on the second mortgage. The income from the apartment building didn't cover his total expenses, and the first property—a nice three-bedroom home where he and his family lived— was not an income producer, so there was no support there. He had placed his holdings in jeopardy by overextending his debt to a point where the income from the apartment building wasn't sufficient to ward off foreclosure.

There is no hard-and-fast rule about overextension. Sometimes it is warranted if you are ready to carry the load until you can increase the income of the property to cover the total cost and, of course, put some money in your pocket.

To be on the safe side, however, in a tight situation you should have a margin of at least 5 percent vacancy in the current existing income from any income property you hope will cover your debt service. It is nice to be able to increase rents, and sometimes the market will go along with that desire. But then sometimes it won't. Be cautious in any lending situation. The total impact of the debt service is the key. Look at it, and then see if alternative mortgage situations are available to reduce it.

Never view any single method as either the best or the most readily available until you have used creative thinking to find an alternative technique that not only will help you attain your goal but will do the same for the seller. Although it is possible that you may never know the primary motivation that is driving the seller, the more you know about the seller's reasons for selling the more successful you will be with the negotiations.

16 CHAPTER

The Private Punt

Private mortgages with kickers have many advantages in tight deals when you have exhausted the usual institutional or seller sources of loans. In a tight money market there are times when you can offer private lenders or even sellers creative benefits to get you the loan. These benefits may or may not be cash and often take other forms of return—"kickers" you offer to lenders. A savvy lender may even spring this concept on you just before she gives you the loan commitment. This chapter can only hint at the creativity of some lenders in their quest to better their investments. In this chapter you will get a heads up approach as to how to deal with the situation when it arises.

THE KICKER DEAL: CLOSING THE LOAN

There are a number of ideas and ways to add kickers to the deal. To see how this works, let's take a look at a few examples. We'll start with Ron. He needed $75,000 cash to close on the apartment building he wanted to buy. He ran some ads in the local papers offering private lenders a blanket mortgage on several properties, including second position in the apartment house. His kicker to the lender was having several properties to offer as additional security to the loan. Because of that, he was able to offer the lender a lower loan-to-value ratio that therefore reduces the lender's risk.

Laura needed only $30,000 cash to close on the North Carolina vacation home she wanted to buy. She offered private lenders a kicker of three weeks use of the home each year the loan remained on the property. Another example is Phil's deal. He needed $100,000 to buy an office building. He offered private lenders 10 percent of all net income in excess of the previous year's rental figure for the duration of the loan.

In each of these three examples, the borrowers were competing with the normal terms of the market. The kickers were offered not only in hopes of softening those terms but to close the loan. Some lenders will take the kickers you offer and not report them as value received, hoping in this way to avoid payment of income tax on the value of the kicker. After all who would ever know about the gift of three weeks in North Carolina?

When offering kickers that give the lender an added benefit that has a real dollar value, keep in mind that the IRS will treat this as an income to the lender. You can report this as an added "cost" to you, and the lender should report the "kicker" as added revenue to him. In the examples just given, Ron's kicker of added security to the loan would not fall into this category.

WHAT KICKERS SHOULD YOU OFFER?

When dealing with the private lenders or sellers of property you want to purchase, you need to feel your way through the deal to ascertain what kind of kickers to offer and what "value" you want to offer. In general kickers vary between hard kickers and soft kickers.

There are several types of hard kickers to offer:

- **Percentages of income.** There are many different ways to set up this kicker. In the previous examples one way used was to offer a percent of the revenue that was in excess to the previous years income. In major joint ventures between developers and lenders, the lender frequently gets a percent of the gross revenue as well as a percentage of ownership of the property.
- **Increases in interest.** Instead of offering a side-kicker, sometimes the loan is set with a bonus to the interest paid. This is a straightforward deal and may come with other contingencies that can limit the viability of the deal. A type of loan that was popular

in the late 1990s and into the new century and still survives is the conduit loan. This loan is generally reserved for large commercial deals, and most commonly has penalties to prevent prepayment of the loan. Here the lender locks up the property and gets a yield management penalty in the event of an early pay off of the loan. The way this works is the lender charges, for example, 9 percent interest on a 15-year loan with a balloon at the end of 10 years. If the loan is paid off at the end of five years, and the prime rate (or other benchmark used in the deal) drops to 7 percent, then the borrower will have to pay a penalty that would amount to the presumed loss of yield for the remaining five years of loan payments from the 9 percent charged to the current market rate of 7 percent. In lending jargon, this is called yield management. It is designed to protect the lender's yield in the event that a current rate drops substantially below the contract rate that you have agreed to pay them. When this happens the borrower is enticed by other lenders to refinance the loan and pay off the higher interest mortgage. By including a penalty to the borrower, the lender can forestall the refinancing of their higher-yielding mortgage than they would be able to obtain by relending the paid-off mortgage.

- **Interest adjustments**. Many lenders prefer to loan on an adjustable interest basis. Here the interest on the loan is adjusted to some benchmark rate, prime for example, so that as prime would change, either up or down, the interest charged would also change. Generally these adjustments occur quarterly or so, as this is a negotiating point. Borrowers can negotiate a cap, which is a ceiling or a maximum in which the interest can be increased. This should not be confused with CAP, which is an investment capitalization rate that is the percent of the yield the investment returns on invested cash.

- **Actual percentage of ownership**. As I mentioned earlier, big deals often mean the lender gets a percent of ownership. This does not have to be limited to big deals as you can offer a seller or outside lender a piece of the deal to entice their participation in the transaction.

- **A piece of other benefits**. Any benefit you can get you can also offer to someone else. This means tax shelter, appreciation of value, equity buildup, and so on. Let your mind roam wild or just sit back and see what the lender wants.

Now let's look at the types of soft kickers to offer:

- **Noneconomic use of the property**. If there are times when the property isn't producing much or, for that matter, any income, then offer them that. The mountain vacation home, your beach condo, and so on may all have noneconomic producing periods.

- **Use of some other property during its noneconomic period**. If you own a mountain cabin, for example, offer time in that facility to the lender giving you cash to buy something else.

- **Professional or craft services that you do personally on some limited basis**. If you are a dentist, doctor, plumber, carpenter, or electrician, you have a kicker to offer that need not take away from your normal economics.

- **Kickers that you can buy at a discount**. You might find that the lender will make the loan if you give her a trip to Paris each year during the term of the loan. If you calculate the cost and then make a deal with a travel agency to give you a commission on the sale of the travel, you can reduce the overall cost to you.

- **A percent of future profits when the property is sold**. This is a hard cost but is softened as it is not paid until the ultimate sale of the property and can be limited.

- **The opportunity to buy at a discount**. If you are building on or redeveloping an existing property and plan to sell units or condos or subdivided lots, you could offer a lender (or seller of the original property) the opportunity to buy at a discount. This cuts into your pocket but generates some sales right away.

- **The right to buy into a future deal**. Some developers might offer to let their lenders come in as partners in future deals.

- **Add other property, either personal or real, to the security of the loan**. This improves your loan-to-value ratio and enhances your opportunity to get a higher loan, a better term of payment, or both.

THE FINE POINTS OF THE DEAL

Before getting into the details of this type of transaction, let's take a look at the private money market in general. In any given society there will be individuals who have a lot of cash on their hands. The tougher the times, the greater the amount of cash some people will accumulate. They will do this out of fear of the market or out of prudence. But whereas having cash at the turn of a sellers' market into a buyers' market will put them on the top of the pile, holding onto cash can be very frustrating. What do you do with it? Long-term, short-term? Stocks? Bonds? CDs? As this cycle develops and as the money market gets tighter, the institutional lenders begin to dry up. They eventually lend only to prime clients, and then only if they have the funds.

Private lenders can be lured into providing the necessary funding for small, moderate, fixed investments by giving them the yields the institutional lenders demand, plus some of the kickers mentioned. A great advantage of dealing with private lenders is the often reduced cost of the loan. Big banks and savings and loans like to collect big points, which are additional interest in the form of upfront expenses. Private lenders can be enticed to reduce these charges, and at best closing costs with private lenders are usually more negotiable than with institutional lenders.

A big drawback of dealing with private lenders can be the nervous nelly who has just made her first real estate loan and will call you every time the wind blows or your grass hasn't been cut for over 10 days. It's easy to say, "Stay clear of newcomers to the lending market," but that isn't sound advice. Some of the best lenders you can develop might make their first loan with you. A few, however, will be so nasty and scared that you will never want to see them again. Remember when you are dealing with institutional money, the people you deal with are removed from the money. After all it isn't their money. On the other hand that private lender has worked hard for her cash and will take a personal interest in having it paid back on time.

Where to Find Private Lenders

Private lenders exist everywhere. They are wealthy people. People with newfound cash. People who like the yields and security obtained through real estate lending. The best way to find them is through lawyers and accountants. Write letters to them, mentioning that, as a real estate investor, you are interested in knowing if any of their clients are potential lenders to good, sound, excellent-yielding real estate loans. In doing this you will also draw out any lawyers and accountants who might have available cash. But don't rely solely on your letters; you should plan to personally visit real estate lawyers and accountants in classy areas in town so you can see each other face-to-face.

Newspapers are a good advertising source you can use. Most classified sections have a column headed "Money Wanted" or "Investment Opportunities," so put your specific ad for the specific deal in the paper. For
example: "Glen needs $50,000 for sound real-estate transaction and will
give the lender great terms with fantastic kickers. Call . . ." On the flip side
some private lenders will place ads themselves, searching out good loans.
Look for such ads in the "Capital Available" or "Money to Lend" columns
of the classifieds.

An active borrower, however, will look beyond newspapers for his
lenders. There are three sources of private money in your neighborhood.

- **Investment Brokers**: These are stockbrokers and other
  investment counselors, and they are easy to find. If you have one or
  two yourself, then those are the ones to start with. Make absolutely
  sure that you are very clear in dealing with these people, however,
  and make it particularly clear that you expect to pay them a fee for
  finding you a lender. The usual fee would be 1 percent of the
  amount of the loan. If they demand more, you must weigh the total
  cost against your need for the funds. In any event be sure to
  examine carefully the total cost of any money you borrow.
- **Accountants**: These professionals know their own clients'
  specific needs and financial capabilities. If you are offering
  secure mortgages and borrowing is usual in your business, they
  will sometimes be of help to you. If these chaps (or any lender)
  think you need the loan to save your butt, then the chances are
  you won't get it—or it will be offered at terms that won't save
  you anything. Accountants should not be offered a fee, but you
  should be willing to pay if they bring it up.
- **Lawyers**: Your own lawyer might be okay, and you should let her
  know that you are looking for private lenders. Other lawyers will
  usually see your need for money as a weakness.

Private money can be very good if you play your cards well. When
you repay the loan, chances are the lender will ask you if you need more
money. If you develop a good rapport with the private lender, she can be a
lifelong partner in your ventures.

You should therefore take care to always be prompt with the loan
payments—even more so with private lenders than with institutions. The
institution has taken into account the potential wait for its funds, and none

of its employees have loaned their own money so there is no one to upset. The private lender, on the other hand, will sit at home waiting for the mail on the first of each month to make sure she has gotten her payment on time.

Keep in mind that the wrath of a private lender can, and usually will, be far more swift than that of the biggest and toughest savings and loan association or local commercial bank.

Why is this? Institutional lenders hate to foreclose because when they do the real estate then ends up as evidence that someone at the bank made a decision that cost all this trouble. The property then goes to the REO (real estate owned) department and must be dealt with by a staff of people, all of which costs even more money. Generally a borrower can get all kinds of concessions from the institutional lender if she is having difficulty meeting the loan obligations. Talk to them early. Let them know you are a good risk. What they hate more than anything is the borrower who just stiffs them and leaves town. That is not good for your reputation, so don't do it.

17
CHAPTER

The Institutional Punt

Much like the private loan, the institutional loan can and does function well when there are kickers added. As money becomes tighter, the big lenders find that kickers are not only needed to entice them into the deal but also that without the kickers their ability to survive the market would be in jeopardy. Some of the kickers that would be in demand were mentioned in the previous chapter. If you have not read it yet, I recommend you do so before continuing with this chapter.

To understand the risk of surviving in the financial marketplace, it is helpful to examine the differences between the private lender and the institutional lender. There are several very important differences between them. Now that I have introduced you to the private lender in the previous chapter, it's time that you had a better understanding of the institutional lender.

WHO ARE THE INSTITUTIONAL LENDERS?

The financial community of lenders centers on the big banks: Chase Bank of New York, Barclays Bank of Tokyo, Bank of London, and Royal Bank of Canada. Each bank is a major factor within its own circle in the ultimate cost of money. New banks are created all the time, perhaps as a buyout of one or more of the existing banks or as a new bank on the block.

Often the new bank specializes in a narrow category of property against which they will loan. Be sure to check them out if you are buying what they like to loan on.

Together the major banks set what is called a prime rate, which is the supposed interest rate that the preferred low-risk clients of these banks must pay when funds are loaned to them. All other clients are of a higher risk factor and must pay over prime.

The savings and loan associations and other savings institutions make up another part of the institutional market. These banks function much as competition to the commercial banks within the usual markets, and have been, in the past, primary lenders in the residential and small commercial real estate market. These lenders are governed tightly by the laws granting them existence and are heavily hurt by declines in the real estate industry, which is their lifeblood of lending.

Nearly all of the money loaned by these two banking sources is money given them in the form of deposits. These deposits are given to the institution for safekeeping and for the interest the institution pays to the depositor for the use of the money. The bank or savings institution then loans the money to others in the form of real estate or other kinds of mortgages and loans including new and used car loans. What is important is that the deposit comes in and within a short time the money is given out. The mortgage loan might be over 15 to 40 years at an interest rate that was fixed for the life of the loan at not more than 3 percent to 5 percent over the rate the bank pays the depositor.

For years this system worked pretty well: You put money in your savings account and the S&L pays you one rate while they lend it out at a rate that is double or greater. As long as the level of deposits continued to grow, the institution could grow. Based on the level of existing deposits, they could borrow additional sums of money from other lenders, namely the Federal Reserve Bank, at an interest charge that is generally lower than what they pay their depositors, and lend out that money, making a nice profit all the while. The institutional lenders weren't lending their money, they were lending the depositors' money or the Federal Reserve's funds. The yellow brick road looked like it could go on forever, but it didn't.

THE LONG-TERM CONTRACT: BOOM AND BUST

The long term of the mortgage loan is what has made real estate financing within the United States much easier than almost anywhere else in the world. An 18-to-35-year loan is not unusual in the United States, whereas 5 to 10 years in some countries is considered a very long term.

As the institutional lenders began to make long-term loans, they discovered that the average loan was paid off somewhere between the seventh and the ninth year. The original term of the loan apparently didn't matter much, since borrowers found it economically prudent (in times of relatively cheap financing) to refinance after seven to nine years. This trend was reinforced by the fact that many people sold their homes, on the average, between the seventh and ninth year. This average loan life prompted lenders to create longer contracts as an enticement to seek out their funds, since it seemed that borrowers preferred long payouts, as the long payment schedule lowered the monthly payment, even if they might choose later to cut them short.

The big problem came when interest rates, formerly held down by usury laws, went up and up as those laws were relaxed. The federal government took economic measures in hopes of fixing the national economy. Interest rates were permitted to rise and in fact were encouraged to do so by a tightening of the Federal Reserve rate to the institutions that needed those funds to survive the ups and downs of their cash flow problems.

As the rates went up, the institutions found they had to pay more and more to their depositors to keep a flow of cash in their vaults and to stem the tide of withdrawals moving into high-yield money funds. By mid-1981 the depositor could get a safe return of more than 12 percent on his certificate of deposit, which was a far cry from the 5 percent or so his savings were earning just a few years earlier. By the middle of 2003, it was difficult to find a bank willing to pay a depositor more than 2 percent per year on short-term certificates of deposit.

Money became tighter and tighter from 1979 through the early 1980s, and a great slowdown within the real estate industry began to develop. People talked about the high cost of borrowing money for buying their home or apartment, and lenders running out of cash to lend started cutting back (out of necessity) the volume of loans they made. This combination of events meant property owners were not going to refinance those low-interest loans they had taken out seven to nine years ago.

History has a tendency to repeat itself, and beginning in 2002 the world has seen the money market take a dive. Interest rates charged by lenders in 2003 were at a 50-year low and billions of dollars of old loans have been refinanced with the new, all-time low rates. The conduit loans that have yield-management penalties designed to "lock" the borrower into the loan for as long as possible are the last to be refinanced, and many of them are still in existence at comparatively high interest rates. Lenders who are sitting on a portfolio of those loans are sitting pretty—for the time being. However lenders who are forced into a fierce competition for places to lend their piles of cash may become locked into low interest rates for long periods of time. History, as I have said, has a tendency to come back to kick us in the shins.

The problem in a nutshell is that institutional lenders loan the money they get from others just like you and me. Then they lend it at a higher interest than they pay and pray that they won't have to borrow money themselves at a higher rate.

Private lenders differ greatly from institutional lenders in that much if not all of the money they lend comes from them since they are their own depositors. They take their own cash and give it to you in the form of a mortgage. You pay them back in the form of loan payments, and that is how they get their cash back. The private lender will never have a run on his deposits unless he has acted like an institutional lender by borrowing the money he lends.

In the vast majority of small loans (small in relation to the size of the lender), the private lender is using his own cash. While this makes for a more stable lender in normal times, it also makes for one who frightens easily and wants to foreclose quickly in tough times.

Taking the institutional lender to task is far easier than with the private lender. In the first place when money gets tight, the logical conclusion is that the institutional lender will become tough just like the private lender. After all it will be the institutional lender who will be losing by having to borrow at rates in excess of those earned on the old mortgage. However institutional lenders have restrictions requiring them to reserve funds for potential foreclosure losses every time they foreclose on a property. In short even though they will threaten it, most institutional lenders will avoid foreclosure, even to the extent of absorbing considerable loss. (They will, of course, eventually foreclose in the end.)

Living with these facts isn't easy for the institutional lender. But they have some tools to fight back with, and they are getting smarter about getting the edge in lending. To simply be a lender will, in the long run, kill you. You have to get some of the other benefits that go along with the real estate, not just the interest on the loan.

With this in mind let's look at some of the kickers that the institutional lender can and will request. If you find one that is more palatable to you than another lender is requesting, suggest a trade-off—don't wait for the lender to bring that possibility to your attention. Lenders are not always as creative as they could be.

KICKERS INSTITUTIONAL LENDERS USE

There are three types of kickers that institutional lenders use.

The Landlease Ploy

This can be a good kind of kicker for both the lender and the investor. Here the lender takes a look at the total amount of funds to be lent, then allocates part of the money to a purchase of the land, which the lender then leases back to the borrower at the same or a slightly higher rate than would have been paid on a mortgage.

Maria needs $1 million to finance the construction of an office building on her lot. A good loan would have an interest rate of 8 percent per year. But Maria has not been able to find a lender who would lend to her on those terms. Instead she is offered (and takes) a loan proposal that will get her the full $1 million she needs; however the total amount is not structured as a loan. The lending documents show Maria sold the land to the limited partnership owned by the lender for $300,000. The limited partnership then leases the land back to Maria for $60,000 per year. The remainder of $700,000 is structured as a regular loan at 8 percent interest.

Maria's total debt service is split between the mortgage and the landlease. It is easy to see that her "interest charge" on the land side of the deal is actually 20 percent of the amount she got ($300,000), which boosts the lender's overall return. Of course unless the loan document requires that Maria buy back the land at some future date, she will never have to pay back the $300,000. She will only need to continue paying the rent. It is important for you to realize that most landleases, have escalators in the amount of rent that is paid. It is very rare today to find a lease fixed in the amount paid, although in the 1960s that was a common event. So Maria's ultimate cost in giving the land as a kicker could be a continuing increase in the amount of rent she has to pay. But she isn't given the alternative option.

Maria looks at the total picture and realizes that she will be faced with increases in the landlease rent sometime in the future. But it is all a matter of economics. The land isn't a tax-shelter item, and it might be good for Maria to take the deal. After all she needs the building and doesn't have another way to go. The loan might actually be great for Maria—or for you if the deal was so good that you could get your profit before the other shoe (the rent increases) hit the floor.

100 Percent Upfront Financing

More and more lenders are coming into deals as partners instead of lenders. They do put up all the cash at times, however, anticipating their judgment of the reputation, character, and creditworthiness of the investor to be prudent and the profit potential sound.

A preference position is a great way to go. A lender or investor (or a bit of both) puts up the money but gets a yield, such as a bonus of income taken off the top before any disbursements to other partners or investors. The borrower doesn't get any return until the lender is paid his bonus yield, and then the borrower receives the next yield until they are equal, after which all is split on a 50-50 basis.

This technique, of which there are many variations, is used for income-producing investments such as apartment buildings, office buildings, shopping centers, and the like. Income on such properties has a tendency to grow over the years, and to be a partner in such a venture can be a great advantage to the lender. As he advances all the cash needed, he is buying the investor's expertise and of course the investor's packaged deal.

Percentage of Income over a Set Gross

This kicker is more common with insurance companies than the previous kicker. Generally insurance companies don't want to become actual partners with builders and investors. They prefer to either own the property or the loan on it. In this transaction the lender advances the agreed-upon sum of money, which is secured by a mortgage, and collects the monthly mortgage payments as in any other loan. At the end of the year—or sometime during the year—the borrower will calculate the gross income of the property (the rents that have been collected) and will pay to the lender a percentage of any income in excess of the ceiling established by the loan agreement.

You want to borrow $1,500,000 for a 20,000-square-foot strip store. The lender (if they want to impose this kicker) calculates the comfortable gross income needed to support the expenses of the strip store. Let's say that the current rent is $270,000 per year and operating expenses are $70,000 each year. This would leave a NOI of $200,000 for debt service and return to the investor. Based on this information the lender would want a buffer between the NOI and the debt service of at least 30 percent. As the debt service on $1,500,000 at the term and interest rate demanded by the lender might be $120,000 per year, that mortgage payment falls within the "safe" amount you should be able to pay.

However, since income is going to go up as rents increase, the lender tells you that to get the $1,500,000 loan you must give them 50 percent (or whatever percent you can get them down to) of all gross income above the $270,000 gross revenue during the life of the loan.

Just remember that everything described within the note and mortgage is generally negotiable. No matter how standard the documents look, you can question and challenge every term and condition. The first draft will be the one that is absolutely their best win if you sign it. The key is to have a good real estate lawyer who is up to date in this kind of legal document. Make sure that you have a lawyer who will give you strong legal advice, answer all your questions, give you his opinion when you ask for it, and leave the decision making to you.

THE FINE POINTS: FOUR KEYS TO DEALING WITH INSTITUTIONAL LENDERS

Remember that institutional lenders differ from private lenders. If you choose to go this route for your deal, here are four key points to remember:

1. The farther the institution is from the actual property, the more information you must give them. This is sometimes not examined too carefully—until you leave out something important.

2. The people you deal with are not lending you their own money. They will therefore have an impersonal approach to the entire situation. Because they do control the situation to some degree, they do at times like to make borrowers squirm.

3. Loan officers don't like to make bad loans because each time they do, they earn red marks on the president's LOFN (Loan Officers to Fire Next) checklist. Therefore they will try to cover their tracks to be sure they don't get burned if your loan goes under.

4. Deal with the president if at all possible. Since he is responsible for the lending institution overall, he will make sure that foreclosure on your loan is the last possible recourse.

18
CHAPTER

The Family Loan

Let's say you want to buy a run-down gas station and turn it into a fast-food restaurant. Have you ever thought about asking your family to finance your loan? The family loan may sound like a simple transaction but obtaining a loan from that single most private source—your own family—can be one of the hardest ways to finance a deal. I say this for several reasons. First of all, asking for the loan might be next to impossible for some people. Second of all, there is frequently a good deal of reluctance from family members to make the loan. You might hear, "A loan? No one gave me a loan when I was just starting out," or "If I give you the $50,000, then what will I have to give to your two brothers and your sister?"

One objective of this chapter is to help you to decide whether you should ask your family for a loan and, if you do, how you should set up the family loan. Another objective of this chapter is to help family members ascertain whether the loan request is a prudent one and, assuming the funds are available, whether the loan should be granted. The natural reluctance to lend should not enter the picture. If the deal is well secured, you should approach the loan with as open a mind and as businesslike an attitude as you can muster.

THE MUTUAL DEAL: SOLVING THE PROBLEM

Paul comes from a nice family in California. Not a wealthy family but a nice one. He has finished college and is working for an electronics company in Utah. He has the opportunity to tie up a small duplex in the Salt Lake City area on an option. Paul figures he can put some money together by the time he has to close on the deal in four months. If he can't he will lose the $2000 he put down on the option.

Paul strikes out at the local bank and everywhere else he goes for the loan. It isn't a question of the value of the duplex, which is sound, and Paul's deal is an excellent one as far as the purchase goes. However the lenders in the area just aren't lending to anyone except their long-standing customers, especially to a young man from another state just out of college. Paul is out in the cold. He figures that he will need $10,000 to close the gap between the money he can scrape up and what he needs. Where should he turn?

"Dad," he says, "I have a proposition for you." He knows something about his father's finances. He knows that good old dad has some cash tied up in CDs and some more in stock. The stock isn't doing so hot at the moment, and Paul is willing to pay an interest rate equal to or better than the rate dad is earning at the bank. In fact, if he must, he will offer dad a kicker or two to entice him into the deal.

Dad looks at the deal and decides he will make Paul a second mortgage provided Paul moves into part of the duplex himself. Dad figures this will cut down on Paul's living expenses, since the apartment where Paul lives costs about $150 more per month than what the small side of the duplex would rent for. In addition Paul will be on the site to fix up the property, which needs some tender loving care.

Each party has approached the loan as a business venture. Sure there was personal interest that went beyond the hard economics of the transaction, but in the end it was a sound business deal that offered real economic benefits to each party. Ultimately a lawyer was hired to draw up the necessary papers at a nominal cost, paid by Paul, and the deal was made.

This example is not typical. Most family loans breach all business sense and end up proving the adage, "Lend to the family and you will break up a family." If you remember nothing more about this chapter, remember that a handshake deal might work with anyone, but it rarely works with a family member. If you do any business with a family member make absolutely sure that every family member knows exactly what the deal is, what the obligations of each person, especially the borrower, are, and what is expected of them. Get it in writing, and get it signed, legally executed, and witnessed. If not, then you are in for an interesting experiment in family discord. It doesn't have to be like that, of course, as Paul and his dad have illustrated. If both parties follow the checklists in this chapter, they will have a clearer understanding of their positions.

THE FINE POINTS OF THE DEAL

As I mentioned, a loan from your family should be set up like any business transaction. So let's look at this in more detail. When should you ask the family for a loan? There are two answers to this question, and they are in the form of questions themselves:

1. Is it better to keep the interest in the family?
2. If all other sources fail, should you give up without trying this last possibility?

Carefully review these questions; there are important factors for each party to consider. In the first question the theory is simple enough: If you are going to borrow money and pay a profit to a lender, why not pay that profit to a member of the family? The theory breaks down, however, in the application of the business sense. If a member of the family turns you down for the loan for any reason at all, the matter should not be taken personally if you are being businesslike about the request. After all, you aren't going to take revenge on the local loan officer if the local savings and loan association turns you down, are you? Any lender must occasionally turn down what appears to be a good loan. They do so because of other commitments, or simply because they don't want the risk at that moment.

The fact that you have sought the funds elsewhere and have failed doesn't mean that the loan is not sound. It could mean that the local lenders you have approached are out of funds. Or perhaps you actually got offers of money, but at terms that strangled the deal. It is one thing to pay top interest and closing costs, but to have to pay through the nose, too, might mean a reassessment of the project. No project or investment can support any debt service. There is a limit. I point this out because any good deal can find funds if you are willing to pay any price for the money. Loan sharks and that sort of moneylender must be avoided, as they are not a good business source of funds.

If you have approached the investment properly, you will have examined several alternative forms of financing to solve your cash needs. This book offers many such alternative forms of purchasing real estate without cash, and some of these techniques used together or by themselves might be your answer. If none of the others produce the funds at a cost that makes the investment a potentially successful one, you then follow up with this technique. On the other hand if you have had some past history of borrowing from the family and you have always been a good risk, then the family might be the very first source of funds to reach out for.

No matter when you go to the family, first or last, the time to do so is only when you can present a prudent risk to the lender. You must be ready to meet the market in interest and terms. You must also be ready to pay the penalty of kickers if that is what the market demands, and accept the punishment of foreclosure if you are behind in your payments.

WHAT MAKES A PRUDENT RISK?

No lender should approach a potential loan without wanting to know the present and potential value of the property and the background of the investor. In approaching your family for a loan, you should be ready to answer these questions in depth and with backup documentation to support your evaluations. Unlike an institutional lender, the family won't have the advantage of an appraisal department to check out those values. If you can obtain an independent appraisal to support your own evaluations, then this will be a good idea. Never use family relations as an excuse for a lack of professionalism in obtaining the money. "Gee, Dad, don't you believe me?" after you have told them the property you are buying for $50,000 is really worth $120,000. It might be, but document it. A bank would want to know so why not Uncle Frank or mom and dad? A prudent risk for a lender, then, is the chance one takes in lending money where the present value of the property will be reasonable security for the amount of money lent if the lender has to take the property back through foreclosure.

If I give you $50,000 in cash, I want to know that, if I have to take the property, a foreclosure sale will return me my unpaid money, plus unpaid interest, plus costs, plus aggravation. Sometimes this all adds up to quite a lot of money. For this reason lenders are careful and some borrowers have to pay high interest to get money.

Naturally the lender looks to the borrower and not just the property. Two people who want to borrow the same amount of money on the same property will be viewed in different perspectives if one is a wealthy well-known owner of real estate in the area and the other is just out of school and doesn't have a job or has just started working.

Since the majority of family loans will be within the secondary loan category, some of the problems of ascertaining the risk are slightly elevated as there is already debt on the property. What mom or dad is asked to do is increase their risk by making a second loan. A secondary loan, by the way, is the placing of any mortgage on a property that has an existing mortgage already recorded against the property. Most investors reaching out to the family for a loan will be attempting to get part of the down payment, leaving intact the existing first mortgage.

Secondary mortgages are riskier than first mortgages because, in the case of a default, the first mortgage is covered in the foreclosure sale ahead of any other mortgage. Sometimes there aren't enough proceeds from the sale at the courthouse steps to cover the first mortgage, costs, and interest, and the second mortgage holder is wiped out or forced to take over the property and deal with the first mortgage lender. This leaves the secondary lender in the terrible position of having to take the loss or go after the borrower by obtaining a deficiency judgment. This kind of judgment is very tough to get in most states and in most circumstances. And even when you can get the judgment, it is tough to collect. So as the risk goes up, the cost of money also goes up.

How to Reduce the Risk or Eliminate It Altogether

Here is when kickers come back into the picture. You can do a lot of things with kickers for a family loan that you wouldn't do with other loan sources. For example, Teresa needed $12,000 to put down on an FHA-financed home. Of the amount she needed she was able to scrape up $5000 of her own money but was still short the other $7000 she needed. She asked her dad for a loan, and the kicker that enticed her dad into the deal turned the transaction into something quite different than what Teresa asked for. The end result was not a loan at all though the end result was the same for Teresa. The home was put in dad's name. The $5000 Teresa had went to dad as an option that would allow Teresa to buy the home in the future. Dad then took the $5000 plus the $7000 Teresa wanted him to lend to her and purchased the home. He then rented the home to Teresa with the option to buy it back. The rent was equal to the monthly mortgage payment. All Teresa had to do was to give her father a down payment of $7000 and a small interest payment at the ultimate closing when Teresa exercised the option to buy the home.

In the few years between deals, dad had an arm's length transaction where he had bought a home and rented it out. If he needed it, dad would be able to get a nice tax shelter on the home (depreciation), which Teresa wouldn't have been able to use anyway as it was to be her own residence. The risk of a loan was reduced greatly in this kind of a deal and worked to solve Teresa's need for a house. There could be other benefits to be shared as well, like splitting the equity buildup when Teresa purchased the house from dad. What Teresa really did was give her father some of the benefits of a real estate transaction and at the same time end up exactly where she wanted to be.

SHOULD THE LOAN BE MADE?

The following checklist should help families faced with this critical decision. There are many aspects to examine that might mitigate some of the potential negative answers you can get as you go through the checklist, and I will elaborate on them at the end of this chapter.

The Lender's Family Preloan Checklist

- ☐ Does the borrower have a history of loan payback? This is a simple question with a tough answer. If the member of the family asking for the loan has never borrowed money before, then there is no plus or minus on this point. However if she has and the results have been late payments or foreclosure threats, this is a definite negative.

- ☐ Examine the investment property data carefully. How well documented is it? If it's sloppy, send it back to be returned as a neat and well-presented package. If other experts are brought in, check their credentials and their willingness to put their spoken words into written words.

- ☐ Ask this question, "Why are you buying this property?" and expect a good answer. If it is a closed restaurant and the idea is to turn it into a steakhouse, then examine the qualifications of the investor to do that.

- ☐ What are the other financing details? If the property has great existing financing, this can make a moderate deal great. On the other hand, if the existing financing is at 12 percent interest per annum with only five years left, there might be a problem of overburdening the deal with excessive financing cost. In that situation look to new financing and the potential of simply becoming a cosigner to the new loan instead of making a separate second mortgage loan.

☐ What investment alternatives does the investor have? What you want to know is whether he or she would be better off buying a nice office building than buying an apartment building. You also are seeking to learn how well the investor has scoured the market.

These five questions to consider will bring items to the forefront the investor herself should have examined. If they are examined, then the answers will be fast in coming. If not, then perhaps you will do the investor a favor by not lending the money until the full background of this investment and the alternatives have been examined.

Another Factor for the Loan

If you have a program of bit-by-bit transferring parts of your estate to your children, then you don't need sound business reasons to make a loan. It is possible, through lending at low rates of interest or at no interest at all, to enable your family members to benefit at a minimum of tax consequence to you. I won't expound on the many ways this can be accomplished, except to say that you should seek the advice of a good tax counselor to set up a program that best suits your goals.

THE LENDER'S VIEWPOINT: WRAPPING UP THE LOAN

In the end, once you decide to go ahead with the loan, make sure you do it legally with a lawyer or a title company and make it simple, clear, and concise. Then live it up. You should have nothing to worry about if your risk in making the loan is compensated for and you can better your yield over other investments you presently have. If it's done in a professional and businesslike way, there is no reason not to lend to a member of the family.

19

CHAPTER

The Presale Refinance

Some buyers have a terrible time getting approval for new mortgages. Perhaps they have poor credit or cannot satisfactorily prove to the lender their net worth or the source and amount of annual income. Whatever the reason these buyers may find it easier to purchase a property subject to the existing financing or even assume existing mortgages already in place.

When using this technique the seller either lets the buyer take over the existing mortgages or arranges for new financing prior to the closing and transfer of title. The buyer purchases the property subject to the new or previously existing financing. While this technique can work wonders, there are several problems that you need to check out first. If the new lender is going to establish a loan with conditions that make it impossible for someone else to assume or if the new owner must be approved as though he had applied for the loan in the first instance, then this is not a technique with much merit. Keep in mind that many existing mortgages may not require assumption. A purchase-money mortgage that is held by a previous owner of the property might be fully assumable with no paperwork involved. Older institutional loans may have a more simplified "takeover" provision that does not require the full-blown loan application process.

It has been my experience that you need to read the full loan documentation package to find out just how assumable existing financing might be. This includes reading the full mortgage and the actual note. All mortgages come with these two parts. The mortgage is what the buyer or borrower gives to the lender. This spells out the terms of the security and the obligations of the parties for the lender's right to place a lien on the property that has been placed as security for the loan. The note is the promise to pay, much like an IOU, and is what is breached if the payments are not made in a timely fashion. The combination of these two documents will give you the full details on what is going on. Copies of these documents should be kept by the borrower (seller of the property), but if lost they can be obtained through public records at the local county records storage or from the lending institution itself. You cannot take the lender's word for any of this. Get the document and read it yourself, or have your attorney do it for you. Why? Because if you call the lender and ask them, it is easy for them to take the easy way out and say, "We always draft our loan documents in such a way that a new buyer must go through the full loan application and approval process to assume an existing loan." That might or might not be true.

THE QUALIFYING DEAL: WHEN THE BUYER CAN'T BE APPROVED

There are several instances when this technique is the ideal one to use such as when the buyer cannot qualify for a new mortgage, or when it is in the seller's best interest to approach the sale this way. For example look at Lou and Bob's transactions below.

Lou had lost two deals in the past three months because he had been unable to qualify for the financing he needed. It wasn't that he was a bad credit risk, only that he was property-poor and had few liquid assets. This scared the lenders, but it didn't scare Lou. He was eager for more property and kept looking.

Soon he found a home he wanted to buy. It was priced at $165,000 in a good area of town, and its zoning would permit professional offices. He knew he would be able to convert the home into a beautiful doctor's office and quintuple the existing rent. The seller owned the property free and clear of any debt and did not want to hold any secondary paper. He wanted to be taken out of the deal with as close to 100 percent cash as he could get.

Lou studied the deal and saw that the seller could get the price he asked and over 80 percent of the cash he wanted if he would simply follow the plan Lou offered him. All the seller had to do was take out a new mortgage, let Lou buy the property "subject to the existing mortgage," and accept from Lou a second mortgage equal to the balance of the funds needed.

Lou calculated that if the seller placed a value of $170,000 on the home, he would be able to borrow $136,000 (80 percent of that value). There would be some closing costs on the mortgage, and Lou anticipated that would total $4000. This then would net out $132,000 to the seller. Lou would assume the $136,000 loan and give the seller a second mortgage in the amount of $38,000.

It looked good on paper. After all, the seller was walking out of the deal with a lot of cash; he could keep his price firm and only had to give in a little on the paper part of the transaction. Lou, by the way, was willing to pay a good rate of return on the second mortgage and that could have clinched the deal right there.

The seller still did not like the idea of letting the buyer walk in with no cash and little risk. To counter this Lou offered two kickers as additional security in the form of a set of sterling silver tableware appraised at $12,000. Lou had been holding the silver for his younger daughter's dowry and decided it might as well sit in a safe-deposit box as security on this paper. He also agreed to give the seller a percent of the income from the office tenants he expected to have within six months of closing the deal. Those two kickers were enough to make the deal work, and Lou bought the house. He kept the silver, of course, since he only gave it as security. As long as he paid the mortgage, the silver remained his.

Bob, on the other hand, was a seller who had a problem. He needed to unload a property he owned because he was short of cash but would have tax trouble if he sold any more property that year. He had a buyer ready in hand to buy the property, which was a small apartment building that was beginning to be more aggravation than it was worth. It needed fixing up, and Bob was on the move all the time and didn't have time to look after it. As he pondered what to do, he remembered that money borrowed is tax-free money. This meant that if he borrowed on a mortgage on the building, then that would generate the cash he needed without the tax worries.

So what Bob did was this: He made a deal with the buyer on an option basis to take over the management of the apartment house with zero cash down. The buyer could purchase the property at the end of one year, provided the terms of the option had been lived up to. These terms were to fix up the property as outlined in a detailed list of improvements that were needed.

Bob then borrowed the cash he needed, and during the year didn't have to worry about the operations of his improving apartment building. At the end of the year, the buyer exercised his option to buy (adding cash to the deal, which he obtained from a second mortgage on the now like-new apartment building). Bob solved his problem and made it possible for another buyer to get a zero-cash deal.

These are just two examples of refinancing prior to a sale to solve separate problems. The use of new financing to help the transaction along can be a marketing technique as well. It is possible for some owners to have so much equity in their property that a sale is difficult. Buyers with a lot of cash are generally the investors who hate to use it. The majority of investors around like to buy in with as little cash as possible. Therefore, investors who have a lot of equity may find that placing a mortgage on the property prior to closing is not only prudent but can make the sale. Keep in mind that the mortgage need not be placed on the property until you know you have a buyer in the wings, but it is a good idea to make sure you have a lender ready to make the desired loan.

THE SELLER'S VIEWPOINT

Any seller who approaches a lender with this technique should be candid with the lender. Tell the lender that your intention is to finance (or refinance, as the case might be) a property you own and ultimately plan to sell. Let him know that you want the loan to contain provisions allowing it to be assumed by a future buyer. The lender may impose limitations on this assumption, such as their approval of the buyer and adjustments of interest rate (contract rate) to a current level. But be honest with them on the ultimate intention to sell. Some lenders may relax the assumption provisions if you agree to remain on the loan. As a seller your risk in this circumstance will depend on the loan-to-value ratio of the mortgage loan, and your trust in the new buyer. If there is substantial equity in the property and the buyer has a good background and you don't believe he or she will trash the property, then the risk by staying on the mortgage may warrant the benefit of having the property off your back.

Whatever the lender will agree to, make sure you get it in writing. It is possible the buyer can come up with the necessary requirements to satisfy the lender without a full-blown loan application. A commitment from such lenders as a savings and loan association or a commercial bank can usually be obtained without cost, and when a lender has made the commitment, the balance of the deal can be put together.

THE BUYER'S VIEWPOINT

Once the commitment has been obtained the buyer can proceed with the purchase. The documentation the new buyer should carefully prepare would be the same in either new financing or assumption of existing financing. This information would include: a net worth statement, verification of income, details on any income property owned showing income and expenses and a rent roll of tenants, plus any other questions the lender may include in their loan applications.

THE FINE POINTS OF THE DEAL: UNDERSTANDING THE DIFFERENCE BETWEEN THE MORTGAGES

One of the toughest things to fully appreciate is the cost of the debt service. This single element, the total cost of the mortgage, is vital in developing beneficial refinancing instead of simply getting new money at future detriment to the investment.

The mathematics of mortgages is such that a $100,000 loan at 9 percent interest per annum payable over 30 years will have an annual payment (combination of 12 monthly installments) of $9660. This payment will continue, in the average amortized mortgage, at the rate of $805 per month for a full term of 30 years, over which time the principal of $100,000 is slowly reduced until it reaches zero. The reason it is slowly reduced is that the bulk of the payments are interest. In fact to pay back the $100,000 borrowed will cost $298,800 over the 30-year life of the mortgage at 9 percent interest and will split as follows: $100,000 of principal and $198,800 of interest. In the beginning the total cost, on an annual basis, of principal and interest is a steady percentage rate of 9.66 percent of the original mortgage loan amount. Providing the loan does not have an adjustable contract rate, which could periodically change, this percentage of 9.66 will reflect partial interest and partial principal. This percentage is called the "constant rate." If you look at Table A in the Appendix, you will find a series of interest rates and corresponding columns of years. A $100,000 loan for 30 years will have the 9.660 percent constant shown in the 30-year column under the column for 9 percent interest.

The annual payment for this $100,000 mortgage, then, is the amount owed multiplied by the constant rate for the remaining term of years. Multiplying $100,000 by 0.0966 will equal the annual payment over the term of 30 years of $9660 per year. This constant payment is multiplied by the loan amount (whatever is the actual loan amount), and the result of that gives you the total annual payment. However as you make the monthly payments divide that annual payment by 12 and you will have the constant payment per month for the next 30 years, which will cover interest and principal.

Back to the cost for a moment. In the very beginning you have a cost then of 9.66 percent for both the principal and interest part of the mortgage. I say in the beginning because as the loan pays off principal, the percentage increases. For example, by the time the loan has five years' maturity, the balance owed is $95,888.78 That's right, five years of payments at $9660 per year for a total of $48,280 and all you've paid off on the mortgage is a little more than $4071.50 of principal. The rest of what you paid is all interest. As the annual payment (total of 12 months) is constant and remains at $9660 per year, the cost relates back to a lower principal, therefore showing a greater annual percent. If you look at Table A's 25-year row in the column for 9 percent interest per annum, you will see the constant rate for a 25-year remaining term loan to be 10.07. The payment for the $100,000 loan over 30 years at 9 percent is a constant of 9.660 percent, which gives you a cost of $9660 per year. A loan that has a principal outstanding of $95,928.50 with 25 years of payments ahead of it, at 9 percent interest will have an annual total (of 12 months) of $9660.

Continue down the years now and examine what happens at the midpoint of this original 30-year loan, when the loan has 15 years remaining. If you look at the 15-year row of Table A at 9 percent interest, you will see that the constant is 12.17 percent. To instantly find the remaining balance owed on the loan, divide the annual payment ($9660) by this new constant rate (0.1217). The answer is $79,375.51. Although the loan is half over, almost 80 percent of the amount borrowed is still outstanding.

When you reach the point where only five years remain of the original 30-year term, things will look even more dramatic. Look at the five-year column at 9 percent in Table A. The constant rate is now a whopping 24.91 percent. Using the same fast technique to find the amount owed, you divide the annual payment of $9660 by this new constant, 0.2491, and come up with $38,779.61 still owed. This amount will be reduced to zero in the last five years of the mortgage at the same monthly payment you started out with.

The point here is that refinancing can bring down the overall cost of the money borrowed even if you have to borrow at a higher interest rate. Borrowing $100,000 at 9 percent, for example, at a new term of 30 years, will cost you $9660 a year in payments of principal and interest. However if there was an existing mortgage of $80,000 but it had only 12 years to go and is at 8.5 percent interest your actual monthly cost will be 13.32 percent constant rate. This is an annual cost of $10,656, which is more than the 9 percent loan of $100,000 for 30 years. If you did not need that extra $20,000 it would be better to take the existing loan and absorb the additional $1000 a year and have the $80,000 loan pay down to zero in only 12 years. If you need the additional cash to close the deal then you might be forced to the lower constant rate (but higher interest rate) in the form of the 30-year loan.

The take-away side of that story, of course, is you have just refinanced yourself back to a 30-year mortgage program from a mortgage with only 12 years to go. However, if the interest market drops, as we have seen during the first years of 2000, you can always refinance to more favorable terms.

It pays to learn about constants as a shortcut to understanding the mortgage market and just where you stand with overall cost. From time to time as the book develops, I'll give you more uses for the constant tables. You will find that they are a marvel at quick and easy calculations. You can invest in an inexpensive mortgage loan calculator that will work these same problems faster and is slightly more accurate for very large amounts of money. However once you get your hands on the mechanics of the tables you can fly right through problems. Full amortization tables that show the declining balance of the amount owed can be worked out on just about any computer, or surf the Internet and you will find sources that will do the calculation for you. Most operating systems or word processing systems also have mortgage and loan amortization software built into their programs.

20
CHAPTER

The Policy Loan

A good source for instant cash can be to borrow against your life-insurance policy. It may be, in fact, the most inexpensive loan available to you. That being the case, it is a technique to check out and see if it works for you. Before we go any further, though, let's look at the reasons not to borrow against an insurance policy. Later in the chapter we'll walk through how this technique works.

It could be that you have overlooked a better source of money. Prior to beginning this book, your repertoire of techniques to finance your real estate purchases was most likely limited. It's growing now, and by the time you finish this book it will be far richer than when you started. But that isn't all there is to the game. In addition to the individual techniques offered here you will end up with literally hundreds of combinations of methods to maximize the use of other people's money (OPM). This is a powerful tool. These techniques, with their blends and variations, will give you hundreds of alternative methods to make your deals work without your digging into your own pocket for the cash to buy.

Don't use your insurance cash value for your loan unless this loan technique provides the maximum benefit. You wouldn't borrow $15,000 against a free-and-clear $100,000 property if you could use a $17,000 property or $20,000 investment as that security.

You don't want to run up loan processing costs, so whatever method you use, make sure you are obtaining all the cash you need. Later on once you have established a "new value" to the property you can always refinance, often reducing the overall constant rate of the mortgages and thereby allowing you to repay borrowed capital and improving the income cash flow from the property. Of course when you borrow from your life-insurance cash value, you do have a freer in-and-out privilege. Usually you can borrow, repay, and borrow again at a high percentage of the cash value building up and at the low rate provided by most insurance contracts.

THE INSURANCE DEAL: BORROWING AGAINST YOUR POLICY

Janice had just about given up trying to find $20,000 to nail down a deal she was putting together. The triplex she had tied up was a real gem and she knew she would be able to turn it over in less than a year at a nice profit after fixing it up. She also had a fallback position because she knew that once she had completed the fix up, painting, and new landscaping, she would be able to refinance the property and recover every dime she had invested. But she was $20,000 short of closing the deal.

She was able to find lenders, but the property already had a first and second mortgage and she was reluctant to add a third. The lenders saw the potential, of course, and thought they had Janice over a barrel. They were hitting her for maximum interest and kickers that made the deal less than attractive to Janice as well as making it a risk Janice didn't want to take. She then remembered that her life-insurance policy had a cash value and that she could borrow against that cash value at a low interest rate.

She went home and, after a few hours hunting around in her office, she found the policy. It was an old one, taken out nearly 20 years before, and there was a provision enabling Janice to borrow up to the amount of the cash value. Let's stop here for a moment. Not all life insurance policies have a cash value. Some policies are what is called "term insurance"; this is written by the insurance company for a specific period of years. Sometimes these can be extended, and sometimes they might be convertible to another form of life insurance. But almost *never* do they have a cash value. So if this is the kind of insurance you have, feel free to discuss this situation with your insurance agent, but do not be disappointed when he tells you that there is nothing you can borrow against.

Janice did exactly this and discovered she had a type of insurance called "whole life," which was one of the kinds of life insurance that would build up a cash value as she made the annual payments. She also found that she could borrow against this cash value at the current borrowing interest rate, 6 percent annual interest.

At first Janice was cautious about borrowing on her life insurance. After all what if she died, or was crushed by the weight of her mortgage payments? Then she put it down on paper. Borrowing money from the insurance company didn't mean she wasn't still insured for the amount of the policy; it meant only that she was getting some of that insurance early and would be able to pay it back at any time plus the interest due. Surely if she was still insured for her policy amount and could borrow the funds she needed now at 6 percent, then that was much better than being held up by a third-mortgage lender at 12 percent plus in the form of part of the future profit in a later resale of the property.

There is no real trick to borrowing on your life-insurance policy, the only question is, can you borrow on it, and how much? After all, as not all insurance policies have a cash value, and not all that have a cash value will permit low-interest loans, you need to know just where you stand with your own life-insurance company.

THE FINE POINTS OF THE DEAL

Before moving forward into this type of deal, take time to reexamine your investing goals. Your long-term goals will affect your borrowing program so it's best to look at the whole picture upfront and make sure your goals and investments are in alignment. If you are interested in buying a four-unit apartment building with the idea of fixing it up for a resale, the method you choose of financing the purchase may differ from the one you would have chosen if your intention were to move into one of the units and keep the property for long-range income. You should be careful to follow this next part. I said *may differ* because you alone don't call all the shots: The deal will be made between you and the seller. It is possible that there will be only one way you can make a deal, that being the seller's way. If that fits your economics, okay, though you will still find that many of the techniques in this book will help you in meeting the economic needs to make the purchase, even on the seller's terms.

For the slow turnaround kind of purchase, I recommend you concentrate on techniques that use the purchased property as security rather than using other property you own first. If you still need cash and are still comfortable with the deal, then you can dip into loan sources such as policy loans. The idea here is to keep the maximum financing on the property you know will take you a long time to turn around. The short turnaround deal doesn't matter that much, and you might rather use a major refinancing to recover your capital if the sales market suddenly goes soft. But long turnaround deals might require extensive remodeling, and this is often best dealt with upfront with the lender. When you can show a lender a good remodeling plan with several prospective tenants ready to go, the positive economic conversion of that property will be attractive to the lender.

Let's say the four-unit apartment building you're interested in is priced at $192,000. It has a first mortgage of $150,000, and the seller has already agreed to hold a $20,000 second. To generate the $22,000 cash to buy it, you might find your insurance policy an ideal source. However that puts you into the apartment building with $22,000 equity (cash you borrowed from the insurance policy). This might be the ideal thing to do, except that when you sell the property you must get that cash back to pay off the loan. Since your plans to fix up the property include remodeling a detached garage and a workroom into another unit to make it a five-unit property, your approach to a new lender might attract most if not all the needed funds. Assume that your remodeling was going to cost $25,000 based on the new income potential that the five units would have a market value of $310,000. You can show the lender that your total investment is $192,000 plus $25,000 plus $10,000 (contingency funds), or a not to exceed total of $227,000. If you ask for 70 percent of your presumed new value of $310,000 the lender would lend you $217,000. If this was the case you could tell the lender that you can come up with the contingency money yourself (from your insurance policy loan).

SHOULD YOU BORROW AGAINST YOUR INSURANCE POLICY?

Now with what you have learned, does it make sense for you to borrow against your insurance policy? It really boils down to the proper matching of what you want to do with what you have to work with. Be sure to include all three of the important elements that you actually have to work with: time, ability, and capital. This matching of ideals with opportunities can rarely be done to perfection, but you can learn to avoid deals that require of you more than you are able to give. The key here is to fully understand what you are able to give, and what you need to get out of the investment in the first place.

There are three questions you should ask yourself before deciding to borrow against your insurance policy. If your answer to one or more of these questions is "yes," then the likelihood is that this is a good way to go. Keep in mind, however, that you must be very honest with yourself in answering these questions.

1. Have I attempted and failed to obtain the funds through the other techniques offered in this book at a cost lower than or equal to the total debt service for the insurance-policy loan? If you have not examined the situation in this totality, do so before going on to the other questions.

2. Is my long-range goal to hold on to the investment? If so, the security for the loan should be the security that provides the lowest loan cost.

3. Can the needed funds be fully attained through the insurance-policy loan? You should not dip into this well for only a portion of the needed funds, unless you already have the balance tied up in the contract or from other sources. Your insurance policy is like cash in the bank and should be looked at as a good source if the deal is good, and you have exhausted all other reasonable alternatives.

21

The Autograph Collector

When you are at your last thread in putting a deal together, you might find that the source for the funds was right before your nose all the time. All you needed was some signature power behind you to clinch the loan. This someone should be able to add credibility to your name and effort and increase your credit rating. In short you need a cosigner. The cosigner may be a person, corporation, partnership, or any entity that will entice the lender into making a loan that would not be made to you otherwise.

Let's say you were using a substitution technique, such as a pyramid, where the seller was holding a second mortgage on another property and you were trying to refinance the purchased property with your savings and loan association. Assume for a moment that the savings and loan cuts you short and offers you less than you have asked for. This is often a ploy on their part to see just how much you will stick to your demands. It is in their benefit to reduce the loan-to-value ratio since that increases their security. But when you really need the amount you have asked for and they turn you down, that can put a major crimp in your plans. If or when that happens, this technique can pull your deal out of the fire. Let's look at this situation in more detail.

THE PENNY SHORT DEAL: GETTING A COSIGNER

Tim was trying to buy a stripmall store. It was 10,000 square feet of local shops and generated a nice income as well as provided a sufficient tax shelter attractive to Tim. The price was $450,000, and the property had a low first mortgage of $150,000. Tim felt that any local savings and loan would lend 75 percent of the value, or $337,500, if he went to them and showed how he was going to increase the income thereby raising the value of the property. Tim figured that there would be loan costs totaling about $7500. He calculated that if he could get the seller to hold a $120,000 second mortgage secured by a farm Tim owned, then the seller would be well secured. After all, Tim had an appraisal showing the farm was worth well over $350,000 and the current first mortgage was only $50,000. In this way the savings and loan would not have an adverse loan-to-value ratio as the $120,000 second mortgage did not directly affect their security in the transaction. Tim would not have a second mortgage on the stripmall store, but on the farm instead. (See the discussion on pyramiding in Chapter 23.)

All was going according to plan until Tim got the results from the savings and loan association's loan committee. They said they liked the stripmall store and would loan $307,500 but not a penny more. That upset Tim's plans, as you can see here:

What Tim Wanted to Do		The Deal After the Loan Committee	
Cash Down	0	Cash Down	$ 30,000
Net Loan	$330,000	Net Loan	$300,000
Seller Takes		Seller Takes	
Second on Farm	$120,000	Second on Farm	$120,000
Price	$450,000	Price	$450,000

Keep in mind that in each of these two examples, the seller will get all cash proceeds above the net loan amount after paying off the existing $150,000. Even so there was no logical reason for the savings and loan to refuse the amount of money Tim needed, except that the current economic times made them reluctant to risk more loans on Tim. They needed to be enticed into the deal.

Tim asked for a conference with the loan officer and gave him some new ammunition to take back to the committee: He had a cosigner to make Tim less of a risk. This gave them a reason to increase the loan to its more realistic level, and the deal was saved. In Tim's case the cosigner might have been a relative, or it might have been the seller. Why would a seller cosign when selling the property? There are several good reasons. One might be that the seller herself likes the deal and doesn't want to lose Tim or Tim's deal. After all, the seller likes the deal, and is happy with the mortgage on the farm. For added security the seller may insist that should Tim ever default on the new mortgage the seller could step in and foreclose Tim out of the farm. Sure this is a potentially tough kicker, but it won't cost Tim anything as long as he lives up to his end of the bargain.

Your transaction won't be exactly like this, of course, but it is possible that you will find that you can and will be able to use the cosigner technique effectively. And remember, as long as you intend to keep to your end of the deal, you won't need to have the cosigner actually kick in.

THE FINE POINTS OF THE DEAL: USING KICKERS

If you know you can lock up the deal by adding a signer to the loan, then look at the possibility of giving the cosigner something for their risk. In the previous chapters I suggested several kinds of kickers you can offer, and they work with cosigners too. Cosigners shouldn't expect much—if anything—but be ready to offer something if you are in a tight market.

In my opinion the best kicker to offer a cosigner, if you have to, is something having to do with a future benefit. It might be a piece of the profit or perhaps some future use of the property. Of course if the cosigner is the seller, often her motivation is best satisfied by the deal closing and her ability to keep track of the deal by being a part of the loan.

The benefit for some parents in aiding their children will be getting them out of the house while at the same time watching their children grow and develop their own wealth. Kickers of this nature can be cultivated. But remember a start in the financial world doesn't just center around the use of another name; that name has to have something behind it to make it worthwhile from the lender's point of view.

What Is the Combined Net Worth of You and Your Cosigner?

This is a question lenders will ask. Remember what I've said about dealing with institutional lenders: You're dealing with people who lend someone else's money not their own. They are responsible for someone else's money so they will make sure that if anything goes wrong and the institution has to foreclose on you, no one will look back at them and say to the loan officer who processed your loan application, "Why did you do that?" To cover his tracks, the loan officer will say, "I can't understand what happened. We made him get a cosigner. Look at this net worth—it's better than our normal loan."

To be confident in that statement the loan officer will have insisted that your cosigner look as good in the credit reports as she does on paper. It's no good getting mom or dad to cosign if they are about to file for bankruptcy or divorce. Also your wealthy partner and cosigner won't do you one drop of good if she is on her way to the penitentiary for grand larceny. Pick a cosigner who can show a better net worth than you. (Your net worth, by the way, is your total assets less your total financial obligations.)

In determining an individual's net worth, there are two kinds of assets that a lender will examine carefully: liquid assets (cash or those items that are just as good as cash, such as gold or stocks) and nonliquid assets. (Real estate is one of the top nonliquid assets around. It can't be quickly turned into cash at its real value.)

Obviously lenders prefer strong liquid assets to nonliquid ones. On the other hand most real estate investors have a far stronger nonliquid asset list than cash equivalency. Since this will become your problem as you develop a real estate portfolio, you will need to make your nonliquid real estate look as important to the lender as it is to you.

All lenders want you to fill out a financial report. Use their form even if you have a dozen of your own. However, never fill out a lender's financial statement without giving a backup package detailing all the real estate you may own. If real estate is the bulk of your assets, you should show the income or profit potential of that real estate in hopes of softening its nonliquidity. Thus, if you own income property, spell out clearly the cash flow you earn and its potential for increases. If you have vacant property, then hint at your intended use or how and why it is going up in value.

The enhancement of your assets may not eliminate the ultimate need for a cosigner, but it will aid both of you in presenting the strongest lending package possible. In this way you will have the greatest opportunity to get the maximum loan at the most favorable terms.

THE SELLER'S VIEWPOINT

If the seller, who generally is the most motivated of all lenders, is balking at giving you more paper, it may be because you are a higher risk than they want to accept. In Tim's case, if the savings and loan association had ultimately turned Tim down on the increase needed or didn't come up to the required level, he could have gone back to the seller and said: "The savings and loan is about to blow your deal. It seems they are just about out of money, and I'm short $30,000 to make the deal work. I'll give you a second mortgage on the stripmall store for $30,000, however, with a cosigner to add to your security. Don't forget, Ms. Seller, you will still get $250,000 in cash when we close." (Of the new loan $150,000 would go to pay off the existing loan, and the balance would go to the seller.) This solution will work only if the new loan lender will allow the second mortgage to be placed on the property. Some will and some will not. If they balk at allowing the secondary financing, then either seek another lender who will, or offer the seller a mortgage position on another property.

FINDING A COSIGNER

So you're ready to sign the deal and you need a cosigner. Where do you find one and how do you go about it? There are many places to find a cosigner. Here's where they hide:

- Home (dad, mom, brothers, sisters, other relatives)
- Office (partners, coworkers, boss, employees)
- Social circle (your bartender, hairdresser, friends)
- Neighborhood (neighbors, shopkeepers)
- Financial circle (the broker, the seller)

For the most part the cosigner is taking little or no risk if they use any prudence at all. For this reason the most useful cosigner is apt to be found at home. If your parents, for example, can improve your future by doing nothing more than placing their names on the loan with yours, then that might work out nicely. If the loan is a low one in relation to the loan value one (unlike Tim's deal, a 75 percent loan-to-value), there is substantial property value securing it. At the same time the lender knows there is a moral obligation on the part of the cosigner to ensure that the loan is more secure, even if in fact there is little or no risk on the part of the cosigner.

22

CHAPTER

The Double-Scoop

When using this technique you get the seller to hold some paper while you finance the rest somewhere else, and usually you end up with cash in your pocket at the closing. There are many ways to double-scoop your purchases. Best of all, the technique is very flexible and can be used in combination with most of the other OPM techniques described in this book. Because it allows you to write your own terms on mortgages that do not yet exist, it gives you considerable control over your total debt service cost. This factor alone can allow you to create substantial value. Remember, in investment property, value is a function of the bottom line that the property will generate. When you can increase your bottom line by reducing your overall debt cost, that savings will generate up to 10 times (or more) into new value. So if you can reduce your total debt service by $2000, as compared to other more institutional financing, the value of your investment property has increased by at least $20,000.

The main ingredient in the double-scoop is a seller motivated to sell the property without the need to "cash out" at closing. Naturally a motivated seller is important in any real estate transaction where you hope to get the upper edge but not all sellers are that strongly motivated. Your job, then, is to either find a motivated seller or come up with a plan of purchase that will motivate the seller to accept your offer.

HOW TO FIND A MOTIVATED SELLER

With this technique you need to find a motivated seller. What makes a seller motivated, and how do you find a seller who is actually motivated? The first thing you need to understand is that motivation comes in many packages. The following is a list of some of the things that create motivation.

The Motivation Checklist

Management Problems. Management problems are the number one reason why small property sellers want to sell their income-producing properties. Some real estate investments are fairly management free and these tend to escape that motivation. Landleases and long-term triple net leases fall into that category. Top of the list of motivation to sell would be any management intensive properties that are not large enough to support hiring a management company. These would include apartment buildings of less than 50 units, small seasonal properties, stripmalls, office buildings of less than 20,000 square feet, and any other income-producing property that does not generate a net operating income (NOI) of $100,000. Understanding this as a potential motivation can help you make the kind of deal you want, especially if it is a double-scoop OPM transaction. Why? Because if you have the management skills needed to take this property and improve it, then by increasing the bottom line you will find it easier to convince the seller of your ability to buy the property. This is the first step to getting the seller to hold paper on some other property. Even if it is one you don't own yet.

Profit. Many investors are solely interested in acquiring a property and turning it around as quickly as possible for profit. Naturally all real estate investors hope ultimately to find a profit in their investments, but when profit is the primary motivation it is helpful for any new buyer to understand this. Why? Because the seller motivated by the desire for profit is working against time. It is like the used car business. Owners and managers of car lots get very anxious when the car has been on the lot for more than 30 days. As a buyer of used cars or real estate (held by owners whose motivation is principally profit) you will discover that your persistence in making offers may convert the early "not interested" into "okay, let's close."

Excessive Debt. There are many reasons why people get over their heads in debt. Whatever the circumstance, this can become a very persuading motivation for any seller. When a seller is facing potential foreclosure many things begin to fall apart. They don't sleep well anymore, their personal relationships begin to deteriorate, they start cutting corners, and the property itself begins to deteriorate. These are prime candidates for any creative OPM deal. The bad side of this motivation is that many of these sellers do not see the handwriting on the wall. Or if they do see it, they struggle along hoping that somehow they will pull the rabbit out of the hat in the end and save the day. By the time foreclosure has been filed it is often too late for an outside buyer to enter the picture. The key for buyers is to look for the symptoms of this motivation. Why? Because the symptoms are usually clearly visible. Look for buildings in good areas that are in need of simple cosmetic update and buildings that have not had any maintenance for awhile. Check the county records advertisements in local business publications for mechanics liens for nonpayment of work done on the buildings. Ask your newly found loan officers in your local lending associations to keep you up-to-date on any problem loans that may be getting dangerously close to foreclosure action. You will be ahead of the pack if you do.

Absentee Ownership. Property owners who live more than a three-hour drive from their investment property will, at one time or another, think how nice it would be not to have to deal with that property. Absentee ownership presents many problems and magnifies even the smallest of them. Often the property owned by the absentee owner is kept up pretty well. This is a defensive move to keep from having to deal with the magnitude of problems that come when you always let a property run to the last minute before having work done on it. The concept of "if it ain't broke, don't fix it" is how many property owners manage their real estate. This is wrong, in my opinion, so when you see a property that is well cared for do not assume that the seller is not a likely seller. The absentee owner cannot hide and is a good person for you to get to know. Best of all, they are easy to find. Why? Because property records will have their address, or at least the address where the tax bill is sent each year. If the tax bill goes to a management company you may not get the actual owner, but properties that are managed by companies and not the owner may indicate an absentee owner. Check them out.

Desire to Be "Free of Property Worries.*"* Every small property investor will have these thoughts, often many times a day. Usually this is a motivation that is given to you when you ask why the seller is interested in selling. These are great sellers because they still want income but without the problems that come with the ownership. Find them and you will eventually have a good seller to deal with. Why? Because they have or are about to lose the joy of property ownership. Develop a relationship with them and one day they may call you to see if you want to purchase their property.

Downsizing Lifestyle. Many people come to the realization that having 100 (or 100,000) employees working for them is too much. Owning a million square feet of shipping center or just 10,000 square feet of stripmall stores is complicating their life. There are many reasons people reach this stage of their life and like the desire to be free of worries, you may not see the symptoms manifested in the real estate. But if you read local newspapers and society magazines you will see the beginning of that trend. Why? Because one of the major reasons people downsize is because of a major and often dramatic change in their life. The death of a family member, the announcement of retirement, being fired, having a member of the family sent on a long, fully-paid government vacation (jail), divorce, announcement of children graduating from college, and so on. All of these are preludes to downsizing of lifestyle.

Personal Problems. The list of personal problems would include everything I have just mentioned and a hundred or more other things that are, indeed, personal. You may never hear or discover the actual truth to any of these because they are frequently manifested in a defensive way. A seller may not want to let anyone know that his property is being sold because he has lost his job, has a terminal illness, or is forced to leave town to seek a job elsewhere. If you do discover this it is often because you have close mutual friends, so be careful. Why? Because you need to protect the privacy of that motivation. Seek to learn what goal the seller wants to achieve. You might be able to help them get it.

The Bottom Line of Motivations

You will be able to tailor your creative use of OPM strategies by understanding the motivations that drive a seller to accept any deal. Often the best way to do this is to start your relationship with that seller in a slow and deliberate way. I have mentioned earlier the importance of the seller knowing you are interested in their property and would like to buy it. If they are really interested in selling they will actually help you buy.

In the end, however there is only one real way to find sellers who are motivated to do business with a hard nut of an investor like you. You must make offers, make offers, make offers, and then make some more offers. By constantly being a ready and willing buyer (on your terms, of course), you will be ready when the seller who wasn't motivated yesterday all of a sudden becomes motivated today.

The basic law of successful real estate investors centers around this simple fact: You have to ask someone to do what you want them to do before they will do it. This works most emphatically for the double-scoop.

Never Forget the Unmotivated Seller

The guy who has overpriced his property may not appear to be a strongly motivated seller, but if it is a property I would like to own, I will not cross him off my list. Why? Because if his property is overpriced, it isn't going to sell. The average buyer will pass it up in favor of a more reasonably priced investment. However, if I like the property, I'll hang in there and make one offer after another, change from one buying technique to another, not in the hope of breaking the seller down to a lower price but to let him know I'm a taker of his property when he becomes motivated.

The double-scoop method works on the motivation of need and the lack of alternatives to which the seller can turn.

THE DOUBLE-SCOOP DEAL

Gregory found a beautiful office building that could be purchased for only $200,000. The building had some major drawbacks, the most important being the fact that it was currently 100 percent vacant. The property had been on the market for over a year, during which time Gregory had watched one tenant after the other leave the building. The price dropped a little each time, until Gregory was ready and willing to step in and make the deal he wanted.

Gregory offered the seller $150,000 in cash, out of which the seller would have to pay off the small $30,000 first mortgage. On top of the

$150,000, Gregory would give the seller a note for $50,000. The note was not secured by the building and was at a relatively low interest rate, but Gregory agreed to pay off the note within five years or at that time secure the note with a mortgage on property worth a minimum of twice the remaining amount of the note (as a kicker) and to then pay off the balance within four more years.

Gregory knew he was making a good deal as he already had a tenant lined up for the building. It was an insurance company that needed just that sort of building. Based on the lease Gregory knew he could work out, he went to a savings and loan association and showed the now improved value (improved because the building would no longer be vacant, but, instead, rented at top dollar). That new value was estimated by Gregory to be $270,000.

The lenders agreed that the rent justified this higher value, and Gregory was able to borrow 75 percent of the new value, or $202,500 net of mortgage loan costs. This gave him a good loan at the best rate of interest. The seller would walk away from the closing with $120,000 cash and a $50,000 note from Gregory. Of that $30,000 went to pay off the existing first mortgage, and Gregory owned the office building. He left the closing with $52,500 (less the closing costs) in his pocket.

Gregory's Deal

Purchase price	$200,000
Cash to seller	$120,000
Note to seller	$ 50,000
Pay off of existing	$ 30,000
	$200,000

Gregory's Investment Position

Borrows from the bank	$202,500
Gives seller	$120,000
Pays off existing	$ 30,000
Puts balance in his pocket	$ 52,500

Gregory double-scooped on this deal because he had over $50,000 cash in his pocket after paying the closing costs on the mortgage and taking title to the property. That $50,000 cash, by the way, was tax free to Gregory and was promptly put to work as a down payment on another property.

THE FINE POINTS OF THE DOUBLE-SCOOP

It's important to maintain an economically strong, successful, and confident composure. These three important images are even more effective if they are more than skin deep, but in the beginning you must at least appear certain that what you are doing is going to succeed. There are also other key factors that will aid you in making your double-scoop transaction successful.

Buy high-equity property. When you are dealing with sellers who own their property free and clear of any mortgages or who have high equity, then you have a greater potential for generating cash for the seller as well as yourself. If the seller has a high percentage of financing already on the property, you need to seek some other method to make the deal work, as there would be little room to refinance.

Find sellers who can't exercise control over their property. If the seller is moving out of town, or can't deal with the public, or has a full-time job that doesn't allow him time to look after his own interests, then you have a seller who has lost or is about to lose control over his property and will more freely accept any deal that will solve his imminent problem.

Deal with sellers who have a distinct and definable need or goal to attain. You have to examine the current times to know who they might be. In tight money markets, they might be builders or developers looking to unload property they don't need to protect their projects. A seller who has had some economic or personal tragedy befall him should not be overlooked.

Buy property that lenders like. You find out what property they like by asking them. Visit mortgage brokers and loan officers and ask that big question, "What is the most borrowable property in town?" Work from that. Smart investors don't buy what they are in love with, they buy what the lenders are in love with. Wise up on this score. Once you are wealthy and can blow your cash, you can spend money on property you've fallen in love with.

Think big and act big. If you've just obtained an option to buy a property for $130,000, don't be afraid to up the value on that property to $250,000 when you approach a lender. Make sure you can back up the new value of $250,000, but never, never point out the increase. Simply say, "The value of this property is $250,000 because I have a letter of intent to lease this building from IBM for $14 per square foot on a triple net lease with cost-of-living adjustments every year over the next 20 years." If that doesn't do it, nothing will. If you point out that this figure represents an increase of value, you tie it back to the old value. The past in real estate is gone forever. Don't raise values, however, on a whim. Have a sound basis for doing it, and stick to it, but be sure you can document it with sound, current, and pertinent information.

Shop around for mortgages. You have to look for financing; it doesn't seek you out. Only really big investors have money barking at their door. Remember what barks also bites. When you seek a loan, visit with a minimum of four savings and loan associations and one or two commercial banks. Start with lenders that are most distant from you (but still within the investment area). Why? You will want to practice your presentations skills on lenders you may not ultimately do business with. Save the closer lenders for your polished presentations.

Do not take the first or second no. When a loan committee turns you down, try to find out why. Then try to counter the objection with a new loan submission. Try a kicker, a cosigner, or something else, but keep at it until you obtain the financing at terms you can live with.

There will be a point, of course, when you must finally take a no gracefully if it keeps on coming back to you. After all you don't want to burn your bridges.

FROM THE BUYER'S SIDE OF THE DEAL

Buyers need to beware the potential overextension of loan to value when using this technique. You will have a mortgage with the lender and another with the seller. If you aren't careful, that will burn a big hole in your pocket in a hurry.

The obvious advantage of the double-scoop is you finance 100 percent nearly all the time and much of the time you can walk out of the deal with cash. There are, however, times when you are unable to do the double-scoop as I've outlined it in this chapter. In fact there are times when the seller will go along with everything except the unsecured note.

When this happens you can fall back on the pyramid and its several variations. In the next two chapters we'll discuss two pyramid techniques that offer fantastic opportunities to launch yourself into sudden equity and greater wealth by leveraging your equity from one property into another.

FROM THE SELLER'S SIDE OF THE DEAL

The seller is taking a risk, of course, by taking a note back on a deal not secured by any mortgage. But some sellers, anxious to get the cash and trusting the buyer, will do just that. In fact if you were a seller you might seek out a prime candidate you trusted and sell him your property just that way.

Risk, after all, is a two-way street. If the seller can get a good price and a lot of cash by taking a risk on a person he already believes in, that isn't such a bad risk after all.

23

CHAPTER

The Grand Pyramid

All pyramid techniques rely on the human tendency to view the grass as greener on the other side of the fence. The pyramid techniques I use and describe in this book are completely legal methods to enable you to get the most out of your equity. In all pyramid techniques, the seller holds some paper or benefit as a part of the transaction. What differentiates the pyramid deal from the usual situation where the seller will take back a second mortgage is that, in a pyramid, the seller holds the paper or other benefit that results from some other property. In short, the buyer gives the seller something other than the purchased property as security on the loan.

THE PYRAMID DEAL

Let's take a look at how this technique works. Eric has found a great vacant lot on which he would like to build a rental apartment building. That is, he will build it if he can put his transaction together in such a way that he can borrow all of the funds necessary to build the building.

The lot is priced at $30,000. Eric will put six studio apartments on the site at a total construction cost of $180,000. He calculates that other costs—such as plans, interest on financing, and miscellaneous items—will bring his total costs for land and building to $240,000. He is sure, however, that by the time the building is rented (and the current low vacancy rate in the area indicates that will happen as soon as the building is completed), the value will be at least $320,000. He quickly found a bank that would lend 80 percent of the pro forma (future value estimate). This gave him $256,000, which was more than he needed; only the lender would only pay the funds over the construction period. This is a normal situation and lenders divide the funds up so that the payments can reasonably go directly to the construction costs. These are called "draws" from the bank. The downside of this is that the lender was not going to advance the acquisition part of the loan but pay it at the end. This meant that Eric would have to pay for and own the lot from day one on. In the final moment, when the loan is fully paid off, Eric will be able to pay all construction and purchase costs and come out okay. But in the beginning he is $30,000 short, which is the amount needed to purchase the lot. So he offers the seller the following:

- $15,000 cash, to be paid out of the first construction draw when Eric breaks ground.
- A note and mortgage in the amount of $15,000 at closing. The mortgage will be on a beautiful three-bedroom home Eric owns in Vero Beach. True, it will be a second mortgage, but it is a beautiful home and the first mortgage is quite low.

The seller really wants to sell the lot, and this deal is a secure and safe one. He gets some cash within a few weeks after starting the construction, and he holds a strong mortgage, even if it is a second-position mortgage. As Eric has no secondary financing on the lot he is buying, the lender will have a first lien on the lot. It is as if Eric has $30,000 equity in the deal. Here is how the deal has shaped up:

At the outset Eric owes $15,000 in cash on the lot but this is not a mortgage, it is a unsecured promise, or might be secured by the home in Vero Beach along with the mortgage on that property. The construction loan is paid over the draws I mentioned earlier and as Eric is the building contractor, he will allocate the draws to cover his ongoing costs, one of which is the first payment to the owner. In essence, Eric will be taking his overhead and profit as a contractor and giving it to the lot owner. When the construction is nearing completion, it is likely that Eric will have already sold the property, at what he anticipated or even a greater amount. The permanent part of the loan will go into place when all the construction is finished, so the would-be buyer assumes or is approved by the lender for that loan and everyone gets what they have been promised.

The use of the pyramid to generate 100 percent financing is a sound way to approach any building program. In Eric's case if he had not sold the property by the time construction was finished, he still had enough money from the payout of the loan to satisfy the loan on the Vero Beach house.

Then there was Mike's situation. Mike wanted to buy a 35-unit motel on route AIA in Fort Lauderdale. It was a nice property and was priced at $1,225,000. The present owners had owned the property for over 15 years and had paid the financing down to only $210,000. Mike saw this as a real opportunity to use the pyramid, so he approached the sellers with this deal:

- Mike calculated he could give them $700,000 cash at closing.
- He would take over the obligation of the existing mortgage.
- He would give them a first mortgage of $315,000 on a large vacant tract he owned near Naples, Florida. The terms of this mortgage were such that Mike knew the sellers would accept them.

The sellers looked at Mike's offer and realized they would get more cash out of the deal than they had hoped for. They had anticipated that a buyer would not come in with more than 30 to 40 percent down, so getting $700,000 cash out of the deal was very attractive. On top of this, they didn't even have to hold mortgages on their motel.

What Mike did next should already be in the back of your mind by now. He went to a lender (who he knew liked motels) and cut a deal to borrow 75 percent of the purchase price. That gave him $918,750 in cash. Out of that he made a deal to pay off the existing first mortgage of $210,000, which was at a very low rate of interest. The holder of that paper was so glad to get cash that the mortgage was discounted down to a round $200,000. Mike then gave the seller his $700,000, paid $15,000 for the mortgage closing, and was left with $3750 in his pocket.

Now watch what goes on when you pyramid. In the first place, there are more motivations at play than just the "grass is greener" one. In most cases the sellers are actually glad they aren't being asked to hold a mortgage against their own property. The reason for this is rather simple. When the seller bought the property, he probably paid much less than he is now asking. In the seller's mind there are mixed emotions. Suddenly he loves the property to death: It is a pot of gold, his diamond, his life and blood; he can't part with it; he'll never find another parcel like it; he'll kick himself forever in the head for selling it. You have either had these emotions or you will at some time of your real estate ownership life. On the other hand he wants to sell, must sell, can hardly wait until he is rid of the dump, can't stand being there any longer, the world is about to end if he doesn't sell. This too is in your real estate future. And yet everyone has told him that if he sells he should never hold a second mortgage on the property he just sold unless he gets a ton of interest per year and has a first mortgage with a loan-to-value ratio of 50/50.

But an ultrahigh second-mortgage interest rate will hamper the sale of the property. This is proven to him as one deal after another is blown because as a seller he doesn't want to hold paper on his property without such compensation and buyers can't make the deal work with such high debt service. On top of that, sellers frequently object to holding paper for another reason. Remember, they paid so much less for the property when they bought it they now have a hard time accepting the fact that the property is really worth as much as it is. I've had sellers who, a few weeks earlier, had ranted and raved how their home was worth over $800,000. Then suddenly as I presented an offer that asked for them to hold a small second mortgage, they looked me in the face and said, "Hold a second mortgage on this dump? That's too much risk."

THE FINER POINTS OF THE DEAL

You don't just blunder into a situation and try to spring a pyramid on the seller. You need to feel out the seller to some degree to get a pulse on his motivations. It would be nice if you could find out just how low he will go in price. Can you break him down on cash needed to make the deal? Your first, exploratory offers should be rather low, just on the chance that you have found a seller so motivated that one of your low offers hits the right nerve at the right time and he grabs the offer then and there. But even if this doesn't happen, a low offer—say, $255,000 on a $375,000 home—lets you out if that is what you want and is a shocker of an offer.

If you are making this offer through brokers, you must tell them you think this property is overpriced but you would like to own it. Be sincere that you are ready to make this $255,000 offer and would like the brokers to present it. The brokers may react to this if they are worth their salt and attempt to dissuade you from making this low offer. At this point you must stand firm. Unless you are paying your real estate agent and have the utmost trust in them, never give the broker or salesperson any indication that you will come up. Never say, "Well, let's see what he says." Just say, "I would like to buy this property and I wish you would present this offer."

Do not worry if the broker tells you that the sellers have turned down more; if they have, it is possible they now wish they hadn't. Simply stick to your guns and insist that you want the offer presented. Don't be nasty about it. In fact if you want to make your point even stronger, write out a check to the broker's escrow account for a modest deposit and hand it to him while at the same time, in a much lower voice than before, you nearly whisper, "We love this property and want very much to own it."

If you have played your role well enough and the broker or salesperson isn't a real nincompoop, he will get the picture. You really do want to own the property. But you haven't given him any indication that you will come up in price.

The moment the salesperson thinks you might come up in price, he will assume you will. That feeling will be imparted to the seller and will come back to you in the form of a counteroffer higher than it might otherwise have been. On the other hand if the salesperson gets the feeling you will buy, he will work harder to bring both of you together, even if he has to take up some of the slack by reducing his commission.

As a salesperson I hate to give away any secrets, but brokers do from time to time cut their commissions. The deals they are most likely to do that on will be the deals they have worked the hardest to make, and in which there is at least one party who appears to be appreciative of their efforts. Keep this in mind no matter which side of the fence you are on, because the opposite is also true: Brokers will stand so firm that their commission blows a deal when both buyer and seller take the posture that the broker is the only thorn in the garden. Alas how easy it is to forget who watered the flowers.

Okay, so you are being nice to the salesperson and he is out busting his buns to make your deal work. If you have done your job right, you are offering less than the seller may take and there is going to be some kind of a counter. That is almost a 90 percent sure thing.

DEALING WITH THE COUNTER IS A MOVE TO THE PYRAMID

When you move into the real nitty-gritty of the purchase negotiations, you should be ready to get serious. Your original offer, if countered at all, will be countered with an offer much higher than you would like. Now you can let the salesperson bring you up, while at the same time you learn more about the seller. Before making your second offer (counter to the counter), which could be your final offer, you should be sure you have the answers to the following questions:

1. **What are the existing mortgages and other financial obligations against the property?** You may have thought you knew what they were. The broker for the seller may have also thought he knew, but sometimes the first offer brings out some hidden mortgages or tax assessments or other frightening things the seller forgot to tell anyone about. You must know exactly where you stand with the actual financing and hidden obligations. You need to know more than just amounts. Who holds the mortgages? What is the payoff penalty, if any? What is the interest rate, etc.? You won't be able to pyramid or, for that matter, use many of the no-cash-down techniques if there is a whopping mortgage that everyone thought could be paid off only to find that it cannot be paid off without killer penalties. Tax assessments are essential, too, as they may require sudden cash payments and might be one of the seller's strongest motivations. After all, neither the county tax collector nor the IRS is a creditor you want to mess around with.

2. **What is the owner's real reason for selling?** The owner of a hotel told me he wanted to sell because he wanted a larger property. I made a thorough inspection of the hotel he wanted to sell and found it to be in horrendous condition. I asked the owner if he knew the condition of the property, and he did know, which is exactly why he wanted to sell.

   You may never find out the full extent of the reasons for sale. Some sellers will be impossible to understand, as not everyone operates logically. But some idea of the reason for the sale might open up alternative techniques of buying that neither you nor the broker would have guessed. If it turns out that a seller wants to get out of his large, electricity-eating house, and move into a more economical property, a buyer can seek out some possible solution to that need. If another seller discloses a desire to travel around the world, the buyer might make that dream come true—not by paying cash but by making travel a part of the deal. Only by knowing where the seller wants to end up, can the buyer fit his buying techniques to the benefit of each party.

3. What are the seller's feelings about holding paper? This one is hard to get at because sometimes the broker asks the question negatively: "You wouldn't want to hold a $40,000 second mortgage, would you?" The salesperson might have to be coached by you on this, for example, "If I gave the seller a mortgage I'm holding on another property, do you think he'd be interested in that?" Sellers will view outside paper in a different way than they view mortgages on what they are selling. But sometimes they don't know how to respond to the question.

4. Does the seller know I want to own his property? This is important. If the seller knows this, that is good. If the seller thinks you are dying to own the property, that is bad. If the seller is insulted that you have made a low offer and are trying to steal his pride and joy, then you have to do something to counteract this feeling. Usually it is a matter of reprogramming the salesperson. "Look, I understand how the seller feels," you say to the salesperson in a low voice that causes him to strain to listen. "You have done a fantastic job in finding us the very property we would like to own. We didn't fully appreciate its value and made a low offer, but please express our feelings that we love the property and wish there was a way to own it."

5. Does the seller know that you will buy something else if you can't work out a deal with him? This is essential: There must be some urgency on the seller's part. There is no need to tell the salesperson this; ask to look at another house or two—even make another offer if you find something else in the meantime. The word will get back to the seller.

In the end the best bet is to let the pyramid offer be the best face-saver they may get. What you're saying is that you're convinced of the value but the deal has to be this way because it allows them to sell the house. Then close with a kicker if you must. You might agree to give an extra 90 days to close so that arrangements can be made to move or secure that second mortgage with property you own (the pyramid), in Belo Horizonte, Brazil. When the pyramid is presented, make sure you have the backup on the "grass is greener" property to close the deal right then.

WHAT KIND OF MORTGAGE SHOULD YOU OFFER IN A PYRAMID?

Keep in mind that when you offer a pyramid, you are writing a mortgage against a property you own (in this technique) and the mortgage does not presently exist. This enables you to write a soft mortgage. This is a mortgage at an interest rate and or terms that are usually below the current market rate. Remember this is a mortgage you are creating. However it is presented to the seller as though it already exists.

For example, earlier in this chapter when Eric made the deal on the lot, he pyramided the seller off to a second mortgage on his three-bedroom home. The amount was only $15,000, but since the security was excellent, Eric may have gotten by with a 6 percent mortgage interest. In a current market of 9 percent interest, the 6 percent rate would have been soft, but, as the seller got his price, the deal was cut without much argument. The seller was more interested in the sale than quibbling over a point or two of interest.

In Mike's motel deal he pyramided with a $315,000 first mortgage on some land. That mortgage could have been at 7 percent interest for a long payout of 20 years with a shorter balloon. The key is to solve the primary motivation or driving force. Sellers always think they want the most money, but when it boils down to it they will relax that demand when they realize the benefit of a quicker closing, a larger front-end deposit, shorter inspection time, longer or shorter secondary mortgage payout, and so on. In the beginning all sellers measure their desired contract against the ideal. But the ideal is rarely offered. As you become a seller you should try to remember this. Each offer that is presented to you might just be the best you will ever get. As you hold out for better this, more of that, and so on you will discover this fact. On the other hand, time, if you have it, is always on the side of the seller. If you can afford spending the time, you can hold on to most real estate until it rises up to your expectation of ideal. But time is money. In the world of secondary financing, time and interest rate combined is everything. I can pay almost any reasonable price if the seller is willing to accept my terms.

If you can get the seller to accept the idea of the pyramid and can agree on everything else, then the final terms of the debt the seller should hold would become the easiest part of the deal to work out.

Show the Seller How the Soft Terms Benefit Him

It is all a matter of economics. If the seller gets his price, you are closing down on the deal. I'm assuming you have gotten to the point where the seller is trying to get you to increase the interest rate on your pyramid, or shorten the terms. If you have played the pyramid properly, this is just where you want the deal to be. Why? Because interest on a mortgage that is paid to a seller is treated as earned income. The seller pays income taxes on it at the highest possible rate that taxpayer is in, according to the tax bracket he is in for that year. On the other hand, the principal part of the mortgage may not be taxable at all. Even if it were taxed it would be at a capital gain rate, which is taxed at a much lower rate for most sellers than the earned-income tax rate. This simple fact, when pointed out at the right moment, will show the seller it may be better for him to be get the price agreed to, at a slightly lower interest rate on a part of the deal (the amount of the pyramid), than to take a lower price and get more interest.

As you have worked up in your offers, the salesperson can honestly say to the seller, "I've got him up." This enables the seller to rationalize that indeed it is better to get a higher price (get the buyer up) and let Uncle Sam pay the difference by reduction of tax that the seller would have to pay on earned income (taking a lower price but higher interest), through the lower tax on capital gains.

Okay, you should have some idea about pyramids. They are exciting and full of benefits for both the seller and the buyer. The seller can use this buying technique to get rid of high equity and turn a difficult-to-sell property into an attractive buy while at the same time enabling the buyer to acquire a property and simultaneously generate additional capital to fix it up, to purchase other properties.

24

The Distant Pyramid

The grand pyramid, as described in the previous chapter, was based on the human tendency to see something we don't have as more valuable than those things we do have. This is often just an illusion, but it is a strong motivator nonetheless. Such motivations can be put to good use when buying or selling real estate. All pyramiding techniques involve moving equity into paper or some other benefit, which is used to buy other property or to sell the paper or benefit being used in the pyramid. Yet techniques based on the pyramid are far more flexible than you have thus far learned, as you will see in the twist described in this chapter. Here you will learn how you can pyramid to paper, real estate, or benefits you don't own but want to.

This technique, called the distant pyramid, is used when you are making two purchases at or about the same time. In this case you will actually negotiate the seller of one property into holding a second mortgage secured by the other property you are in the process of purchasing or plan to buy. It is possible to double the distant pyramid by setting up the purchase so each of the two sellers will end up with a down payment in the form of a second mortgage on the other property. In this OPM transaction you can make two deals without spending any of your own cash.

THE CONDITIONAL DEAL

Phil wanted to buy a five-unit apartment building and a small commercial building. His big problem was that he didn't have the cash requirement for both. He approached the situation using an offer containing provisions that gave him time to make various inspections and check out the condition of the property without having to commit in advance to purchase the property in its "as is" condition. Often the buyer must seek a zoning change or obtain a permission to construct a specific project. Some cities may require special exception approvals be granted for certain kinds of businesses. Buyers facing this kind of situation may need to go through considerable preparation and expense to obtain these permissions. While this is a normal process, it can be relatively quick or it can drag out for weeks or even months.

Phil felt he needed 45 business days to accomplish everything he needed to do. The conditional contract gave him several outs that in effect prevented anyone else from buying the property; with the property firmly locked up, Phil was ready to proceed. Note that I used the term *business days*. This is the usual way time is stated in the most recent form contracts. The agreement will usually have one paragraph or section that defines the terms used in the agreement. It will be in that section that the agreement will say something like this: Time periods exclude weekends, bank holidays, and other national or regional holidays. Then throughout the balance of the contract it will simply use the word "days" as the time for buyer or seller to accomplish their tasks as will be called for in the terms and conditions of the sale. With this in mind make sure you understand that 45 of these kinds of days can be nine weeks or more in duration.

Let's take a look at terms of the purchase of the commercial building. The price of the building was $205,000. This included the existing financing of which Phil could assume of $130,000 payable over 25 years at 9 percent interest. This left the seller with $75,000 equity.

Phil pays as follows:

Purchase price	$205,000
Assume the existing	$130,000
Cash at closing	$ 25,000
Second mortgage on other property	$ 50,000

Enter Phase Two: The Apartment Building

With the contract on the commercial building tied up, Phil next went to the seller of the apartment building and negotiated the following deal, using a similar conditional contract as with the first property. The price was $200,000 subject to a first mortgage of $45,000, which Phil could assume. In this transaction the seller's equity is $155,000.

Phil agreed to pay equity as follows:

Purchase price:	$200,000
Subject to the first mortgage	$ 45,000
Cash at closing	$ 65,000
Second mortgage on another property	$ 90,000

Now armed with these two deals, Phil proceeded to put his transaction together. The first step was to find out how much new financing could be placed on the $200,000 apartment building. This was quickly ascertained through a few calls to some loan officers at three of the local savings and loan associations he customarily dealt with. If the appraisal checked out, Phil could anticipate a cash loan of $160,000 on the apartments. The closing costs of the loan would total about $6000, so Phil would net $154,000 from the closing of the loan on the apartment building. Since he knew he would have to pay off the existing first mortgage of $45,000, he could figure on having $109,000 left over. Of course he would then give $65,000 to the seller, leaving himself $44,000 cash to play with.

The second step was to work up a nice pro forma on the commercial building and take it to the apartment owner. The pro forma showed the rents and other facts about the building as they actually were, but showed the projection for the future and a higher value based on the projection. The seller of the apartments studied the pro forma, looked at the building, and agreed to accept the second mortgage on the commercial building. In essence the apartment seller agreed to hold a $90,000 second mortgage on the commercial property.

Phil then went to the seller of the commercial building and asked him if he would take a $50,000 second against the apartment building. Phil explained that there would be a new first mortgage in the amount of $160,000 and that his mortgage would be second to that lien. The answer again was yes.

Phil arranged a simultaneous closing with both parties to pass title. From the loan proceeds on the apartment ($44,000), Phil paid the commercial-building seller $25,000. The $19,000 cash left over went into the bank to pay for the improvements Phil planned to make on both properties to quickly improve their appearance so he could increase rents.

In working a distant pyramid the key is control of the property you are buying. You cannot effectively work the deal with less than a signed contract binding the seller to close on the deal if he approves the security on the second mortgage he is to take. The motivation on the part of each seller goes through a sudden transition the very moment a contract for sale has been signed, and this will work to your benefit if you understand it. Once there is a contract of sale, most sellers will psychologically let go of the property they are selling. Remember up until the time they have sold the property, they are the owners and maintain 100 percent control. Keep in mind that this period of time can be one of mixed emotions for the sellers: to sell or not to sell. The seller may wake up the following morning with what is commonly called "seller's remorse." This will happen to nearly every seller. Did I do the right thing? Did I get enough? Should I have held out for more? And so on. When you are working with a conditional contract, you must make sure that your control period extends beyond the usual period of seller's remorse.

HOW TO HELP CURE SELLER'S REMORSE

Seller's remorse is an illness that will kill your deal if you don't take preventative measures to stop it. There are several things you can do to help the seller over his bout of remorse, and you should anticipate this as a natural sequence for you to follow.

- Make sure you have no direct contact with the seller during the conditional period. You are honest and don't want to be put into the position of having to avoid a question you don't want to answer. Your business is your business, so keep it that way. Avoiding the seller, however, must be done in such a way that the seller doesn't become worried about where you are. You don't want to see the seller (or talk with him directly) until you are ready to get his approval on the security of the second mortgage.

- Be sure anything required of you in the contract is carried out promptly. If you are using an inspection of leases or of the mechanical apparatus of the building as a way out of your agreement (you have to have time to have them inspected, then to approve of the inspections), then be sure someone is actually inspecting the items in question.

- Instruct those actually doing the inspections not to raise doubts about the inspections. You don't want the termite inspector, for example, to walk around shaking his head and stomping on the ground like he is killing insects. Likewise, the accountant or apartment manager you have looking over the leases should not comment at all on the condition of the leases. A smile, a kind word about something, will smooth ruffled feathers even if there are problems.

Keep in mind that if there is something wrong, you need to know all that's wrong before you attempt to adjust the contract in anyway. In the meantime the seller's motivations must be cared for and you want the seller to recover from that bout of seller's remorse. The big reason for this is that another seller's illness enters the picture.

SELLER'S ANXIOUSITIS

Once the seller recovers from seller's remorse, *anxiousitis* sets in. This is when the seller starts to think, "Okay I've sold the property, now when are we going to close?" Sellers move from one mental state to another. They've now made a deal, they will live with it; only when do they get their money, so they can go out and spend it? In fact many sellers have lined up their next purchase by the time seller's remorse ends (it helps them get over it).

It is toward the end of anxiousitis that you want to plan your appointment to present the property on which they will hold the second mortgage. By this time the motivations are well in your favor and you can get an approval that you may not have gotten the day you presented the offer. You must be careful, however, as anxiousitis will revert back to seller's remorse if you let it go on too long. Both of these illnesses can be reduced if you have a good broker who is working for you. This situation is called a "buyer's broker" and the seller should be aware of this arrangement from the very beginning of the transaction. Your broker can be your point person and can keep the seller informed as to what is going on, without you having to do it yourself.

Phil's transaction was an extreme use of the distant pyramid. Frequently the technique is used in long-term-option properties, as in the following example. Trevor had tied up a vacant tract of land two years ago on a long-term lease with an option to buy. He wanted to close on the property as it had appreciated tremendously, but he was going to be short on the cash he needed to tie up the loose ends to the deal. The reason for this was that, although the property value had increased from the $50,000 option price to $110,000, no lender wanted to make a loan on the vacant tract at terms that were realistic.

Trevor decided to look around for a property to pyramid with, to create a first mortgage for the vacant land. He discovered a nice $200,000 industrial building that was free and clear (without any existing financing). He offered to buy the property by giving the seller $100,000 in cash and a $100,000 first mortgage on the vacant land mentioned before. The seller accepted.

This allowed Trevor to go to a lender and offer the industrial building as security for a loan. The lender liked this kind of property and agreed to give him a total loan of $165,000. Trevor financed the industrial building, netting out after loan costs $150,000. This gave him all the cash he needed to close on both properties.

It should be obvious that the longer you can benefit from appreciation without having to pay for the property, the greater your leverage in any form of financing tool. Trevor's option on the vacant land could have been part of another deal not connected directly to the vacant land at all. It is not rare to buy one property and at the same time ask for an option to buy another property from that owner. In leasing office space or commercial space, you will find that if you ask for an option to buy the building you are leasing, sometimes it will be granted. Sellers who are anxious to make one deal will frequently offer the option as an enticement to a would-be buyer: "Buy this and I'll give you an option on that." Look for these opportunities in every transaction.

THE BUYER'S VIEWPOINT

For the investor the drawbacks of this pyramid technique are few. Most drawbacks are centered around that symptom of bad times where there is too much debt to be serviced and not enough income to accomplish it.

The ease with which you will make 100 percent zero-cash deals will astound you when you use any of the pyramid transactions correctly. Your finesse in moving into the pyramid, and in some cases getting the seller to suggest the pyramid, will take practice. For example, "I sure would like to own your property, Ms. Wright, but as I've told you, I'm property-poor. I have several nice properties—you must have seen my home over on the Intracoastal, or the office building on Commercial Boulevard, and, on top of that, last year I purchased over 80 acres of pine forest near Disney World, but the one thing I'm short of is cash." A short pause as you show the 8-by-10 color photographs of your properties to the seller of whatever it is you want to buy. "And I've built up a lot of equity in these properties. The 80 acres is free and clear. I'd sell that land to buy yours, except I know it is going up in value too fast to sell right now. I wonder if there isn't some way you could be protected in selling your property to me without my having to give you more cash than I can generate from the refinancing of your low mortgage?" If you say this (in your own words, of course) you will find some bright seller responding, "Why not let me hold a first mortgage on that 80 acres?" If that 80 acres is everything you have said it is (otherwise you shouldn't have said it), then that seller might have just made the best deal in town.

THE SELLER'S VIEWPOINT

In a pyramid where the buyer has real equity in the other property, the risk of holding paper on a second property may be less than holding it on the seller's property. Risk is the enemy of profit, so reduce a lender's risk and you improve the chances of making the deal even though you might reduce your profit at the end of the day.

On the other hand, if there is no real equity in the other property and the buyer is trying to shove off a lot of risk on the seller, the risk has multiplied substantially. Sellers must be cautious about the stated value of whatever the property or benefit that is offered in any kind of "second property" security. In many instances it will be relatively easy to substantiate this value. If the buyer is proposing a first mortgage on vacant land, a local realtor can search the sold and active properties of similar nature in the area and can arrive at a market value based on these comparables. If the mortgage offered would be in a second position, then the key is what is the first mortgage amount and its terms. I stress the word "terms" because it is possible to have a property with a recognizable value of $200,000 that only has a $100,000 first mortgage on it and the buyer of your property is offering you a 10-year second mortgage at 10 percent interest. This might be a great pyramid. But if the first mortgage is at 10 percent interest on a zero coupon payout that began 10 years ago, things are not what they first appeared. Zero coupon format is where there is a debt that has no payment until the end of the term. Interest builds up as does interest on that buildup. The amount owned on this specific first mortgage would grow 10 percent per year and would have a payoff due at the end of the tenth year of greater than the $200,000 present value of the property. Always know the terms and full payout of any existing mortgages.

For this and other reasons sellers should approach the pyramid with caution. But do not avoid the pyramid just because you need to be cautious. Real estate values can be verified and existing mortgages can be studied and checked to be sure they are current and not already in default. This kind of strategy can actually save your assets in the long run. In fact for some sellers the use of the pyramid is the only way to get equity out of the deal and soften the debt service, enabling a difficult property to sell. Review the example of the seller's use of the pyramid in the preceding chapter. In simple terms the pyramid is a fantastic way to use a basic motivation of people, which is to get a piece of something someone else has.

25
CHAPTER

Junk Versus Antiques

Anything you own can be used to barter for real estate in lieu of cash. Many zero-cash real estate investments are made by the buyer giving the seller something other than cash. In the last two chapters, for example, the buyers gave the sellers notes or mortgages secured by other property to keep from giving cash, which they may not have had in the first place. Many real estate investors don't want to use real estate or cash as a means of securing the deal unless it is absolutely necessary. Instead they make their deals using items of a non-real-estate nature. These items are called "personal property."

THE JEWELED DEAL: IDENTIFYING YOUR PERSONAL POSSESSIONS

Barbara desperately needed to get her own place to live. She was sick to death of renting and was constantly being asked to leave once the owners realized that she loved dogs and had 12 of them. Dogs were Barbara's life. She raised them for a living and was well known as one of the finest dog trainers in the southeastern United States. She had a good profession, but she couldn't hang onto money, so she was always short of cash.

She told her broker that she needed a home with a large backyard but had no cash. The broker was smart enough to ask Barbara what else she had. Together they made a list of her important possessions. The list included several blue-ribbon show dogs, but Barbara couldn't bear to part with them since breeding time was only a few months away. Also on the list was some old jewelry that Barbara had been keeping in a safe-deposit box at her bank. This treasure consisted of a few bracelets and rings she had been given by her mother.

The broker suggested a current appraisal and, sure enough, the jewelry was appraised at a substantial value. Barbara's first thought then was to sell the jewelry and use the cash to purchase the needed home. But the broker wisely told her that selling the jewelry would be a mistake. The broker knew that buyers of such merchandise would pay less than half of the appraised value; it would be better to exchange it for the desired property if possible. In essence he suggested that Barbara use the jewelry as the down payment on whatever real estate she wanted to buy. An OPM deal in the making.

Of course, many investors don't have a safe-deposit box full of valuable jewelry. They may have a Rubens hanging on the wall instead and not know it. What do you have?

TAKE STOCK OF YOUR VALUABLES

If you have something you don't use and you derive no benefits from its current value, use it to buy something else—a real estate investment or even a personal holiday somewhere. It doesn't matter if you're short of cash or not. What is important is this: Do you no longer get any benefit from what you have stashed away in that box? If not, and if there is no emotional tie to the item, or if there is no reason that it is going up in value more than what you might exchange it for, then get rid of it. Exchange it for a real benefit that will help you move closer to your goals.

The first step is to make a list of what you own. It isn't a bad idea to have a list of all your personal property anyway. You never know when some nut will break in and rob you, a fire will destroy all your possessions, or your spouse's divorce attorney will want to know what you've purchased for the family over the last 20 years. So make a list.

The best way to approach such a list is to first decide that you will not exclude anything. If you try to list only the important things, you'll find it too difficult and will probably overlook the very thing you would give up in an exchange. The best approach is to list everything.

How to Make a List of Your Personal Property

It's best to make a list of your possessions in one fell swoop. Do it over a long weekend if you have a lot of stuff, or if not, do it in one evening. Don't do it bit by bit. Don't try to do it one room at a time or every Saturday until you have finished. This allows more room for errors. You will either overlook a lot of stuff or count things twice. Do your inventory as a marathon, however long it takes.

1. List everything in each room. You can transfer categorized items later on cards or sheets as you mark them off the room list. For example, like me, you may have lots of books. Mine are scattered all over the house, with the largest concentration in my office at home and at my real estate company. If I tried to list "books," I'd go from one room to another with a lot of wasted effort. In your case you might have an art collection whose pieces are displayed in various rooms of your home or apartment. List first by room, then transfer to the category card.

2. Give sufficient description of the item to remind you later what the thing was. For example, writing an abbreviation such as BVM might tell you that it is the blue vase from the Ming dynasty, but five years from now you might forget that code. Avoid too much shorthand and abbreviations in making the inventory.

3. Put some current estimated value on the item or items and the price you paid. If it is recent, as well as the date you acquired it.

4. Subdivide the list into separate lists of those items you still need and use, those items you are keeping as investments, and those items you would just as soon not have.

5. Add to each list as you purchase items, including date and price.

You will be shocked at the cumulative value of your personal property. Items add up: books, rugs, silver pieces, or just tools in the garage. They are all items of value to someone, if not you. As you go about the task of packaging some of these items into real estate transactions, don't work only from your list of things you can do without; the list of items you are keeping as investments is equally important. If you can improve an investment by letting its appreciated value allow you to buy real estate, then that is a decision you should consider. Investors will always exchange one investment for a better one if the real motive for holding the item is profit.

One buyer friend of mine used $7000 worth of sound-recording equipment as the down payment on a duplex apartment building. The seller happened to be a noted speaker who was motivated by the idea of making his own tapes to be sold at his lectures.

Another buyer, who was a client of mine, gave a seller $50,000 worth of gem-quality opals for the purchase of a deepwater home in Pompano Beach, Florida. The seller, a wealthy man who was getting top dollar for the home and lots of cash (from the buyer's refinance of the home), was motivated to take the opals by the "King Solomon Syndrome." This is an illness that hits some people when you offer them jewels or jewelry and other riches. I've seen the toughest of all sellers turn to butter when the small sandalwood box was opened and inside, sitting on blue velvet, was the most beautiful of all yellow topazes surrounded by a pool of half-carat diamonds.

Jim Wolf, a broker friend of mine, made a lot of deals with furs. He uses the furs he obtained from another deal to buy real estate—a lot of real estate. Mike Regas, a former partner of mine, bought a car with a bracelet. Then he gave the car to someone as a down payment on a one-week time-share in Orlando.

All of these examples ended up to the betterment of both parties. There was no forced emotional situation here. It was pure and simple: I like what you have better than what I have. The list of deals that can be made with personal property instead of cash is as endless as the kinds of personal property that can be owned.

THE REASON PERSONAL PROPERTY WORKS

Why does using personal property work? Most of the time because sellers want to save face. You are using basic motivation again. Sellers who want or need to sell but cannot get their terms in the usual market can become frustrated. They don't want to drop their price or compromise on the terms they feel they must have. They will, however, supplement things within that formula, so long as they end up pretty much at the same place they wanted to in the beginning.

This "Please let me save face in this deal, so please buy my property" is a major reason why some real estate investors are able to make deals that astound other investors. In the first place the average real estate investor has his priorities wrong: Most investors think that the critical element in buying and selling real estate is the price. Nothing could be further from the truth. Price is not the most critical aspect in making successful purchases or selling at the best benefit to you. Price, in fact, gets in the way of your making a deal. Many buyers or sellers don't understand this simple fact: It isn't the price you either pay or get that is important, but the benefits received or given. You must look to the benefits.

Benefits, Benefits, Benefits—the Three Most Beautiful Words in Real Estate Jargon

The area of benefits, then, is where the seller can save face if you let him and if you motivate him in that direction. A seller might think he wants or needs $15,000 cash down on the sale of his vacant lot, but in reality he is looking to some benefit that the cash is going to give him. It might be that the seller feels he must get that much cash to secure the mortgage he will be holding on the balance of the deal. Another seller might be trying to raise the cash to pay for a vacation, or a doctor bill, or to buy a car. They have transferred the benefit into a dollar amount. Money will only get you into trouble. Look for the benefit that you want or that the other side of the transaction really wants. Not the dollar amount.

I have discussed with you the reasons to understand the other side's motivation. The more you know about the seller and the benefits he wants to end up with, the better your opportunity to give him a benefit instead of cash. The seller then saves face by allowing himself to substitute items or benefits for cash. And because he doesn't have to "give in" on that part of the contract, deals can be made.

A writer friend of mine had twice as many books in his library as I did. So many, in fact, that he offered to give one seller $4000 worth as part of a deal. The deal was a big one, and while the books were of no real interest to the seller from an educational point of view, he did want to sell the property and $4000 was only 3 percent of the total deal. It was, of course, 50 percent of the total down payment, and the seller could not in good conscience sell the property with only $4000 as the down payment. The other $4000 in books were a face-saver and made the deal. Just as my writer friend did, you must make sure that the values you put on your personal property are realistic. This means keep them as high as you can possibly justify.

THE FINE POINTS OF THE DEAL

The way you make your personal property deal is important. Frequently the best way to use personal property is in a counter of a counteroffer, after making an offer that didn't include any personal property at all. The down payment in your first offer might have been too low, and the seller realized that you were using some other technique to generate the cash and you weren't investing any real equity of your own. The seller then will make a counter, asking you to improve the deal you originally offered. The seller is telling you that he wants to sell, but you and he haven't gotten your mutual benefits clearly in view for the other to see.

Let's say you wanted to buy a condo apartment near Chicago. You offered the seller $100,000 for a property priced at $140,000. You might be using a pyramid technique, where you want the seller to hold a first mortgage on some land you own in an industrial area of Chicago while you refinance the apartment to generate $80,000 cash for him. This is a zero-cash deal for you, and not a bad deal for the seller as he gets $80,000 cash but not the $20,000 pyramid mortgage on the industrial property. He wants a higher price and counters at $120,000 with you securing the remaining $40,000 in paper payable to him over the next five years.

In your personal property list you have a beautiful diamond ring, valued at, say, $20,000. You go back to the seller and say, "Okay, you've convinced me that the value of the unit is more than I've offered. I will pay you $80,000 in cash at closing, and I will give you $15,000 over the next five years, and in addition, I'll give you this beautiful diamond ring."

This technique won't work all the time, and in fact you might find that you have to go down your list of personal property items as well as real estate you can exchange, to motivate a seller. If you have cash and do not want to go through this bother, then don't. But if you are out there trying to get your first deal, then stick with me on this, because it will work.

THE SELLER'S AND BUYER'S VIEWPOINTS

In reality there is no disadvantage to this technique from either side of the fence. Buyers will have the advantage of unloading personal property they don't need, or taking one investment and converting it into a more usable investment. The seller who ends up with the personal property will do so because he either wants the personal property or has substantially gotten his price in the sale and can "play" with the items offered.

As a buyer the biggest problem you will have in using this form of purchase will be the offer itself. Investors who use brokers (I recommend you do, even if you have to educate them from time to time) may get some resistance from them and their salesmen. This resistance can be well founded, since the seller is apt to want the broker or salesman to take the personal property as all or part of the commission. For example if Collin wanted to give the seller a two-year-old Mercedes as part of the purchase price, the seller may want to take the deal because of the other terms offered by Collin. However the seller might tell his broker that he will take the deal only if the broker takes the Mercedes as his commission.

It might be a good deal for both the buyer and the seller—and if it was always a Mercedes, not that bad for the broker. But from time to time there will be items offered that the broker just won't want to get involved with, and this reluctance on the broker's part can create an impasse up front. This is another reason why the personal property should be introduced in the counter of the counteroffer: It is too late for the broker to object; by then, he has invested time and labor and can be enticed into bending a little.

Some brokers, however, recognize that they might be able to do better in their profession if they encourage buyers to make offers of personal property. These brokers and salesmen know that if they can sell more real estate, they will make more in the long run, even if they take an occasional Mercedes or two. In fact, a Ford every now and then is okay too.

26

CHAPTER

Future Sweat: The Do-It-Yourself Down Payment

The future sweat strategy is a sweet way to make your OPM deals fly. In this technique you offer the seller your ability to improve the property as the down payment for your purchase. We are dealing in real benefits here, so do not think for one moment that the seller is not getting real value. Nor, for that matter, that as a buyer you are not giving a solid value. The seller gets the improvements and benefits in three ways. First, the sudden improvements in the property can allow the owner (seller) to increase rents. These additional rents will be his or hers until you close on the sale. Second, you have given the seller increasing security that you are a genuine buyer as you complete every improvement promised. Third, there is the hope that comes with every deal like this that you will ultimately fail and not purchase the property. The seller then ends up with an improved property that he or she might be able to sell for more than your offer.

To initiate this kind of deal, you would make an offer explaining that you wanted to buy the property but, due to its condition, couldn't unless the current status of the property was improved. You would propose that you make the improvements and permit the seller to gain some benefit from those improvements, after which you would buy the property without any additional cash outlay on your part. The seller usually would take back a mortgage in the full amount of the agreed purchase price.

209

Using future sweat isn't for everyone, but it can be most useful when a property you are contemplating buying needs extensive repair and improvements, or when you would be remodeling the property for some other potential use anyway after you bought it. The technique works in its own right as an OPM transaction, as well as a way to reduce your total expenditure of cash. This technique can also double up your benefit by ultimately allowing you to take home cash at the closing.

The flexibility and variation of this technique is very wide. This chapter is dedicated to giving you several different twists on using future sweat. We will also discuss adaptations that sellers can use to aid in the sale of their run-down property.

THE FUTURE SWEAT DEAL

Let's take a look at some examples of future sweat transactions and how they work. Adam is a carpenter by trade and has general jack-of-all-fix-it-up abilities. There isn't much he can't do when it comes to building or repairing, so using future sweat is as natural for him as using cash is for a millionaire. Adam looks around for any kind of improved property that is either in gross need of repair or in fair condition but so ideally situated that a change of appearance would allow an increase of rental income. When he finds such properties, he "tests" the owner to find out if the property might be for sale.

Adam has discovered that many property owners don't have the time to look after their own interests. They may be businessmen or professional people with too many things on their minds to watch their own store. These people often let their property get behind on maintenance, and frequently let old tenants renew at rents that are too low for the current market. Adam has also discovered that many times these owners realize they probably should sell their property but never get around to doing that for much the same reason that they haven't painted the building in the last 10 years.

Therefore Adam never lets the absence of a "For Sale" sign slow him down. "Mr. Seller," he'd likely start out, "you have a fine property which I know you'd be proud of if it were in the kind of condition it should be in." This is bound to get any property owner's attention.

Adam would continue. "I've made a list of all the work the apartment building you own over on Tenth Street should have to bring it up to standard condition. Mind you, this list is just from my inspection from the exterior. I am sure that there is more work needed inside to put this property back in shape. What I'd like to do is to accomplish this list of repairs and improvements at my expense. I will do this because I would like to own the property, and the only way I can do that is to offer you these improvements as my down payment."

Adam will go on to show that his proposal offers the seller the benefits of whatever increased rents the seller can get for the remainder of the 12-month option period Adam needs to accomplish the full list of repairs. He promises, however, to have the major, most beneficial changes and improvements finished within the first three months.

Adam realizes that his approach must convey the impression that he is going in on this deal with all his ready cash tied up in the improvements, since this will spark the strongest of all sellers' motivations—greed.

Greed Is a Many Splintered Thing

Some sellers will view this kind of sale as a proposition where the seller "can't lose." For some sellers it is a bag of mixed emotions: "I'm sad he isn't going to buy but I'm happy that he has done so much 'free' work on my building."

But, if Adam does exactly as he promises and fixes the building as the list of improvements he made earlier indicated, the seller will have made a fair deal with little risk. The improved property should have sufficient new equity over and above the mortgage the seller will hold in the deal to provide a buffer between the seller and default. But then there is always the greed effect that all will be okay even if he goes away.

Adam would be well advised to be careful to include as many of the improvements as possible in the list, and to be as familiar as possible with the rental market for the kind of property he acquires so he'll know how to improve not only the physical appearance of the property but its economic picture as well. What is essential, however, is that neither Adam, nor you, should ever put something down on the list of improvements promised, unless you are sure you can accomplish the work in time and as indicated.

Adam's total investment consists mostly of his time. Naturally there are some materials needed (paint, nails, lumber, bricks, etc.), but they represent only a small percentage (usually around 25 percent of the actual value intended) of what the seller will have to spend if he wants to keep the property.

In another example, Lenny is a general contractor who, in the down periods of his profession, looks around for major properties he can fix up for later rental or resale. He is well known in the lending circles of town and combines future sweat with several other techniques to make his OPM deals.

In one method he starts off much like Adam except that he offers the seller some cash as a part of the down payment. Lenny has discovered that, for him, location is the most important factor. He wants good sites and he knows that to get top locations he needs to be able to choose from a wide selection. To do this, he has to add some cash to his deals. Keep in mind that this does not mean he is giving his own cash.

Lenny starts by finding a property, perhaps a run-down shopping center on a prime commercial corner. A center 25 to 30 years old, which has not had good maintenance for the past five years or so, is going to have rents well below the "like new" centers. Best of all for Lenny, many old shopping centers are full of tenants whose leases are running out or have already expired and they are on month-to-month leases. This is an essential situation for any developer who wants to convert the center to something else or do a major rehab on the property. Properties with a majority of long-term tenants whose leases run for five or more years can be expensive to remove, usually so much so that it is not economically feasible to do so without careful analysis of each tenant and their lease. There is always the possibility that there are tenants happy to get out of a 10-year remaining lease so they can move their business elsewhere.

Lenny begins his offer sequence by making a lowball offer somewhat within the realm of a bona fide steal should the seller accept. His cash down part of the offer is also very low—if, in fact, he offers any cash at all on the downstroke.

In the counteroffers, when the broker (Lenny always uses one) attempts to negotiate the deal to a successful conclusion, Lenny allows himself to be worked up on the terms. The points the seller is winning, however, might be at the sacrifice of losing some points to Lenny. In the end, Lenny, if he must, will agree to spend considerable time, money, and labor to improve the center during an option period prior to the culmination of the transaction. This option for the purchase of the property will not be exercisable by Lenny until the option term has run its course and Lenny has completed the improvements.

Lenny counts on the same seller's motivations that Adam does, and also on the factor of time. Time is on the side of the optionee, and in this case the natural appreciation of the property, due not only to the improvements but to the time factor, will provide Lenny with a much better opportunity to finance the deal when he is ready to close on the option and to buy the property.

Now let's take a look at another scenario. Susan isn't a carpenter or a general contractor, but she knows something about decoration and is a natural-born color coordinator. She looks for properties that are basically sound but present themselves in a bad light due to a lack of good taste in decor or style.

It is relatively easy for a talented person like Susan to cosmetically turn a dog into a gem. When she needs some heavy work done, such as carpentry or brickwork, she hires people she has gotten to know for that part of her future sweat. She has found that some real estate owners are reluctant owners and are actually silently begging people like Susan to come around and enable them to sell their property. For Susan the use of future sweat is a simple and far more profitable use of her time than her old job as a legal secretary. She used to make $600 per week, and now, with half the effort, she makes $50,000 and more each year, buying and selling to and from her own real estate portfolio.

THE FINE POINTS OF THE DEAL

As you are developing expertise in the presentation of your offers with the previous techniques illustrated in this book, you should see the pattern of letting the other side win points by appearing to manipulate you into exactly the position you wanted to end up in the first place. You allow the broker to "get you up" as he wins points for and with the seller, and then you clinch the deal by allowing the seller to save face while he "gives in" to your ultimate demands.

This is the ideal situation, of course, but in reality it doesn't always work out quite that way. Nonetheless in the use of future sweat, your own style of this fantastic technique will depend on your economic ability to back up the sweat with cash. Because some cash in the future sweat deal gives you broader opportunities in property selection, the technique is often used along with other techniques that, on their own, generate cash. Investors who have cash and plan to use it in investing will be surprised to find that using future sweat will buy them the time to turn a good deal into a superb one. In short any investor who anticipates any improvement to a property has the opportunity to use this technique.

Another point is that some sellers are doubting Thomases. They might say something like, "Mr. Cummings, with all due respect, what assurance do you give me so I will know that you will make the repairs you say you will?"

I have several good arguments for this one. First my past performance: "Look at my success here and there." Sometimes this is more than enough to satisfy the seller. But if not, then I would point out that I will lose my option to buy if I fail to do what I say I'll do. Some sellers will still balk, because they fear that I might not be able to live up to the letter of the contract in their minds, and that courts might be needed to settle that kind of dispute. Indeed, sellers who fear such things will want to avoid such potential problems. They would rather walk away from a potential sale rather than risk future problems.

Thus when I know I have to spend money on repairs, I might fall back on this: "I'll tell you what I'll do, Mr. Seller. I'll put up, in an independent escrow account, the sum of $20,000 to be used solely for those repairs. I'll present bills to the escrow agent, which you can verify as being invoices for work or material used on those repairs I promised to accomplish. Naturally I won't present a bill for my own time and labor, so I don't need to place that cash in escrow."

THE SELLER'S VIEWPOINT

In developing your use of this tool, you will find that you can, as a seller, utilize future sweat transactions to your advantage. Here's an example.

Harry owned three duplexes in an older part of town. The duplexes were showing their age, and the yards around them were overgrown with weeds. Harry knew he would never get full value out of a sale of these properties and that all he had to do was spend some time on the site with a few day laborers to straighten out the matter. But he didn't have the time, so nothing happened.

He then learned about future sweat and decided that the best thing for him to do was to set up a situation where a buyer could benefit. He ran an ad offering to sell one duplex to the right person for nothing down. The buyer had to be handy with carpentry tools and have a green thumb when it came to landscaping.

Harry found a buyer who fit the bill, and they set up the deal. In return for the opportunity to use future sweat as his down payment, the buyer would not only fix up the one duplex that was for sale, but, as credit on the sales price, re-landscape and fix up the adjoining two duplexes Harry owned but wanted to keep for a while longer. He figured he could always sell them at a later date if the need occurred.

Harry's benefit was clear and his ultimate profit increased due to the improvement of the duplex he sold, as well as the two he held on to for a while longer. The buyer also got exactly what he wanted. He made a great deal on the purchase of a duplex, and on top of that, he improved the neighborhood (and thus the value of his duplex) by fixing up the adjoining properties. Best of all, he got paid for that work, through credits at closing of title on the first duplex.

THE BUYER'S VIEWPOINT

In fact future sweat can be risky if you haven't selected your property correctly. If you are using future sweat as your down payment, not just to buy time, then the property you buy must be improvable within your means. The danger lies in anticipating that you can turn a property around with 100 hours of your own work and $1000 of paint and lumber, only to find that a 1000 hours of labor doesn't show any real improvement and you could spend thousands of dollars on materials just to fix the broken and rundown results of deferred maintenance.

It is all well and good to fix up property and make profits when you are able to do both. The problem, of course, in this quest for profit is that the real estate and the time don't always cooperate. The real estate can become a hole that will gobble up both your effort and money, and the time can turn a market from one of sure profit to one in which it's impossible to finance a new buyer into your pocket.

With this in mind, all investors contemplating any of the sweat-equity forms of investing should pay close attention to the potential losses they can suffer in attempting to improve real estate. Review the following checklist whenever you anticipate buying any real estate with the idea of fixing it up.

The Prepurchase Checklist

☐ Does the area warrant improvement to this property? You don't want to take on a property that is already priced above the average for the area. What you want is a property that can be improved to the point where it is still not the top property in the area but close to it. The spread of values in the area will give you some hint as to whether you are looking in the right neighborhood. If the price you must pay is not at least 30 percent below the prices of homes in the same neighborhood of similar size but in top condition, then you may not have room to profit from your improvements.

☐ Is there a good seller's market for top-condition properties in this area? Some nice neighborhoods just aren't in demand, so avoid them and look in the areas where buyers go to find their investments. You will want to sell for top dollar, and you need to be in a strong seller's neighborhood for that.

☐ Have you done your "sold" and "available" homework? In short have you found out what similar properties have sold for in the past 12 months? If not, then do so. Your broker can help there, so use his services. Make a list of all properties sold that are either similar to the one you're contemplating, as it is now, or similar to the property as it will be when you finish with it. Check available properties as well: What is on the open market? How long? If they haven't sold in some time, try to find out why. Once you are up on what is going on in the marketplace, you can have more confidence in your judgment in buying selected property.

☐ Is the property you plan to buy structurally sound? You may not be able to tell. I can't so I hire an expert to check out the foundation and other structural parts of the building. But don't stop there: You want to know about the wiring, the plumbing, the heating, the boiler, the air conditioning and, of course, one of the most important of all for many areas of the United States, if the property has termite damage, and if so, if there are also live termites present.

☐ Will time work for you or against you? If you make your purchase option too tight, you will run into trouble. Investors using future sweat will typically anticipate that weekends of work on the property for a couple of months will be enough, only to find that 50-hour weeks for five months would just about do the trick.

☐ Will you have to hire everyone, or what? If you can't do anything yourself and have to hire decorators, carpenters, etc., you might still do all right, but the spread between profit and loss narrows. If you are inclined to this kind of investing, then move into it slowly or get some experience working within the building trades to learn what to do.

Mind you, you generally won't find any of the structural or mechanical items in like-new condition. In fact, you should expect to find them in relatively poor condition, which will account for your good buy. However it is important that you know just how bad "poor" can be. You don't want to get in over your head on repairs and find that you have to spend more than you have only to lose your option and have the owner reap the benefits of the work you have done up to that point.

Despite the potential dangers of biting off more than you can chew, future sweat is still one of the more creative methods you can use. It is so adaptable that it can clinch many deals that start out with other techniques. It should be considered anytime there are repairs needed, or when you need to buy time. Your abilities can be your best asset.

27

CHAPTER

The Partial Interest

When you offer to exchange something in a real estate transaction, never give up all of your benefits when a fraction of those benefits is sufficient to make the deal. The concept here is to offer the seller the smallest portion of the benefit that is enough to entice the seller to sign your offer. This technique works as a solid zero-cash dealmaker on its own or can be used as an adjunct to some other technique where you need kickers to close the deal.

The mechanical function of this technique is to come up with something you can give the seller and still keep as much of that "thing" as possible. As you will see there are many different kinds of things you can offer. Lets start with the term I used in the first paragraph: "benefits." There are three basic benefits that are generated from many of the items you own. These are ownership, use, and economic benefit. Consider a vacation condo you own on Hilton Head Island in South Carolina. You could offer full or partial or limited ownership of that condo as an exchange item in a transaction. Or you could simply offer a period of use, say two months a year for three years, as a benefit with verifiable value, to a seller as a kicker in a deal. Or you could offer a percentage of the revenue that property will generate for the next year or more. It is clear that the most definite of these three benefits is the first one, which would be full ownership of the condo. Do that and you will never be able to use that condo in any more transactions. Logically you will avoid offering that. If you offer specific periods of use, then you are getting the idea of how to give up some benefits while keeping the greater bundle for yourself. When you do this, however, you need to make sure that both parties understand the rules of that use. You would want to have very tight rules of the exchange that would spell out what fees are not included, such as cleaning charges, linen and towel changes, phone and utility charges, and so on. If you give up a percentage of income, you would need to have a new set of rules that spell out how management fees, reserve for replacements, and other charges are deducted from the gross revenue before a sum available for distribution is calculated.

THE PARTIAL INTEREST DEAL

Because the piece-of-the-pie technique will lend itself to the partial division of benefits, lets look at some examples of how this works. Mel wanted to buy a waterfront home. He and the seller had met on a fair price of $250,000. The seller had agreed to accept a pyramid first mortgage in the amount of $40,000, which Mel was going to create on a vacant lot he owned. Mel hoped that with the equity in the pyramid he could obtain new financing on the house and net out the remaining $210,000 so he could pay off the existing financing on the home ($110,000) and pay the seller the balance of $100,000 in cash. If this worked as planned, Mel would not have to put any of his own cash into the deal.

Unfortunately the local savings and loan didn't agree with Mel's plans and approved a loan netting him only $190,000 after loan cost. This meant that Mel was $20,000 short on the needed amount to close. Mel needed to make up the difference and was about to strike out.

Then he got a brilliant idea. He had learned that the seller was an avid sportsman and liked to hunt and fish. Mel owned a condo in the Abacos in the Bahamas, which he had traded into several years before. He didn't want to sell the condo as the current values in the Bahamas were on the uprise, so he offered the seller use of the condo for 20 weeks spread out over the next four years as a part of the purchase on the waterfront home. All the seller had to do was let Mel know several months in advance when he wanted to use the facility and it was his for up to four weeks at a time, with at least eight weeks spread between uses. Anticipating the seller's potential objection, Mel put in the agreement that if the unit were sold or no longer habitable, Mel would owe the seller a pro rata portion of the difference. In essence Mel set a value of $1000 per week for the use of the condo. Mel was sure that if the owner checked with a rental agent in the Abacos he would discover that price was a bargain, even in the off-season.

In essence the seller was being asked to accept $20,000 less cash at closing in exchange for partial (and limited) use of the condo in the Abacos. The seller, who was not out of seller's remorse and into anxiousitis, saw this as a way to keep the deal alive and at the same time have some fun. There was no doubt that the use of the facility for 20 months was a good economic exchange for the $20,000.

Ruby and Bob owned a small citrus grove near Orlando, Florida, which was generating a good income for them. They wanted to buy some real estate, so they took stock of what they had to work with. They had some cash set aside for investing but wanted to hold on to that if at all possible. They also had, of course, lots of oranges each year that just never seemed to get sold, or, at best, were picked for cattle feed at the end of each season.

They decided that they would have no difficulty giving up part of their orange crop each year, for some limited time, of course, to keep things simple. Therefore they sought a seller who might be inclined to be a taker for their partial crop. Not wanting to spoil any of their usual buyers of oranges by offering the oranges on a real estate deal, they crossed off the obvious takers for their oranges and looked elsewhere. A new market was a possibility, but so was a potential large user of their produce other than the vendor.

They ended up going to one of the state's larger real estate developers and making a deal where they would supply that developer with sufficient boxes of fruit each year for the next five years to more than equitably match the down payment on that developer's condo they wanted to buy. The developer used the boxes of fruit as Christmas presents for preferred clients for those upcoming years.

Ron owned a sailboat that he used a few weekends a month, some months of the year; the rest of the time it sat there using up more of his time in normal upkeep. Ron didn't want to sell the boat, but, when it came time to make an investment, he had no hesitation in offering a part ownership in the boat as part of the deal. Later Ron discovered that his talent as a boatman was pretty good, so he made up a business card and made a few deals using his boat (he still owned most of the time), giving sailing lessons.

Larry did much the same thing with his aircraft that Ron did with his boat. He simply realized that his social circle consisted mostly of aircraft people, just as Ron's centered on boat people. This gave him a natural opportunity to deal with people who would be receptive to what he might have to offer a part of. You will notice the same thing happening to you if you dig down deep.

PARTIAL OWNERSHIP OR PARTIAL USE

When you are about to give something to someone, make sure you aren't giving the wrong thing. There are two basic forms of partial interest: partial ownership and partial use. The basic and most important difference is that when you give up a portion of the ownership, it is permanent: The other party is now the owner of that portion of the property and has, in essence, become your partner. This means that as the value goes up, they participate in the profit; and as the value goes down, they take their portion of the loss as well. In the meantime, of course, your new partner in ownership should carry his or her load of maintaining the property. In a co-ownership of a home, boat, or aircraft, this can be substantial and when something breaks on your watch (while you are there) there is a tendency for the other owners to blame you. "Hey, you broke it, you pay to fix it." Be sure to build in a reserve for replacements to keep this kind of argument from happening.

The main pitfall of sharing ownership is the possible difficulty in dividing the maintenance cost. In the condo or vacation home, it might be relatively easy to say you would each have equal time to use the facility and then simply split things down the middle. In theory you can use this same formula for anything; but when you get right down to it, use will rarely be so equitably divided. Invariably, one person will get more use, no matter how well you plan things out. In fact you will find that in shared ownership of something you use, having more partners will be more equitable than just two, because you can so severely limit use that each partner is more apt to use his time than not. This has given rise to a rising number of private time-share transactions, where several friends and acquaintances get together to own a vacation house, each taking a month of the year, renting out any leftover time.

The form of ownership you set up can be critical. This is especially important if you are offering a partial interest or ownership to someone you don't or hardly know. If at all possible it will be more practical if you divide the property itself. Of course there is no way to make a 40-foot sailboat into two 20-foot boats, but you can divide up a duplex or a three-unit property. If actual use is not a part of the deal, then a division of income is a good way to go. No matter what kind of division you do, be sure you have everything in writing and that you have used a good lawyer to properly form this joint ownership to the best interest of all owners.

The advantages of joint ownership will depend on the deal you have just made. It is possible that the only way you can make your transaction is to give up a preferred interest in some real estate you own and will continue to operate or manage. Many real estate investors like to do preferred deals, and they can be very enticing to both sides of the fence. Indeed, this form of investing will work wonders for you as a buyer or seller, so make a special note to yourself that this is one of those big-boy techniques that will work for you on any level of your wealth-building career.

Giving Up Use, Not Ownership

For some kinds of property, the use of it is more attractive than partial ownership. From the user's point of view, there is only enjoyment with no worries about maintenance or upkeep.

From your point of view, you keep the appreciation and only give up partial use, which, if planned carefully, won't be missed at all. As a seller, you might keep this in mind and look for buyers who are owners of things or places you can use. Any time you can give an investor an OPM deal, you improve your chances of selling.

For example, I was offered a block of 10 weeks of charter time in a 42-foot trawler-type yacht out of British Tortola in the British Virgin Islands. The offer was to exchange for a condo I had previously exchanged into some years earlier, giving the then-owners an emerald and diamond ring for their equity. I had been renting out the condo, and had built up equity of around $12,000. The first thing I did was check out the charter rates and discovered that if I was able to get the benefits offered it was a good deal. At the time I made the deal I fully intended on spending those 10 weeks (over several years of course) in the crystal waters of the Virgin Islands, but as it turned out I never made it there. Instead I traded those charter weeks off on two separate purchases I made a year later.

THE PREFERRED DEAL

Normally the preferred transaction is viewed as a buyer's technique, so let's look at it that way first. Preferred buying is where the buyer comes in and says he will buy your property at a good price, but, instead of buying all of your interest, he only wants half. The amount of cash offered, however, is frequently more than half of what you might have taken if the buyer had purchased 100 percent of the deal. For example, if you wanted to sell a shopping center for $1,000,000 and would take $250,000 down, a buyer who wanted to lock up a 10 percent preferred position would offer you something like $180,000 cash down for only half interest in the property.

The advantage to the buyer is what happens next. The buyers will tell you that they want you to keep the other half of the ownership and to stay on as manager of the property, for which you can take the normal management fee off the top of the net income. From the resulting bottom line that would be the net operating income (NOI), the preferred investors would expect to get the first $18,000 of disbursement. This is the 10 percent preference on the invested $180,000 cash down. You, as the other half owner, would then be entitled to the next $18,000 of revenue. Any revenue after that would be split 50/50. Keep in mind that these percentages of preference and split are all subject to negotiation.

One reason buyers like this technique is that it can make an honest man out of a seller who has been puffing the income of a project. If the seller knew that the above property would never make more than $30,000 for the next 10 years, he'd refuse to go into such a transaction. If he did go into it, the buyers would have a lot of insurance that their return was protected.

Buyers also like the fact that there is a great incentive for good management. After all, the buyer's partner will be underwriting the investor's yield. The investor is pretty much assured to get their demand yield (10 percent in the example above), even if the income drops to a NOI of only $18,000. Whatever the seller expected to get would be wiped out by a bad year.

Sellers often jump at transactions like this—sometimes out of desperation, sometimes out of good sound business sense. It all depends on the circumstances and the faith the seller has in the potential of the property to generate sufficient income to give each a good return and then some. It should be obvious that if the seller can get nearly as much cash selling only half of the project and still have the growing benefits of the other half, then it's a good deal.

This is a brief look at the buyer's use of this technique. Now see how you can turn this concept into a different form by being the seller when you buy something else giving up part of the ownership in your property.

A BUYER BECOMES A SELLER

Bill owned an apartment house and lived in one of the units. It provided a comfortable income and required little management on his part. He wanted to get more real estate, but had little cash. He was thinking of selling his apartment house to generate capital to invest but feared he would also have to then find another place to live. He decided he would "sell" part of the ownership in the apartments either outright, or in an exchange. A short while later he found an industrial property he liked. It was grossly in need of repair and partially vacant. The remaining tenants were paying half the rent they should in the current marketplace. Bill discovered this was mostly due to the absentee ownership of the property that had not been taking care of the basic maintenance the building needed.

In exchange for the owner's equity Bill offered the owner of the industrial building 40 percent ownership of the apartment complex Bill owned with a 9 percent preference return in the income of the apartments. Bill had come up with this set of percentages, as he was sure it would give the seller a similar return as he was currently getting from the industrial building. The real bonus to the seller was there would be no management problems. Bill included in the transaction the right by either party to buy out the other within two years with a 90-day notice. There was a formula on the buyout price, which was tied to the current income the apartments were throwing off. Bill was to stay on as manager of the apartments and receive the usual management fee, plus the use of his apartment free.

In return Bill took over the existing loan on the industrial building and received 100 percent ownership of that property. He invested some time and a little cash to fix up the building, quickly increased the rent the existing tenants were paying, and filled up the vacant square footage in the building.

A couple of months later Bill refinanced the building and the new loan generated sufficient cash to replace what he had spent on the fix up, as well as to allow him to give the 90-day notice to his "new" partner in the apartment building, that he was exercising the right to buy him out.

Bill could have approached this seller in any one of several different ways, and he had weighed several techniques before ending up with this one. The above transaction suited Bill because he didn't have to leave his own apartment building. He got part of the appreciation of the building, which he knew was going to be substantial over the years, and with an OPM deal he ended up as 100 percent owner of the industrial property. At the time he made the deal he was not sure that he would be able to buy out the "new" partner so quickly, so that was a very special bonus to him. As for the absentee owner, he knew the rules of the contract and had agreed to the buyout in the first place. He was able to get a good, all cash price, in the end, and had no complaints.

THE FINE POINTS OF THE DEAL

There are several things you need to watch in using this technique. Review the following list.

- Make sure you know what you have to give. You might find there are more things you can give up than you think. Piano lessons? Why not, if you can?
- Make sure you don't offer too much. When you do that you cheapen your product or service.
- Make sure you offer only the interest necessary. Avoid giving ownership unless it is important and beneficial to you to do it that way.
- Get legal advice in any partnership or joint ownership of any property.
- Have everything possible written down about the costs and use of the property. Memories will not work since they are horrible when the repair bills come in.
- Have a plan to either buy out or divide. Properties and partnerships have a tendency to become too valuable from time to time, and some formula is needed up front to cover possible disputes when you have joint ownership.
- If you are giving use, make sure that use is specifically defined and that there are some limitations to notice of when the use will take place, how long it can be, and how many people are to be accommodated. If you want to sell tomorrow and have given up one week in January for the next five years, you may have a problem in selling unless you have a way to pay off the remaining time. Remember the condo in the Abacos? Set values and if you cannot deliver, you owe real money for a change.

- ■ Seek sellers who are potential users or takers for what you have, and then make offers.

You will find that this chapter has presented several interesting and varied techniques under the guise of giving up a partial interest. Like the preferred deal, the partial interest technique will have wide appeal to many buyers and sellers alike. Use it to reap big profits.

28 CHAPTER

Soft Paper Option, Hard Paper Sale

This is one of those techniques that can quickly build equity and also get you 100 percent financing, plus cash in your pocket. The technique uses two separate events to create the profit-making magic. The first is the option of soft paper. This is when the investor obtains an option to buy a property on easy terms. The option you negotiate must allow any debt the seller holds to be assumable by a future buyer (the investor). This single element is absolutely a must to properly use this technique. Once the debt is freely assumable by a new buyer, you can re-package the transaction and offer the property for sale with different terms that generate a profit to you.

This technique enables any investor to tie up a property with a binding option and then sell the property, or "flip" the contract to another buyer at the same price she paid for it, making a substantial profit. Naturally astute investors will look to make an instant profit by selling at a price much greater than what they have negotiated. Let's look at several kinds of transactions using this technique.

THE OPTION DEAL

Wendy found a home that was in poor condition but in a very good part of town. The yard was a mess, the shutters were hanging askew, the paint was peeling off, and there was a burned-out car in the carport. The seller was receptive when Wendy asked for an option to purchase the property at a fair price for the property, providing the seller held 90 percent financing at a rate slightly below the market rate. The price was good and, as Wendy pointed out, the interest, while low, didn't upset the seller's income tax situation. It was more important for the seller to get a higher price than the interest rate she might hold. The seller had lived in the home three out of the past five years so he qualified for up to $250,000 of gain without having to pay tax on that gain.

The option Wendy negotiated gave her some time to do some fix-it work on the property. The seller had also agreed to this, of course, as it benefited him in case Wendy later backed out of the deal. What Wendy did was fix up the yard, repair the shutters, paint the house, hang a new front door, and remove the burned-out car from the carport. Then she put a "For Sale" sign in the yard.

Let's take a closer look at the option Wendy arranged. Her option to purchase was good for six months. Payment for the option was the repairs Wendy had promised. This was detailed in a three-page list of the specific things Wendy said she would do. Wendy also had the right to do other work to the exterior without the seller's approval as long as it did not change the structure of the building.

Price	$120,000
Cash Down	$ 12,000
Mortgage Balance	$108,000

The mortgage was to be held by the seller for 25-year amortization with a 15-year balloon. The interest rate was 5.5 percent per year. Payments would be $663.30 each month until the balloon of $61,086.72 was due at the end of the fifteenth year. This interest rate was higher than the seller could get if he put the money in a money market fund.

Wendy spent $2000 on the home improvements, which she added to the price. She then offered and sold the property on the following terms:

Price	$122,000
Cash down	$ 14,000
Mortgage balance	$108,000

Instead of letting the buyer assume the existing mortgage that Wendy had negotiated on her purchase, she created what is called a wraparound mortgage. This is a technique that has many interesting benefits to both a buyer and a seller, and occurs when the "new" mortgage wraps around existing financing. In this example the mortgage is the same exact amount as the mortgage the seller gave Wendy. The only difference is the amount charged on the interest.

Wendy's wraparound mortgage is also $108,000 and is a 30-year amortization with a balloon payment due at the end of 15 years. The interest charged by Wendy is 9.5 percent interest. A buyer (from Wendy) would pay to Wendy $908.10 per month for 15 years at which time that mortgage would have a balloon of $86,968.87 owed to Wendy.

So how does Wendy profit from this transaction? Each month she collects $908.10 from the buyer and pays out in return $663.30 to the original seller. She puts $244.80 in her pocket each month, or $2937.60 each year (not counting any interest she earned on that in the meantime). If she holds onto the mortgage for the 15 years to the balloon date, she will collect $86,968.87 in the form of a balloon payment from the buyer she sold to and will have to pay $61,086.72 to the original seller on the remaining balance of the mortgage.

Her total cash benefit is shown here:

What Wendy Collects	What Wendy Pays Out	Wendy's Benefit
Mortgage Payments per Year $10,897.20	$ 7,959.60	$ 2,937.60
15 Years of Mortgage Payments $163,458.00	$119,394.00	$ 44,064.00
Balloon Pmt at End of 15 Years $86,968.87	$ 61,086.72	$ 25,882.15
Total Net Cash to Wendy over 15 Years		$ 69,946.15

Keep in mind that Wendy's gain is a complete OPM deal. The little amount she put into fixing it up she got back when she sold her option. She never really had to close on the house at all as her option and sale to a third party closed at the same time. Her profit comes from the benefit of her financing.

The first question you should ask is: Why would a buyer pay Wendy 9.5 percent interest? The answer is because Wendy took the initial risk and invested her time and some cash in fixing up the property. The new buyer was never offered the opportunity to purchase the property at Wendy's original deal.

Had Wendy been as smart as you will be, she would also have raised the price even more than the $2000 she had invested in the fix up. Wraparound mortgages were hot items in the late 1960s, before the banks and other institutional lenders discovered how investors were profiting on their existing low interest rate mortgages. Most institutional lenders now include provisions in their mortgages that prohibit secondary financing without their approval. So wraparounds began to wane and almost disappeared. However there are millions of purchase money first mortgages held by former sellers. Many of these mortgages do not prohibit wraps and as long as you buy a property that has such a mortgage or you can insist that the purchase money mortgage held by the seller of a property you are acquiring allows assumption without their approval and there is no prohibition against you holding a second mortgage behind their existing first, then wrap all you want.

The only downside to a seller when the person he sold to resells the property with a wraparound mortgage is the mortgage they gave to their buyer will remain on the property until paid off. The original seller remains in the same position to lien the property and to foreclose as before. The economic backing of the new buyer might be less than the old buyer but that should not be too critical.

THE DOUBLE OPTION DEAL

Do you have a free and clear property you want to sell? If you have a property that has been on the market for a long time and you own it free and clear of any debt, you can create a fantastic way to turn this technique into a real selling machine. This example will use a free-and-clear property, but you can also make this work well as long as you have a lot of equity in the property. Small moderate interest rate mortgages can be incorporated into what Jim is about to do.

Jim was into fixing up small income properties like duplexes and four-unit apartment buildings. He liked the manual labor aspect, and it was easy to hire experts for the really tough jobs. He also discovered that high-school kids were good, affordable labor on weekends and after school for painting and yardwork.

He was building a sizable basis for a future net worth of millions. However, he was always short of cash, since his whole plan was to plow the money right back into the property. To top this off Jim owned a free-and-clear farm that he had purchased some years ago. He had paid off the original mortgage from a modest rent he collected from the tenant who ran the farm, but Jim's original intent when he bought the farm was no longer in his goals. He wanted to get his equity out of the farm. The market for farmland was not real strong, and banks did not like to make large loans on them; when they did, it was usually at a higher than usual interest rate. These situations did not help the sale of the property. Jim knew he could sell, however, if he was willing to hold a 10-to-15-year loan at an interest rate lower than what lenders were offering. If he could generate 75 percent financing on the farm, he could hold a small second and sell the property for as low as 10 percent down.

The farm was worth $300,000. What Jim wanted to do was create $225,000 in debt at a low enough interest rate to attract a buyer. Has something come to your mind yet? Here is what Jim did. Since Jim was always on the lookout for property he could buy and fix up, it did not take him long to find several candidates for purchase. One was a 20-unit apartment complex in a nice part of town that obviously had a management problem. He had his realtor contact the owner to see if the property was for sale. It was not. Instead of being disappointed, Jim was elated at this fact. This meant the owner not only did not understand the condition of the property, but he did not know what to do about it.

The realtor told the owner that she had a client who would like to own that property and could he please give her some details on the rents and financing. The property had a small first mortgage that had a high constant rate payment due to the fact that it had been a larger mortgage at one time and now had only five years to go. The amount of that mortgage was $75,000 and its annual payment was $18,700. Of the 20 apartments in the complex one of them was occupied by a manager, another by the landscape gardener, and two were vacant. The 16 remaining units, as well as the whole building, were in need of some repair. The rents on those 16 units averaged $500 per month. Jim calculated that the owner was likely pocketing around $50,000 after making the mortgage payment, paying taxes and insurance, and paying other upkeep and operation expenses in the property.

Jim had his realtor send the owner a letter indicating that her client was prepared to make a formal offer on the property if the seller would consider a purchase price of $450,000. A few days later the realtor called the owner to discuss the offer. The owner said he had not answered the letter because he felt the offer was way too low. The realtor asked the owner how low. The seller indicated he could not consider less than $550,000 for the property.

Jim then offered as follows:

Purchase Price	$525,000
Cash at Closing	$225,000
Assume the Existing Financing	$ 75,000
First Mortgage on Jim's Farm	$225,000
Total Purchase Price	$525,000

Along with this offer was an aerial photo of the farm, along with full details on the improvements on the land, current rent, and potential income in the future. The mortgage was to be a 20-year term at 5 percent interest with no amortization for the first five years. This meant that the payment would be $11,250 a year for 10 years then revert to a 10-year amortization at which time the payment would go to $28,647 a year. Jim structured the mortgage this way for two reasons. He had discovered that the owner was well off financially so might like the interest rate, which, although low from a mortgage point of view, was higher than what banks and money markets were paying. Also, the seller won the battle of counteroffers and had successfully gotten Jim to come up in his price, paying the full $550,000 with $250,000 cash at closing. The real closing point was the fact that those last 10 years of payments would come in handy at just about the time the seller would have college expenses for two of his children.

There were several counters and counters of counteroffers and Jim eventually went up to $250,000 cash at closing, based on Jim having a four-month option so that he could make some improvements to the apartment complex. Jim outlined exactly what he wanted to do and assured the seller these improvements would be out of Jim's pocket and that if he did not close, the seller would benefit from those improvements. All the other terms remained the same.

Jim had time to do some work on the apartments, which he wanted to do prior to going to his lenders to refinance the deal at the closing. By the time he did close, the property looked 100 percent better and there were already tenants in the vacant units, with a waiting list for another five units. One of the vacant apartments had become a model right away, and Jim planned to repaint every apartment, add ceramic tile to all the ground floor units (the building was two stories), and install new carpets to second floor units. His asking rent was $675.00 a month. At that level of rent, with a full 20 units to rent out, he would have a rent roll of $162,000 a year. With conservative operating expenses and with a reserve for replacements of 45 percent of gross income, Jim knew that he would have a net operating income (NOI) of nearly $90,000. This would give him a new value of at least $900,000 based on a capitalization rate of 10 percent. (If the investor wanted to make 10 percent on the cash he put into the deal, he would pay $900,000 to make $90,000 per year.)

Jim was able to obtain a commitment for $630,000 net of loan cost. With this money he was able to pay the seller the $250,000 cash at closing, retire the $75,000 old existing mortgage, and spend $60,000 in remodeling the units. This left him with $245,000 tax-free cash in his pocket. He set aside some of that money to make mortgage payments on the "new" first mortgage on his farm.

Jim immediately put the farm on the market for $325,000. He offered the property with a down payment of $50,000 and total financing of $275,000 by adding a $50,000 second at the same terms as the mortgage he had created when he acquired the 20 units. He received an offer from a buyer who had a duplex that had a fair equity of $50,000. Jim took the duplex because he knew he could fix it up and profit even more.

Ending Up with a Landlease

Monte took an option on a small office building he liked. Like Jim, Monte knew the rental market well because he made a habit of noting every rental sign in the area, frequently stopping in to talk to building managers, etc. He knew he could increase rents in the office building by simply telling the tenants to vacate if they weren't willing to pay a more realistic rent.

He gave the seller a check for $25,000 to be deposited within 45 days if Monte was able to find financing for the building. The price of the building is not important in this example because of the soft-to-hard-transaction bid. The deal, however, was at a fair price, based on the existing low rentals in the building.

Monte went to the tenants and told them he had a deal on the building and needed to know if they were going to sign a lease with him at the terms he was offering them. He presented the facts clearly and honestly: If he closed on the building, which he fully intended to do, they would be out if they were not willing to pay the fair and realistic rent he was offering them right then and there. Monte was not greedy; he offered them a more than fair rent, knowing they couldn't find a better deal and that the aggravation and cost of moving wouldn't be worth the hassle.

Based on the new rental pro forma, Monte offered the owner the same exact price he paid, with Monte assuming the same exact terms that Monte had assumed with the first seller with just one difference: Monte kept the land by adding a landlease to the terms. In essence Monte bought the building for $300,000, sold the building for $300,000, and, in the exchange, set a $10,000 per-year landlease on the building. This meant that Monte was now the owner of the land and would collect $10,000 per year. This technique of selling the building and keeping the land is used nicely with the soft buy and hard sell. It worked for Monte just as it can for you.

THE FINE POINTS OF THE DEAL

The more you know about the other techniques in this book, the broader your application of this quick turnaround of property. Your use of combinations of techniques will constantly expand as you see new ways to adapt them to your own needs and desires. Practice will not make you perfect, only profitable.

The most important thing to remember in the use of this technique is never let greed guide you. It can destroy you and your deals faster than anything you can think of. Greed comes in when the soft-buy, hard-sell investor tries to buy too soft and can't ever make those deals gel or when the investor tries to sell too hard and blows that side of the fence.

These transactions work nicely and reliably when the investor turns over the property quickly and at a modest profit. Let the cigar-chewing boys in the back room who have a hard time sleeping at night make the real nail-biting deals where everyone counts their fingers after the handshake at the closing. The very best advice I can give you is to try to establish a reputation of being honest, fairminded, and not greedy. Greedy investors end up at the slaughterhouse.

PITFALLS IN THE SOFT-TO-HARD DEAL

The pitfall in this kind of deal will be your failure to make the deal gel on the selling side. It will be relatively easy to tie up property once you know your backyard. The key is to be sure you have been honest with yourself. If you become emotional about the property, you may not be able to set the harder terms that will enable you to sell. Your terms should be softer than those of the open market as this enables you to turn over fast, and fast is the name of this game.

You can, of course, lessen the danger by being ready and able to actually buy if you have to. If you run out your option and know you have a good buy but you haven't been able to find a buyer to take you out of the deal at a profit (due to the times), then it's helpful to have a plan to fall back on. One such plan might be to actually shop some financing, as Jim did where he had pyramided off with the seller. He probably could have found some local financing to enable him to buy the eight units himself. As long as he didn't go in the hole each month, he could wait out the tough market and then sell in better times.

As a seller you might find it to your distinct advantage to encourage a buyer to take the property off your hands by offering him soft terms. After all, when you must sell, the major benefit might be to be rid of the property and to let someone else who can benefit from the property make a profit. I frequently recommend this technique to owners of buildings they have not been able to sell. By offering soft terms, they become decoys that attract (or seek out) those investors who see an opportunity to take advantage of these motivated sellers for a quick profit.

29 CHAPTER

The Soft-Purchase Double Exchange

This technique has the same origins as the one described in Chapter 28. Here, however, you use the option to purchase a property with soft terms, restructure the financing to your benefit on a sale at hard times, and then exchange (or sell) each element of ownership: the mortgage, the equity, and the property itself.

Let me break this technique down to its most basic elements. First there is the option to buy on soft terms. There are many ways to accomplish this, as you have seen in some of the previous examples. The objective here isn't to keep the property but to turn it over in a relatively short period of time. You may have a second fallback position but let's keep with the primary goal: a quick sale. Because of this there can be cash included in the purchase price, as long as you keep in mind that you don't plan on taking title yourself. To expand your market on the rollover, you will want to keep the cash side of the purchase at a minimum.

Second, you restructure the financing, usually with a landlease, a wraparound mortgage, or another technique discussed in this book. If you have pyramided the seller off to hold some paper on another property, your flexibility is increased as you have greater equity in the mortgage.

When you restructure the financing to a wraparound mortgage, you build in a future benefit. With the wraparound you will have surplus revenue over the debt service on the existing financing. The surplus or bonus gives you increased equity in that mortgage, and this equity can be one of the elements you will use for exchange.

The third element you can deal with is the appreciated value in the property. If you have an option to purchase a property for $60,000 but in reality you feel that the property is worth $75,000, then there is a $15,000 instant appreciation to your equity in your option. In essence if you closed on the property for $60,000, you would benefit by this new value to the tune of $15,000. However, instead of this, you may elect to make a few improvements thereby increasing the value even more, then sell or exchange this appreciated equity.

Those are the basic elements of the soft-purchase double exchange. Now let's look at two examples of this technique in action.

THE WRAPAROUND DEAL

Harry found a vacant industrial building in a good part of a commercial area of town. The previous occupant had been in the building for over 15 years and had finally outgrown the building and moved across the street to a new complex. The owner of the building had all but forgotten about the place for 15 years, doing little but cashing his rent checks. Now the building was a worry since it was not only vacant but also needed considerable maintenance. Harry offered to paint the exterior of the building and fix it up so it would be easier to rent out. This work was to be his option money for a 12-month option to purchase the building.

The deal was structured this way: Harry would buy the building for $200,000 with $25,000 cash down and the seller would hold the balance of $175,000 for 15 years, at interest-only payments of 10 percent per annum. This meant Harry would be obligated to pay $17,500 per year in interest on the debt after he closed on the deal. (This was equal to the rent the owner had been getting from the previous occupant.)

True to his word, Harry painted the building and then some. He added a fence to one side and some bushes along the front to make the property look nicer. Harry knew that even industrial users like their property to have some appeal. And within a short time, a buyer came along and wanted to rent the building at nearly double the rent the previous tenant had paid.

Harry then structured a new set of numbers on the building. First he decided that, based on the new income generated by the new tenants and the reduced operating expenses because the leases were true triple net (tenants pay taxes, utilities, and maintenance), the property was worth $350,000. To reduce negotiation from prospective buyers, Harry knew that if he offered the property with a large, relatively easy-to-pay mortgage, then the buyers could only negotiate with the equity position of the deal. To establish this Harry set up hypothetical financing this way: He structured a wraparound mortgage in the amount of $300,000 (around the seller's $175,000) interest-only mortgage, and put the interest at 10.5 percent per annum on the wrap with a balloon in 15 years. He then offered the building for sale at $350,000 and stated that he was flexible and would exchange into other real estate, or sell outright. A new owner would make monthly payments on the wraparound, which was $300,000 at 10.5 percent interest only. This meant the new buyer would pay $31,500 a year for 15 years then, if he still owned the building, owe Harry the principal amount, which was still $300,000. From this collection Harry would make the interest payments to the former owner of $17,500 a year and at the end of 15 years owe the former owner $175,000. Harry will benefit substantially from the difference in these two mortgages.

Let's take a look at Harry's wraparound structure:

Harry collects $31,500 a year on the $300,000 mortgage he holds.

Harry pays out 17,500 on the $175,000 mortgage he owes.

Harry keeps $14,000, which is the difference between what he collects and what he pays.

At the end of 15 years Harry collects $300,000 on the payoff of the wraparound.

At the end of 15 years Harry pays off the existing first at a cost of $175,000.

Harry keeps $125,000, which is the difference between the payoff of the two mortgages.

Harry didn't want to close on the property, but since he had plenty of time he could be somewhat selective in what he got for exchange, though he was still very flexible. He was able to generate substantial interest within the exchange community and was offered many different kinds of deals. He settled on a free-and-clear tract of land worth $25,000 plus $25,000 cash. The buyer then took over the "newly created wraparound" at its face amount of $300,000.

When Harry decides to unload the wrap, he can exchange it with someone else. He does this at a later date, however, as there is no rush to make the exchange now that he has rolled over the property prior to closing. Any investor looking at a possible purchase of Harry's wraparound mortgage will consider it as an income stream of $14,000 a year with an ultimate pay off of $125,000.

THE LEASE-PURCHASE DEAL

Jasmine made a much smaller deal. She saw a vacant lot she knew was going to go up in value, so she tied it up on a lease-purchase basis. She leased the lot from the owner for a term of one year with the provision that if she purchased the lot at the end of the year, the lease payments would apply toward the purchase price. The rent was reasonable and just about paid the seller's holding expenses for the year.

During the year of appreciation and contemplation, Jasmine decided how she was going to profit on this deal. She estimated that the value of the lot had gone from $35,000, which was her option price, to about $55,000. Based on this evaluation, Jasmine went back to the owner of the lot and asked if she would extend the lease for several more years. The owner agreed only if Jasmine would forfeit the future rent paid and not credit it against the purchase price. The rent was only $2500 per year but Jasmine hesitated so as not to let the seller know just how reasonable that was and then agreed. In essence Jasmine now had a lease with an option to purchase whereby she could buy the lot for $32,500 (she would still get credit for the first year's rent). In the meantime she would rent the lot for $2500 per year. (The rent, by the way, was less than 7.25 percent of the purchase price, so that was a very good deal for Jasmine in a current market where interest on mortgages for vacant land was at 9 percent and higher.)

Jasmine now had two elements, each of which had a value.

1. The leasehold, whereby Jasmine had to pay $2500 per year for the use of the property.

2. An option to buy at a $32,500 figure, which was well below the current market.

Based on this Jasmine could keep both, sell, or exchange either, sublease the lot, and keep the option. Her flexibility in this transaction was ideal since she had expanded her options. The fact that she had changed the lease terms to forfeit the rent didn't hurt much either since the total rent would be deductible as a business expense.

THE FINE POINTS OF THE DEAL

Know your alternatives, study your options, and maintain flexibility— three important factors in any real estate investment but even more important when you are attempting to set up a rollover prior to having to buy the optioned property yourself.

One factor, however, which stands out in dealing with options, is to maintain the proper profile of an investor throughout the deal. If you go into one of these transactions telling everyone how you plan to tie up the property for a quick rollover, you will end up sitting in your corner sucking your thumb. Only you are to blame. Just remember, your business should stay your business. Never telegraph your plans for making a quick profit because you might educate the other side of the fence to do the same. At best no seller wants to make your profit for you by accepting the risk of time and the loss of a more genuine market.

To get the upper hand in these soft-paper purchases and hard-paper transactions will depend on your ability to spot that opportunity in the first place. The old grass-is-greener motivation, which can be used in your favor in the pyramid, will work against you if you stray from your comfort zone and investment area you know so well.

Many investors seek to own property outside where they live; they want to move up, away, and to different surroundings. But the fact of the matter is that your own backyard is probably the single most important place for you to seek out your investments. It does you little good to worry about what is going on in the Salt Lake City market if you live in Washington, D.C., unless you plan to move to Salt Lake City. This should be clear in your mind. But confine it still further. Suppose you live in Miami or even more specifically Miami Beach. Your market, then, is there in Miami Beach and not Coconut Grove, though it is only 10 miles away. You will be advised to stick to what you know well, and avoid the tendency to see something else as a greener pasture. If you want to go elsewhere, do it after you have mastered that area as a new comfort zone and expanded investment area.

Risk in investing is inversely proportionate to the amount of knowledge you have about the area and about the type of property in which you plan to invest. Know a lot and your risk is reduced. Know only a little and you'll chance losing your shirt. You can gain this knowledge by following the hints and clues scattered throughout this book.

PITFALLS OF THE SOFT-BUY DOUBLE EXCHANGE

The only pitfall to you as the originator of this transaction is if you are unable to find a buyer at a price that will give you a profit, or if the buyer milks the property and leaves you with expenses to bring the property back to its original value when you acquired it. However, these are situations that can occur in many other deals as well, and the whole premise that if you buy right you can make a profit holds true. In this kind of transaction you are risking mostly time and effort and are dealing with pure profit. Your margin then is in the profit. As long as you can drop your price and soften the terms to make a deal and still come out ahead of the game, then you can not go wrong. If you get in an upside-down position (a car dealer's term meaning you owe more than the item is worth) you simply did not do your proper due diligence, or you got caught in a sudden downturning market. This can and will happen and when it does, the savvy investor makes an instant decision. Do I bail out and cut my losses now, or do I hang in for the long run and wait for the turnaround of the market? The more you know about that market, the better you can make that decision. Keep in mind that even a loss is not the end of the world as you generate a tax credit against your gains, and you have learned a valuable lesson, providing you can identify where things went wrong, and will accept the blame if you made a mistake.

30

C H A P T E R

The Three-Party Blanket

You have seen that when you use other people's money, all the cash you need may be obtained by way of relatively simple 100 percent financing. Essentially you assume the existing mortgage or take out a new first mortgage, and all the seller has to do is hold all of the balance of a purchase price as a second on another property you own. This formula has been shown already in this book in several different formats. Yet already we have looked at situations where a seller is reluctant to enter into a deal where the buyer has not invested any of his or her own cash. This reluctance even extends to situations where the seller gets substantial cash out of the deal. Using any form of creative financing may require you to illustrate that it is okay for the other party (either the buyer or seller) to benefit from the technique. Fear of something unique is not unusual and there will be times when the seller will walk away from anything but cash . . . even if he loses the property through foreclosure later on.

Motivation, as I have stressed, is always a key to the buyer or seller striking the best deal. Buyers and sellers who understand that deals end with a win-win for both sides is the best possible situation. Your goal therefore is to choose the best technique for the transaction at hand. The strategy that helps the other side move closer to their own goals while it also advances your position will also move you both toward that win-win closing.

The three-party blanket is one of those strategies that will help you close the gap with sellers who are skeptical about this idea of creative financing.

A blanket mortgage is a mortgage that has one set of terms with more than one property as security. For example, at this writing, I am negotiating on behalf of a client of mine to acquire three hotels owned by GE Credit in the Orlando, Florida, area. We have offered them $25 million for the three if they would hold a three-year blanket first mortgage in the amount of $18,000,000. This single mortgage would lock these three properties together until we either release one or more of them with a release of security agreement, or until the mortgage is paid off. I only want three-year terms for two reasons. The first advantage is that the properties need work, good management, and a new image. This takes time, and my client estimates that within two years he will have turned the properties into a gold mine easily worth $40,000,000 to $50,000,000. The second reason is because three years is not such a long time for GE Credit to hold the paper. The time is essential because my client feels that if he can buy this time now, it will be easy to refinance a hotel package that will be worth at least $40,000,000 at the end of these three years. Part of my strategy is we have a fallback position, which is the three-party blanket. If I must, I can offer GE Credit other property as security on the three-year blanket I have already proposed.

USING THREE-PARTY BLANKETS

You will not need to look for "desperate" sellers, and in fact you will be able to make OPM deals you never thought possible. Best of all you will not have to look for multimillion-dollar transactions either.

The use of the blanket mortgage involves offering the seller some other property as additional security on the purchase-money mortgage the seller is holding. In essence you buy a property, give the seller a mortgage for his equity, and offer two or more properties or items (chattels) as the total security for the deal. In most of these transactions the seller or the seller's advisors may recommend that if the seller is to do this, then the buyer should also cross-collateralize the transaction with a secondary position on the existing property being sold. When you cross-collateralize any debt what you are doing is binding more than one property or benefit as the security for the loan. This is important for you to be comfortable with because there are many different kinds of cross-collateralization and this concept may come up in many situations where you are a buyer and when you are a seller. So lets take a moment and see how cross-collateralization works.

Cross-Collateralization and Blanket Financing

Julie wants to buy a duplex and she and the seller have come to an agreement whereby she will put some cash down, take out a new first mortgage, and the seller will hold a small second mortgage. All is okay until the seller's lawyer gets into the action and will not let the seller sign the contract unless Julie puts up some additional security for the second mortgage. The only thing of substantial free-and-clear value that Julie has is a 2003 Mercedes, which she got as the divorce settlement from her former husband a few months earlier. Okay, the lawyer says, tie that Mercedes (cross-collateralize) to the second mortgage. What this means is if you stiff the seller holding the second mortgage, the seller will have the right to lien the property as well as the Mercedes. In the end Julie's lawyer also got into the picture, and the two lawyers came to a settlement. If she made half the payments without any unusual default (late over 20 days), then the Mercedes would be released from the security.

I helped Purvin assemble three apartment properties in an upscale residential area of Fort Lauderdale. The sites are contiguous and front on an ocean access canal. This waterway is called "deep water," which in Florida terms means there are no fixed bridges between the site and the Atlantic Ocean. This is an important and very valuable element in a community where there are many large yachts and sailboats capable of going from Purvin's site to Europe and back.

By the time we came to close on the third site, Purvin was running short of immediate cash. However, he did have lots of other real estate and was in that twilight zone where he owed lots of money (millions) but also owned lots of real estate (more millions). So he went to a lender and took out a line of credit on a package of his properties. This line of credit was secured by blanket financing with four properties all tied to the security of that line of credit through a cross-collateralization provision. As it was his intention ultimately to develop the property by removing the existing structures, which were a mix of 30- and 40-year-old small apartment buildings, and build ultra-high-end luxury condominiums, he needed to be able to release at least half of the assembled property prior to fully paying off the funds borrowed against the line of credit. This created no problem and the bank was pleased to do so because they were well protected with the amount of security they held.

A Release from Cross-Collateralization

In the examples of both Julie and Purvin, there was a method to release part of the property that was tied by cross-collateralization to the overall security of the mortgage or debt. In Julie's case the primary reason for the extra security was to test her ability to meet the mortgage obligations. After two years if she had been prompt in meeting her payments, the holder of the debt let the Mercedes out of the bind and ended the cross-collateralization. In Purvin's example he needed the flexibility to allow development. If any buyer has plans or anticipates a reason why the added property to the blanket (therefore cross-collateralized together with another property as security for a mortgage or debt) will need to be released, they should make sure that provisions for this are built into the original mortgage. Keep in mind if the buyer anticipates the need to sell the recently purchased property (or is forced to do so), then the mortgage that is cross-collateralized will have to be paid off. This situation would also occur if the buyer wanted to refinance the recently purchased property. Because there are many different reasons why a buyer would either want to avoid cross-collateralization altogether or to have a way to end security agreement, look to other techniques covered in this book, such as the sliding mortgage, to aid that problem.

Because cross-collateralization is a real circumstance, I will include it with most of the examples in this chapter, but keep in mind that extra provision may not be necessary or ideal for the buyer. If you must have it, then be sure to have a method to release all or part of the purchased property.

THE TWO-PARTY BLANKET

The two-party blanket is the first and most basic use of the technique. Let's look at how it works.

Connor is attempting to buy from Bill, but Bill won't accept Connor's offer to assume Bill's existing mortgage and give Bill a second mortgage for the balance of the price. Bill does want out of the property, though, and doesn't want to lose a prospective buyer. So he tells Connor he will take the deal providing Connor secures the second mortgage with some other property plus the property being purchased. If Connor has some property he isn't using and doesn't mind tying it up in this deal, he is apt to go along.

What makes this deal a two-party blanket is this: The deal involves only Connor and Bill, two people, two parties, two properties.

MOVE UP TO THE THREE-PARTY BLANKET

The three-party blanket introduces you to a new element of real estate financing: You don't have to own the property you are using as security in a deal. In some situations you can use someone else's property to make your deals fall into place.

In the three-party blanket all that is necessary is a ready and willing property owner who will agree to allow you to tie up his property as security on your mortgage with the seller. You may have to pay a kicker for this use of property, but since the risk may not be too great to the owner of this other property, the kicker may be an acceptable cost to you.

Let's look at these two examples of how it works. Lawton had tried just about everything he could to make the deal he wanted on a small three-unit apartment building. The seller had agreed to a most attractive price, and Lawton liked the low-interest assumable mortgage. On top of this the seller was willing to hold some paper. However, he wouldn't let Lawton sign the contract that left him holding all paper to cover his equity. The seller's point of view was well-taken and quite understandable: He simply saw no future in holding 100 percent of the equity in paper with no additional risk on the buyer's part.

Lawton didn't have any other property to pledge as additional security, so he had discounted the idea of doing a blanket. However, he remembered that his dad had a lot in North Carolina. Lawton then made a deal with his father to put the lot up as additional security on the apartment building. As a kicker he offered his father a piece of the ultimate profit when the apartments were sold. The deal was set up so that the lot could be removed as the additional security once 25 percent of the principal originally owed had been paid. At that point the seller would have the security the lot represented, so it would no longer be needed in the deal. Lawton might have added another provision to the transaction that would allow him to replace the North Carolina lot as security to the transaction provided that the seller agreed to the replacement, or provided that an appraisal showed the value of the replacement property to exceed a certain ratio of value to equity with a minimum value of, say, twice the amount of the secondary financing the seller was holding.

Nevin, on the other hand, was trying to buy a lot in the Florida Keys with the idea of building a home someday in that part of the world. He didn't have the cash the seller wanted, but he was able to make a deal with the owner of the adjoining property (who was a friend of Nevin's and the reason

Nevin wanted to buy there in the first place). The deal was this: Nevin's friend would put his lot and home up as additional security in Nevin's blanket mortgage to the seller. The friend would be able to use Nevin's lot as though it was his until Nevin decided to build. In addition, if Nevin sold the lot before building on it, the friend would get a piece of the action. The whole deal was then covered with Nevin giving his friend an option to buy the lot in the event Nevin defaulted on the mortgage, at a price equal to the mortgage balance at the time of the default. This was not a bad deal for Nevin's friend because if Nevin paid off part of the lot and then defaulted, he would likely pick up a bargain right next door to his home. Nevin's friend might have lived a hundred miles away with another property to be used as security, so don't think you have to limit your search for investments to those that are next door to your friends.

In each of these two deals, the investor had to give up something to make the deal. The borrowing of this security from a third party made the seller more secure in giving the investor an OPM deal.

THE FINE POINTS OF THE DEAL

This is a technique that few people use or even know about. This generally works to your advantage, since a seller may never have been approached this way before. Remember, however, that you must appear to be very sincere in your approach, and it is wise not to start out with any blanket approach unless you know you are dealing with a seller who has seen everything before. Why? Because you do not want to appear to be out to make a "strange" deal. Sellers and seller's lawyers don't like that approach. However, once you have shown that you are a real buyer and are making a counter to the seller's counter of your first offer, bring on the two- and three-party blankets.

There are two elements to this kind of transaction that you should pay attention to in order to gain the edge with this technique. The first is the way in which the approach is made to the seller, and the second is that you can profit from actually being the third party and not necessarily the investor.

In the first instance there is no need to tell the seller that the property you are giving him as additional security to his mortgage isn't owned by you (unless that fact makes the deal even more secure for the seller). In most instances the fact that you are putting up a property as security that is owned by someone else might scare the seller. A more straightforward approach is simply to say, "In addition to the property I'm buying, Mr. Seller, I'll secure the mortgage with a first position (first mortgage) on this beautiful commercial lot described in this brochure."

Some sellers have never heard of a blanket mortgage and must be carefully approached. Terminology is most crucial, so never get technical without making sure that you are being understood. Real estate terminology is not universal, and some people think a wraparound mortgage and a blanket mortgage are the same. (They can be, just like all the dogs in this room might be Dobermans but not all dogs are Dobermans.) Also a first mortgage isn't a first mortgage just because the document says it is; a blanket mortgage is what it is, not what the term calls it. Never assume that anyone understands any real estate term you use; give examples to make sure. Because terminology can confuse people and the last thing you want to do is to confuse the seller, be careful to explain precisely what is going to happen. By the way for a first mortgage to indeed be that, it must be recorded as such, generally in the county where the property is located, ahead of any other mortgage. It is possible for a person to lend money thinking the security is a first mortgage only to discover the person had borrowed money from five people that same day. Only one of them would be lucky enough to get his mortgage recorded ahead of the others. I recommend you always use a good real estate lawyer or escrow or title company to close your transactions.

"Mr. Seller, in this offer I want you to notice that, while no cash will change hands at the closing, you will have a large increase in the security backing the second mortgage you will be holding. As your property has an existing mortgage that is being assumed in the purchase, you will hold the balance of the price in the form of a second mortgage. Naturally you want to see substantial security backing that mortgage. This offer gives you additional security on the second mortgage. That security comes from the first position you are being given on this other property described in the attached report. In essence if there were to be a default on your second mortgage, you would have the right to foreclose on both properties."

It is easy for a broker, in making this presentation, to point out the potential benefit to the seller in obtaining a good price in the deal with strong security. Remember that the real motivation that is driving the seller may not be the price. Often it is some more basic need that must be met. The need for cash is often far less of an issue than the need to be sure that once the deal has closed they, the seller, will not have to worry about getting the balance of the deal. Here the strongest element is the need for security. A broker in any transaction can be beneficial to the investor if the broker is a good one and understands what is happening. When using a blanket or pyramid technique where there must be some validation of some other property's value, a broker can discuss that value much more easily than the investor can. Sellers are biased in the natural tendency to distrust whatever someone tells them when that someone is trying to buy their property for nothing down. Use a broker who understands blankets and you will have a better closing ratio.

The second area I told you to pay attention to is the possibility that you might want to be the third party. You will recall in the two examples cited earlier that both the third parties got something. If you have some unused real estate lying around, you can become a silent partner by lending your real estate to a security position from time to time. These situations don't just fall into your lap, however, you need to look for them. They are found through your broker or through deals that start out as partnerships but often end up this way.

If a friend comes to you and asks you to join in a purchase with him, you might examine the deal to see if you can become a partner by lending your unused real estate to a security position. "Look, Ben," you tell your friend, "I'll take 50 percent of the deal. In fact, I'll show you how we can make the deal with you putting up less cash than you wanted to in the first instance." You can leave out, for the moment at least, "and without my putting up any cash."

USING THE BLANKET TO YOUR ADVANTAGE

There are several elements of a blanket you need to know about and incorporate into your deals. The proper use of any blanket, both two and three-party mortgages, will require that you include the following three in the contract to buy. They should not be left up to the usual "legal aftermath" that often occurs in normal mortgage situations. Blankets are not normal mortgages, so to avoid trouble use this checklist.

The Three-Point Blanket-Mortgage Checklist

1. The contract should carefully describe the position of security that is being given up in the other property. It is possible to give a second position behind an existing mortgage or to build in a subordinated position behind a future mortgage to be placed on the other property. In the subordinated position, the investor (or

owner of the second property) is permitted to obtain financing in the form of a first mortgage on the property even though a blanket mortgage has been given prior to that time.

2. Provide for a release of the additional security. You don't want to lock up your property (or someone else's) for the duration of the mortgages. The seller can usually be convinced that, once you have established equity in the deal, there is no need for this additional security. If you don't provide for such a release, then you will lock up the other property until the mortgage is satisfied. A release provision is simply stated: " . . . and when the total mortgages on the purchased property have been paid down to a total outstanding balance owed of $45,000 [or whatever], the additional property as indicated herein, which is covered by this blanket mortgage, shall be released from this mortgage."

3. Be clear on the form of amortization used. Most mortgage payments are a set amount each month and those payments include interest on the unpaid balance and some portion of principal. These are normal amortization where the payment is constant, but the amount applied to interest or principal pay down changes slightly every payment period. In some mortgages there is a third element, which is a combination of real estate tax and insurance. The first two elements, principal and interest, are at times the culprits that can mess up any mortgage amortization if the mortgage is written differently than you intended it to be. For example, if a $50,000 mortgage is amortized over 10 years with equal payments of principal plus 10 percent interest on the unpaid balance, the annual payment would be $10,000 for the first year. This is because there are 10 equal principal payments of $5000 each. Added to each of these payments will be interest on the balance owed at the contract rate of 10 percent. In this kind of mortgage the payment will decline each time be the amount of reduced interest as the balance is paid off. To this extent each year thereafter will have a slightly reduced payment. By the time of the fifth annual payment the buyer will pay $7500 ($5000 principal + $2500 interest = $7500) and the final year only $5500 ($5000 principal + $500 interest = $5500). On the other hand, if the payments were to be 10 years of equal payments of principal including interest, each year would be $8137.50. This kind of mortgage payment schedule is the most

common and is based on the constant monthly payment, which is
the combination of principal and interest that will amortize the
loan over the specific term with every payment the same. Some
lawyers (and investors) like this first method because it is simple
to calculate. On the other hand if cash flow is important, equal
payments of $8137.50 each year for 10 years might be far more
attractive and is calculated using Table A in the Appendix or by
obtaining an easy-to-use financial calculator. Some mortgages
may call for interest only with a balloon payment at the end of a
certain period. This kind of mortgage has a set payment but does
not pay off any debt. Balloon mortgages can be a sudden blow if
the economy will not let you refinance the property sufficiently
to pay off the mortgage now due. I like to put the actual
payment, as I understand the contract, in the contract. This does
not allow any fussing at the closing table as to what principal
and interest should total.

PITFALLS IN THE THREE-PARTY DEAL

From the seller's point of view, the use of a blanket mortgage aids in his
security and reduces the risk of an OPM transaction. All sellers, however,
should be careful in accepting the other property and should make a thorough examination of the title and value of this second property. There is
no benefit or added security in taking a worthless or heavily over-mort-
gaged property as part of a blanket.

One disadvantage to the buyer using this technique is that the property owner supplying the other property to the mortgage gives up some, if
not all, of his freedom to use this property to generate other financing.

If you are using another person's property in a three-party blanket,
the owner of that property may have risk of considerable loss if you default. Anyone considering becoming a third party in a three-party-blanket
deal should first check into the amount of risk. As in every kind of real estate transaction, if the risk is justly compensated for, the deal may be warranted. Because of this, most three-party blankets will be made between
an investor and a third party who are closely related or connected in one
way or another.

31

CHAPTER

The Discounted
Paper Swap

Many investors hold mortgages that they will gladly sell to you at a discounted value, provided you give them cash. One day you might be in this same boat. This situation occurs because sellers often take secondary paper as a part of their transaction. They do so because they anticipate that they will be able to either pass off the paper to someone else when they purchase another property or sell the paper at a discount. Naturally, some sellers will just sit on the paper and collect the interest, but most second and third mortgage holders will sell their paper at a discount, if you make them an offer.

The discounted paper swap is a multiple event enabling you to generate instant profit and use this profit to buy something, which you hope will increase that profit even more. The technique often involves the use of cash, and many investors who are heavy with cash will purchase mortgages at a discount and then use this technique to get extra mileage out of that cash. In this book, however, I will show you how to use this method to gain a foothold in real estate without any cash.

THE SWAP-OUT DEAL

Let's say you want to buy an inexpensive $70,000 vacation condo. The property has an existing first mortgage of $22,000, and the seller indicates she will hold a second mortgage if you give her at least $10,000 cash in the deal. You know you can refinance this property with a 95 percent loan. This would give you $66,500 less the cost of the loan, approximately $2000. From this loan you would net $64,500, which still leaves you $5500 short of making your OPM deal come together.

However, as you know all about the discounted paper swap, you have been looking around for investors with mortgages to sell. A mortgage holder has offered you the opportunity to purchase a second mortgage at a discount. This second mortgage has a $34,000 face-value still outstanding at 10 years to go at 9.5 percent contract rate. You have calculated the current value of the mortgage, if purchased by you for cash at a price that would give you a 15 percent return if held through the full 10 years remaining. That value is $27,270.25. You arrived at this amount by using the discount formula and checklist supplied in this chapter. The owner of that mortgage needs cash and agrees to sell you the mortgage for the $27,270.25.

You tell the owner of the mortgage you are about to do a deal and ask if she'll sit still on the paper for a few days to enable you to firm up the home transaction. While the mortgage owner is anxious for cash, you are the only buyer so she is willing to wait a few days.

Before going to the homeowner, you survey what you have. You know now that if you give the mortgage owner $27,270.25, you can become owner of a mortgage with a face value of $34,000. This difference would give you an instant equity of $6729.75. You also know that you can borrow 95 percent on the vacation condo and end up with net loan proceeds of $64,500. Looking back over the rest of the deal, you decide as follows:

If the seller of the house will take your about-to-be-acquired mortgage at face value of $34,000 and you pay off the existing mortgage of $22,000, you can give her $14,000 cash, which is $4000 more than she wants. Now in actual negotiations you would not offer her that extra $4000 right upfront. You might ask her to hold an additional $4000 in the form of a personal note signed by you. But your endgame is to end up as shown here.

The vacation condo seller ends up with the mortgage face value of	$34,000
You pay off the existing debt on the vacation condo of	$22,000
You give the vacation condo seller the balance in cash	$14,000
Total value to the vacation condo seller	$70,000

That looks simple so far. But just how did you do this without spending any of your own cash? In this transaction you actually made money in the end by buying the discounted mortgage, which you used as a form of a pyramid, and refinancing the balance of the deal through a local lender to generate the cash needed to pay off both sellers (the mortgage and the vacation condo). The two sellers were each motivated by cash. The seller willing to discount the mortgage gets around 80 percent of the face value of the mortgage ($34,000), and the vacation condo seller gets $14,000 and satisfies another motivation: She sells the vacation condo and gets out from that headache and the debt she owed on it.

How You Financed This OPM Transaction

You will get a new mortgage on the house of	$66,500.00
But you have to pay the loan cost of	$ 2,000.00
This leaves you with a net loan proceeds of	$64,500.00
You pay the owner of the face-value $34,000 mortgage the agreed cash amount of	$27,270.25
This leaves you with a remainder of	$37,229.75
From this you pay off the existing mortgage	$22,000.00
You are then left with	$15,229.75
Then you pay the seller the balance owed	$14,000.00
You have enough left for a housewarming party	$ 1,229.75

THE FINE POINTS OF THE DEAL

There are many fine points to dealing with mortgages you may want to buy. Using them in this kind of buying technique is just one of many opportunities to profit through discounted mortgages. Because of the great flexibility you will have in dealing within the mortgage arena, it is important for you to have a quick and easy way to calculate the value of a mortgage at any rate or term. I will show you the key points to look for in the actual value of a mortgage later in this chapter, but first let's look at the actual discount of the mortgage itself.

Constants are a simple shortcut to discounts. To find a mortgage discount, you must either have in-depth knowledge of the mathematics of finance or have a simple constant table such as Table A, which is provided for you in the Appendix of this book. This table shows constant interest rates that relate to the most common form of mortgage amortization: monthly payments that stay the same for the entire life of the mortgage. This table provides for interest rates and terms of years. Simply match the interest rate column to the term of years in the rows and you will have the annual constant rate that conforms to 12 monthly payments a year.

Once you have found the constant rate that meets the terms of the mortgage you are dealing with you would multiply the constant rate by the actual balance of the mortgage. This will give you the total amount of the total payment for a 12-month period. Dividing that amount by 12, you get the monthly payment. The term "constant" refers to the fact that once you begin with this mortgage the actual payment, which is the combination of principal and interest, remains the same amount for the entire life of the mortgage. However the part of that constant payment that applies to principal or interest changes every time a payment is made, only the total of the two will remain constant.

For example, look at Table A in the Appendix. Under the column for 9.5 percent interest in the row for 10 years you will find the percent shown to be 15.53. If the mortgage in question were $10,000 with a payment schedule spread over 10 years at 9.5 percent interest, you would multiply the constant (15.53 percent) by the mortgage amount ($10,000) and end up with the total annual payments of $1553.00. (Don't forget that when you use a percent in a math problem it must first be converted to a decimal. You do this by moving the decimal that shows in the table two places to the left.) If you divide the annual amount of $1553.00 by 12, you end up with a monthly payment of $129.42, rounding up from $129.416.

The thing to remember is that you can find the annual payment of any mortgage (and then the monthly payment) by knowing the interest rate, the years to term, then finding the corresponding constant and multiplying it (as a decimal) by the mortgage amount. Remember that Table A relates to monthly payments, however, and the annual amount must be divided by 12 to end up with the correct figure.

This is the specific function of the constants table, but understanding this function will enable you to do many other things with these tables. One of these things is to easily calculate the discount of a mortgage.

THE FORMULA FOR FINDING THE DISCOUNTED VALUE

The use of constants will enable you to arrive at a value for any mortgage, based on the return you would demand for that mortgage. In essence mortgage values are a function of the return that the mortgage will show the holder of the mortgage. By this I mean that if you want to buy a mortgage you will want a specific yield on your money. As we saw in the earlier example, the mortgage holder of that $34,000 was willing to discount his 9.5 percent yield mortgage at a discount to give the buyer a 15 percent return. Just because a mortgage has a set contract rate (in that case 9.5 percent) you can adjust the structure of the mortgage to give you a higher yield without changing what the borrower is paying. Let's look at the economic side of the picture.

The contract rate on any mortgage is the interest the mortgagor pays by virtue of the original loan agreement. While this interest may fluctuate, the contract rate will always be a rate that is described in or a function of the original or modified loan contract. The 9.5 percent interest rate previously mentioned would have been considered well below market in the mid-1980s if the mortgage were in a second or third position. A lender would demand a much higher rate, and 15 percent would be considered more acceptable. To force a 9.5 percent mortgage to return you 15 percent over a term of 10 years, you would have to pay less for the mortgage than the current unpaid balance. How much less? You must take the following steps to find out.

Five Steps to Finding the Discounted Value

1. Ascertain the "demand rate" you want to earn. This will set the stage for the discount value of the mortgage. This means simply decide what yield you will be willing to make if you pay cash for this mortgage. You may find that your offer may not be accepted and you will end up paying more, which will give you a lower rate of return than you hoped for. But if some of the other, noneconomic circumstances are right, you may well accept a slightly lower rate than your initial demand. In the case at hand, we are assuming your demand rate is 15 percent. As you want to make 15 percent on this (or any) mortgage and you know the term of years, you must now go to step two.

2. Find the constant rate for your demand rate. You want to find the constant rate for the remaining term of years of the mortgage you want to discount, at the demand rate. Since the mortgage in question has 10 years to go, and your demand rate is 15 percent, you look in Table A and go to the 10-year row, and follow it over

until you reach the column for 15 percent. The resulting constant percentage rate is 19.36. This is the demand rate you want to make after you purchase the mortgage.

3. Find the constant rate for the mortgage at the contract rate (9.5 percent). In the same row for 10 years go to the column for 9.5 percent interest. This will be 15.53 percent.

4. Find the current unpaid balance of the mortgage. Usually you, or the mortgagor, will know this by examining the mortgage amortization schedule. If this amount is not known, you may have to reconstruct the events dating from the start of the mortgage. This involves having a copy of the mortgage contract to know the exact starting time, the original principal, and the number of months that have passed.

For example, if you read the mortgage document and see that the mortgage has a contract rate of 9.5 percent interest for 12 years with equal monthly payments, you can look at the 12-year row next to the column for 9.5 percent interest to see a constant of 14.0 percent. This amount multiplied by the beginning loan amount (shown in the contract) of $37,718.94 would give an annual payment of $5280.65, which when divided by 12 gives the monthly payment of $440.05 that the mortgage will carry for the full 12 years. A quick check on this will prove out by matching the payments you might have been given. Remember, however, that you are using principal and interest payments here and some mortgages will add taxes and insurance and other items to the total payment. You must discard all added figures and work solely with the principal and interest portions. Once you find the original constant, you can then go to the constant closest to the present time. As a buyer of discounted mortgages, you will select the half-year point already past if you cannot fall right on a time span shown in the tables. In this case, however, you notice that exactly two years will have gone by from the original start of the mortgage to the date when you would become the owner.

As you are trying to find (or test) the actual remaining principal outstanding, you locate the constant at the actual current date that you did in step three. Since you know, or have calculated, the actual mortgage payments, you divide the annual payment by the constant.

ORIGINAL ANNUAL PAYMENT $5280.65 = $34,002.90
with 10 years remaining

Divide $5280.65 by CURRENT CONSTANT of 0.1553
and the balance shows as exactly $34,002.90. For the
balance of this example I will round this to $34,000.

The $34,000 then is the remaining balance of the mortgage.
Whichever method you have used to find the current
unpaid principal, you can check it with the other way.

You are now ready to move to step five.

5. Calculate the discounted value. The discounted value can now be
found by using the formula shown below. You have all the
necessary elements to put into the boxes.

ACTUAL TOTAL OF ANNUAL PAYMENTS: ($5,280.65)
DIVIDED BY THE DEMAND RATE AFTER
DISCOUNT: (.1936)

5280.65 divided by .1936 = $27,276.08

The DISCOUNTED VALUE is $27,276.08

By following this formula you can arrive at a discounted
value for a mortgage. It is also possible to discover the actual yield
from a mortgage offered to you at a discount in a similar way.

FIND OUT WHAT A DISCOUNTED MORTGAGE WILL ACTUALLY YIELD

Let's assume you are trying to buy the same mortgage in this example. You
know the current principal outstanding is $34,000 and the annual payment
totals $5280.65. In the negotiations with the holder of this mortgage, you
make a lower offer than the seller wants, only to find you are able to buy
the mortgage (if you want) for the reduced sum of $25,000.00. You know
that this will yield you more than 15 percent, which was the discounted
sum the seller offered. But what is the yield?

You need to find out what constant is represented by this amount. In
short, you divide the annual payment by the price at which you are able to
buy the mortgage. Annual payment ($5280 rounded off cents) divided by
the amount you pay will give you the constant rate for your new yield
percentage.

$5280.00 divided by $25,000 = 0.2112

This will give you 0.2112 which, when represented as a percent (by
moving the decimal over to the right two places), gives you a 21.12 constant

rate. As we are dealing with a 10-year mortgage in this case, you simply move across that row (the years remaining) to the closest possible constant. You find that 21.12 corresponds to between 20.86 for 17 percent interest and 21.62 for 18 percent interest. This mortgage at this price then, would return slightly over 17 percent to you if you purchased it for $25,000.

This is a lot of math just to set the stage for this technique, but it is essential because you will never be able to effectively negotiate for mortgages unless you can properly discount them to current values. You will find, however, that the actual math is very simple and that the cheapest of all electronic calculators should do the calculations effectively. One note of caution: You must make sure you are using a calculator that does not round off decimals to three or four places. Test this by multiplying 0.1234 by 0.1234. If you don't register 0.0152275 as your answer, it could be that your calculator is dropping the 4 or even the 3 from the multiplication problem. This kind of calculator will be of little use to you in finance. Also, keep in mind that the most accurate method of doing any of these calculations will be with a financial calculator. The tables I have provided are quick and easy, once you get the feel for them, and they tend to make the payments a bit lighter than the financial calculators will because my tables do not extend past four decimals. This is accurate enough for most mortgages, but if you are dealing in mortgage amounts above $500,000 the payment amounts could vary slightly. For example my calculator shows a $500,000 mortgage over 30 years at 8 percent interest to be $3668.90 a month while using Table A shows a monthly payment of $3670.83. Not much of a difference, but be aware of these differences. A closing agent will use his own calculator and not my tables.

FACTORS TO EVALUATE IN MORTGAGES

There are several factors that contribute to the value of a mortgage and make the discounting of mortgages very profitable to those people who know how to evaluate these factors. Understanding these elements will better enable you to know when to keep the mortgage being offered to you at a discount and when you should simply use it as an element in the discounted paper swap. These factors of mortgage values are as follows:

1. What is the mortgage's loan-to-value ratio? This is a key factor in any mortgage situation. What is the value of the property, and what is the total loan circumstance? If the property is

conservatively valued at $100,000 and the total loans on the property are $80,000, there is an 80 percent loan-to-value ratio. The amount of equity the owner has in the deal decreases the risk on the part of the mortgagee. Low loan-to-value ratios are therefore better than high loan-to-value ratios.

2. Where is this loan in the total picture? It is possible the property has more than one loan outstanding. If you are buying the first mortgage, you want to know the loan-to-value ratio as it pertains only to the total loans but not including any loans behind, or junior to, this one. If there is a first mortgage of $20,000 and a second mortgage of $60,000 and a total loan-to-value ratio of 80 percent, but only a 20 percent loan-to-value ratio for the first mortgage, it is easy to see that the second mortgage is riskier than the first.

3. What do you know about the owners of the property? This will tell you a lot. If the owner is anticipating an addition, or a possible refinance of the total loan structure, or a sale of the property, these elements can cause a sudden and premature payoff of the loan. This creates a bonanza, as you will see.

4. What do you know about the property itself? Examination of some properties will show that they are ripe for redevelopment. Trends in the area might dictate that only the foolish would hold the property in its present status for very long.

A study of these four elements will often reveal a potential early payoff of a mortgage. You should be aware that it is rare for any mortgage to run for more than 10 years, no matter what the original contract. The need for funds, a new buyer, redevelopment, additions, etc., all cause the property to be refinanced. The advent of new federal savings and loans provisions in their first mortgages, requiring adjustments or refinancing in the event of a sale or other disposition of title, will trigger early payoffs of junior mortgages.

THE PROFIT DUE TO EARLY PAYOFF

Let's look at the mortgage you bought in this chapter for $275,000. Originally you tied up this mortgage with the thought of using it in the discounted paper swap, but then you realized the owner of the real estate that secured the mortgage was going to pay off the mortgage early. Perhaps you discovered this when you went over to look at the property and noticed the "For Sale" sign being taken down and the new buyer told you he was going to remodel the whole property. Remember the face amount of the mortgage still outstanding is $34,000. If you can buy the mortgage for $25,000 and within a month or so have it paid off for the full $34,000, you will profit to the tune of $9000. This is a healthy yield of 36 percent even if it took a full year for this to occur and that would be in addition to the interest yield you would earn from the mortgage payments (remember that was slightly over 17 percent by itself). This is not bad at all, and it shows some of the potential in discounting mortgages.

MAKING THE DISCOUNTED PAPER SWAP WORK

Getting back to the technique at hand, you will find that sellers of real estate will allow the pyramid to work for you in this kind of deal because of that grass-looking-greener-on-the-other-side-of-the-fence syndrome I've talked about before. The fact that you will give a seller a mortgage at its face value when you have bought it at a discount doesn't matter: You aren't offering an alternative, for one thing; and, if the seller doesn't find that the totality of your offer does something for her, she will turn it down.

The motivation of the seller to sell and get a good price is the major point for you to work on. You must never allow yourself to get caught in the trap of making comparisons between what you are offering and what the seller wants. The only comparison that is valid for either you or the seller is to compare what you are offering to what has been offered and what is currently still open. In essence, you compare what you want to do with all the options open to you.

Many sellers turn down the first and best offer they will ever get, only to take something less later on. Time works against many sellers who are motivated by the need to make a deal as soon as possible. Their need for cash makes this and any real estate deal easier if you make use of the techniques offered in this book that enable you to generate cash (none of it yours) to the seller.

PITFALLS IN THE DISCOUNTED PAPER SWAP

There is no pitfall to the investor who ties up some paper at a discount and then uses the appreciated value to generate the cash or equity he needs to make a deal. This kind of transaction creates pure profit up front. The equity you obtain in the deal is yours to work with and is the same as cash when the seller takes at face value the mortgage you bought at a discount.

The pitfalls for the seller can be many, however, and all sellers taking any mortgage paper must follow business prudence in making sure that the mortgages are sound, the security isn't over evaluated, and the real risk of having the loan wiped out in a foreclosure of a senior mortgage is low. This will require that the seller taking such paper examine the situation carefully. The pitfall can be a sudden and drastic loss of 100 percent of the value of the mortgage in a foreclosure that cannot sustain the values of the debt outstanding.

Proper evaluation of such risks, however, will enable sellers to use this tool to their advantage. There is nothing wrong with a seller taking good paper providing the total picture is worthwhile. If the cash the seller is getting is sufficient to satisfy the seller's need for cash, and the total price on the property is above what the seller might have been forced to take had time eaten her up, then the total goal of the seller might be well serviced. In fact many such sellers find that taking discounted paper where they don't get the advantage of the discount is not only easy, it is downright rewarding.

32 CHAPTER

IRC 1031: The Greatest Loophole Left

The Internal Revenue Service (IRS) gives and takes away. The Internal Revenue Code (IRC) 1031 is the section of IRS code that deals with tax-free exchanges. While this code deals with exchanges of many different items, it is also pertinent to certain real estate exchanges. If you use it properly, it can help you not only make OPM deals, but also allow you to save on taxes at the same time. Keep in mind that any rules or laws having to do with taxes is subject to change. Some past changes have caused dramatic negative impacts on the taxpayer, especially the real estate investor. Other changes have relaxed earlier slammers. As of this writing President Bush has announced new sweeping tax plans that will have some very positive impacts on interest, dividends, and capital gains treatment. Like a lot that comes from Washington as we approach an election year, much of this kind of talk is political hype either to sway or to confuse voters. However, changes happen all the time, and it is important for all investors in any commodity to be mindful of the current and pending laws (voted in but not applied as yet) that are likely to affect you.

First let me set the record straight. Not all exchanges you make will qualify under IRC 1031. This doesn't mean those exchanges will not be of benefit to you since any exchange that moves you closer to your goal is a good exchange. The benefits of IRC 1031 exchange are basically that you can postpone or even avoid tax you might have to pay in the event of a sale. When you use the benefits of IRC 1031 you can save on the amount of the tax you would have had to pay in the event of an outright sale. Those are attributes for a seller. As a buyer this strategy can work for you in enticing a seller to "take" your property in an exchange because of the tax he will save.

THE SAVING GAINS TAX DEAL

Alan owns a hotel in Hilton Head, South Carolina. He wants to sell it and has negotiated with Toby for a final, not-to-go-lower-than price of $2,500,000 after all closing costs. Alan's tax basis (book value) in the hotel is $1,000,000. He has a first mortgage of $500,000. If he sells for the price he wants, he will have a gain of $1,500,000. Assume he will have a tax of at least 20 percent of the gain. (This is based on past tax law, and depends on Alan's total overall income tax rate and his possible offsetting tax losses.) At this rate and gain he is looking at a potential tax of $300,000 ($1,500,000 gain × 20 percent = $300,000). Out of the $2,500,000 sales price he will get, he will have $1,700,000 left to reinvest. (Sales price of $2,500,000 less mortgage of $500,000 leaves $2,000,000, then subtract the tax of $300,000, and we have the remaining $1,700,000.)

Let's take a look at Toby's deal. Toby finds out Alan wants to sell the hotel because he would like to move to Fort Lauderdale to own a hotel. Toby's broker gets some more data on this, and Toby looks around and discovers several prime hotels are available in the Fort Lauderdale area. Toby goes to Alan and offers him the $1,850,000 equity in one of the hotels as a full and direct exchange for the Hilton Head hotel.

Toby's broker explains to Alan that if he sold his Hilton Head hotel at his asking price of $2,500,000 he would not have sufficient cash to purchase this Fort Lauderdale hotel because of the tax he would have to pay. But if he made the exchange, he could be the owner of the property in 60 days. Today Alan and his father operate a prime hotel overlooking the Fort Lauderdale beach front.

THE WORLD OF REAL ESTATE EXCHANGES

Real estate exchanges are simple to accomplish, but most people never get involved with this exciting part of the real estate profession or end of investing. There are several reasons for this, and it is important to recognize what these reasons are so you can cope with them when they confront you. Here are the six reasons people avoid real estate exchanges.

1. **Because they don't understand them.** It is human nature to avoid something you don't understand. But remember this about your comfort zone, and it works both for you and against you. As a real estate investor you must strive to expand all those areas and techniques that can increase your profit potential; one such technique is the use of all kinds of real estate exchanges. When you know the strategies of this kind of investing, you no longer can use the excuse you did not know. But in dealing with people ignorant of exchanges, you will have to go slowly to avoid giving the "sharpie" looks to what you are proposing.

2. **Because they believe that one party to an exchange gets the raw end of the deal.** I won't say this doesn't happen from time to time, but it can happen in anything you do. How many sellers feel they receive the most money the buyer would pay? How many buyers feel they paid the lowest price possible? The client of mine who tells me that he will make one offer and it will be a take-it-or-leave-it would be most chagrined if the seller said, "Okay, I'll take it." That buyer would forever wonder if he hadn't offered too much.

    The more you know about exchanges, the more you will realize that for some people the exchange is more beneficial than a sale. In fact some sellers will accept in an exchange a property they would not have purchased (given a wide selection and the cash to make the purchase), because the exchange was offered to them and the cash was not.

    Your use of exchanges will show you that both sides of the exchange can and most often do come out smelling like a rose. The best proof of this is that most exchanges occur between members of the real estate profession brokers and salesmen exchanging real estate in their own portfolios with other brokers and salesmen. These exchangers form clubs and networks where they deal with each other. The slipshod or shifty dealer is quickly recognized and is "dealt" out.

3. **Because they believe people who exchange set two prices.** One price is for the exchange and a real one is for cash (which is much lower). Now this point is often true and to me is one of the

drawbacks of the exchange side of investing, unless you know how to deal with it. The basic reason some people set prices this way is that most people don't understand that since exchanges can save you tax money, if there were to be different prices, the exchange price should be at a lower value. As the exchange saves you on taxes, you can benefit more from the exchange than the sale. After all I'd rather have a $40,000 lot in exchange (if I wanted the lot) than $45,000 in cash with a $9000 tax to pay. Other people set higher prices on exchanges than on cash sales out of defense. Personally I like to quote one price and then stick to it. However you can easily counter the double standard of pricing by never asking someone the value of the exchange, but, instead, always ask what the price is for sale. Work from that evaluation every time.

4. **Because they believe that you never get exactly what you want in an exchange.** Part of the problem here is that most people don't really know what it is they want to end up with. Do they end up with exactly the amount of cash they wanted in a sale? If you truly understand your goals, you will have an easier time with this negative view of exchanges. A clear view of your end goal will enable you to see when the exchange is taking you closer to that goal. You do not need to make the jump from San Francisco to New York in one exchange. It's not that such an exchange isn't possible, only that you are far more likely to get to New York if you take Phoenix, then St. Louis, and then Washington, D.C., on your way to New York. When it comes to real estate exchanges, you have to be willing to give up something that is not doing what it should or what you need to progress toward your goal, in exchange for something that will. Remember that any exchange that moves you closer to your goal is a good exchange.

5. **Because they can't accept the thought of owning something they don't want at all as an intermediate step.** This is often very difficult to explain, though it appears simple enough. The professional exchanger will frequently take a client through a multileg exchange to end up with a beneficial exchange. For example, if I want to acquire a duplex, I might offer the owner of the duplex cash (which I'll get from refinancing the duplex) and some vacant land out of my Armadillo Ranch near Naples,

Florida. If the duplex owner doesn't want my vacant land, the deal could die right there. But it probably won't if I explain that he doesn't have to keep the vacant land. I will make my deal contingent that we can exchange it for something he does want or is more willing to take if he will allow me the time for the extra legwork. If he agrees to allow the deal to be tied together (binding us both to the exchange if I can dispose of the vacant land for him by bringing in something he will take), then I can work out the rest of the deal. He might say he would take a vacant lot, but only if it were in the Florida Keys. I might find a lot he would take, but that owner doesn't want the vacant land in Naples, Florida. I keep going until I find someone who will fit the slot and make the whole jigsaw go together.

I'm not sure what is the world record of legs to an exchange, but I know of one that had seven different steps before it was finally put together. Patience and a determined broker are essential to exchanges.

6. **Because people think you have to own something to make an exchange.** The answer to this paradox is that you can exchange property you don't even own. How? Wait until Chapter 33 for that answer.

The fortunate thing about real estate exchanges is that you will have the opportunity to use this strategy as a buyer as well as seller.

THE BUYER'S VIEWPOINT

When you learn the motivation of the seller, you often realize that the exchange might be your way to do one or several of the following things:

- **Get rid of something you don't want to keep.** If the seller of what you want is highly motivated, he is apt to be willing to take as part or all of this equity something you have in exchange.
- **Motivate the seller because of tax benefits**. The seller hanging on the fence might be motivated by the tax savings you can show him through the exchange you are offering.
- **Bring added equity into a transaction that satisfies the seller.** This is especially important if the seller has been asked to hold some secondary financing. By adding something of equity to the

transaction you show the seller you are willing to put more real value at risk. What you add to the transaction may be less important as the item, as it is the value. A diamond ring, a timeshare apartment, a lot in North Carolina, equity in a condo in Naples. Look at what you own that is doing nothing positive for you. Put those items to work.

THE SELLER'S VIEWPOINT

As a seller, there will be times when you have to dig deep down to the bottom of your soul and come up with some powerful methods to bring a buyer to the table. After all not all real estate will sell itself; sometimes you have to find a "taker" for your property, as that is often the start of a deal. A "taker" is anyone who will, in the right situation, become an owner of your property. The opposite side of that is the "haver" who is anyone who has something an investor would take. "Wants" are what "takers" are looking for. A "haver" could be you if you are trying to sell something.

When you offer your property, or part of your equity, for an exchange you broaden your market. There are buyers out there trying to find what you have, only they don't have money. Try to show them how to make an OPM deal that satisfies their investment wants while it also solves your needs.

If you find a "taker" for your property, you have generated additional options for yourself. When someone says to me, "I'll take your property and assume the new mortgage I can put on it (giving you 80 percent cash) if you take this lot for your remaining equity," I would review that deal carefully. If I take the offer I now have cash and a piece of land, which I can keep, exchange, or offer to someone else on the same basis (I'll hold the mortgage and take something for 20 percent of the lot's equity).

I've made million-dollar exchanges that started out a lot of exchange and little cash and ended up with a small portion of the transaction as exchange and the majority of the deal as cash and mortgage. One such exchange arose out of my desire to sell a large tract of oceanfront land I controlled in the Vero Beach area. My marketing program didn't produce a buyer no matter what I did. Then I decided to open the property up for exchange. Not that the exchange was the most desirable or the most practical thing to do because of the nature of my partners in the ownership of the property. Nonetheless, I knew if I could find a "taker" by suggesting an exchange, it might be possible to find a person who would discover the ocean front property was such a great buy that the exchange idea would either disappear or become just a small part of the deal.

Shortly after placing the land on exchange, the offers began to come in. A large villa in Spain, an orange grove in Florida, and other proposals. Then there was an offer to take some vacant land, free and clear of mortgages, for the equity in the oceanfront land. This offer came from a highly qualified buyer who thought of himself as an exchanger. Through four months of negotiations (nothing else was happening on the property anyway), the deal was concluded. We accommodated the buyer to a small degree by taking some of the vacant land offered (which later went to the brokers as their commission). The exchanger saved face by giving up some vacant land, and we got cash and mortgage for the balance. What started out as an exchange with no cash ended up as a cash deal for the sellers, and the brokers got a large tract of land as a commission they would not have made otherwise.

When you find a taker for your property, you have the choice of moving on your own property or moving off the exchange property. For example if I offered you a small duplex as part of a deal to buy your motel, you might say: "I'll take the deal if I can find a buyer or other exchange for your duplex, as I don't want it."

If I'm motivated to take your motel, I'll sit still for a while and let you go in two directions. I can't stop you from making a deal without me if someone else comes along to buy your property. I'm at the mercy of your intent to try to move off my duplex onto something else. I can, of course, try to find a buyer to take the duplex out of the picture and give you cash. If I know that you and I have a deal, and I have not gone as far with you as I might have, such as pay you more for the motel, I can sweeten the duplex deal for a buyer of that property by lowering the price, reducing interest on a mortgage, or other things we have discussed before.

All sellers should investigate their opportunities and examine the value of an exchange. Even the seller who says "I can't exchange, because I need cash" might find there are no buyers for what he has to sell and that his only way out is to exchange for something that is sellable.

THE MECHANICS OF MAKING EXCHANGES

There are several essential mechanical aspects of making exchanges. The first is the balance of equities. The others relate to presentation and the maximizing of gains. All exchanges must have a balance of equities. There are three ways to achieve this balance: the cash balance, the mortgage balance, and the combination balance.

The Cash Balance

Assume that you own a duplex worth $75,000 and owe $50,000 in a first mortgage against it so your equity is $25,000. You want to exchange for Peter's apartment building, worth (to you) $200,000. Peter has a first mortgage of $130,000 on the building, giving him equity of $70,000 based on your evaluation of the property. You want to make the exchange and will balance the equities with cash, as shown in Table 32-1.

T A B L E 32-1

Cash Balance of Equities

	YOU	PETER
Property given up	$75,000.00	$200,000.00
Less outstanding mortgages	$50,000.00	$130,000.00
Equity	$25,000.00	$ 70,000.00
Cash balance (who gives cash)	$45,000.00	0
Balance of equities	$70,000.00	$ 70,000.00

The Mortgage Balance

If you don't have enough cash to balance the equities, you might try a mortgage balance, as shown in Table 32-2.

In balancing equities with a mortgage, you add an additional mortgage to the property you are to take. In this case you give Peter a $45,000 mortgage against the property you are taking from him, or use the technique where you place the debt on some other property you already own.

T A B L E 32-2

Mortgage Balance of Equity

	YOU	PETER
Property given up	$75,000.00	$200,000.00
Less outstanding mortgages	$50,000.00	$130,000.00
Equity	$25,000.00	$ 70,000.00
New mortgage owed to Peter	0	($ 45,000.00)
Balance of equities	$25,000.00	$ 25,000.00

The Combination Balance

In the combination, you might give Peter $10,000 in cash and $35,000 in the form of a mortgage. Or you could augment your equity by adding other properties. Nothing will keep you from offering Peter the duplex, a gold watch, and seven partridges in a pear tree in addition to some cash and a mortgage.

PRESENTING THE EXCHANGE

A key to all exchanges is the presentation to the other party. Does this sound familiar? It should, because so much of your success in real estate investing depends on the tone set at the time the original offer is presented, and how well the pressure of the deal is both maintained and accepted.

If you are dealing with a real estate broker who has not dealt in exchanges, you are apt to have some problems from the very start. For the same reason, however, it may be difficult for you to make your own exchanges at first. So your first step is to acquaint yourself with someone knowledgeable in exchanges in your area. I'd suggest a call to the local board of realtors, a look in a newspaper for a real estate exchange column, or just calling several brokers and asking them whom they would recommend you talk to. Since having the best representation won't cost you any more commission than the worst—and the worst can be more expensive in the long run—try to find the best in your area. I stress this last part because finding a great buy 1000 miles away won't do you a dime's worth of good.

Seven Keys to Presenting Any Offer

1. Work only from the "for sale" value the other party has given you. To ensure that you have not been given an inflated value for exchanges only, do not initiate any contact with an exchange offer. If you happen to see a property advertised in an exchange column in the newspaper or some other media, have someone else call (your wife or business associate will do) and ask if the property is "also for sale, and if so, how much."

2. Always assume the other party may ultimately accept an exchange. It will do you no good to presume the other party will turn down a valid proposal. It may become your obligation to prove that the exchange works for you both.

3. Keep the initial contact and presentation as simple, but complete as possible. Simply say, "I want to buy your property, Mr. Seller, and I'll give you five acres of pine woods and $10,000 as my deal. Let me show you a package I have that shows the five acres in detail together with comparable values of land in that area." Sounds much better this way and won't upset a never-before exchanger.

4. Always have a professionally compiled documentation for the property or items you are offering in the exchange. Have some backup package on what you are offering too. If you let your broker go off without a package, you will lose the edge.

5. Be persistent with your offers. Make them until you are blue in the face, but don't be too conciliatory too quickly. "Look, Mr. Seller, I'm very interested in your property and will keep coming back to you if I can think of something to make this deal work." No genuine seller will want to turn you down too flatly since you are demonstrating that you are a taker and you might come up with something. The seller that tells you (either directly to your face or through your broker) he is insulted by your offer should be reminded that: (a) You are attempting to demonstrate that you like their property enough to make an offer, and (b) If they want to be insulted they should consider all the people they know who have not even made them an offer. As I learned from a carpet merchant while I was working in Tangier, Morocco, "all deals have a beginning that must start with something in mutual. A prospective buyer of my carpets must first want to enter my establishment, then must do so, and must want to own one of my carpets. Now there are two things we have in mutual. He wants to own one of my carpets, and I also want him to own one of my carpets." No seller should be too quick to shut the door to any prospective "taker."

6. Be flexible when you negotiate. Exchanges are a new, wide-open game for many people. You might be turned on by an offer for an around-the-world cruise on the QM2 as part of a deal and who in the world would have thought of that? Options that are opening up to you will be exciting. Live with them for a while. The more you get the other party to invest time in what you are proposing the better your chances are that a deal will be made. There can be a limit to this, of course, as you do not want to spur on a horse that is already dead. There will be "waste your time"

people everywhere you go. When you are sure you have found one, move on.

7. Close doors very softly. It is all right to ease them closed: "I'll say no to this, as it doesn't solve my problem, but I do appreciate your interest and I hope we can work something out. Perhaps you will come up with something else that may be of interest."

THE BENEFITS OF THE 1031 EXCHANGE

The IRS Code 1031 says that if you make a like-for-like exchange, you don't have to pay the gains tax at the time of the exchange. This is true as long as you have done everything properly, have not received any boot, nor had net mortgage relief and have met all the rules and regulations that apply. Of these rules there are two that are most important. First of all each property in the exchange must be within the United States. This is a change to the old rules and may change again. But right now the United States only is the rule. The other critical element is that the exchange must be like for like.

Let me explain these different terms. Like-for-like in the bottom line simply means "investment for investment." You can't exchange part of your inventory as a builder for an investment or part of your parking lot for an investment, and have a 1031 exchange. Investment for investment is the major thing for you to remember. No matter what kind of real estate it is, if you owned what you gave up as an investment and are acquiring what you get as an investment, then it works as a 1031 exchange. Be careful with your documentation of any 1031 exchange transaction, because if you get audited by the IRS you will be asked to prove that what you gave up and what you received meet the "like-for-like" requirement.

"Gain" on property is the sum of everything you get in a sale (or exchange) less your adjusted cost, which is your basis. Your gain, or profit, is thus the price you get less the price you paid, after the net sales receipts have been adjusted for depreciation or improvements.

The basis is like book value. When you buy a property, it has a value. You can add to the value by building something on the property. You can take away from it by certain deductions, such as removing part of the improvements, or depreciating the assets over the years as allowed by the IRS.

Remember that depreciation is the technical deterioration or aging of an asset. The tax code allows annual depreciation for certain assets, when held for investment or used in a business. There are specific mathematical methods that can be used depending on the asset, and these methods are subject to rule changes. The final result of allowable depreciation is that it creates a "paper expense" for the taxpayer. This "paper expense" is not the actual expenditure of money, but the deterioration of money previously spent when the asset was purchased. This "paper expense" is allowed as a deduction from earned revenue to arrive at taxable revenue. When such allowable depreciation is taken the taxpayer does not pay tax, that year, on the amount of paper expense, and can, therefore, put that savings in his or her pocket. However as the value of the asset has been decreased, the basis of the property is decreased as well. Because gain in a sale is all that is above basis, the total accumulated depreciation gets added back into the gain.

Let's take a look at an exchange example using the IRC 1031 loophole. You purchase an apartment building for $500,000 cash with no debt. Of that amount there is $450,000 of building, furniture, and other equipment. Your gross income is $80,000 and you have operating expenses of $30,000. Your net operating income (NOI) is now $50,000 and this amount would also be your potential taxable income. If this income pushed you into a 35 percent tax bracket your tax on that portion of your gross income would be $17,500. You hold onto the property for five years and sell the property for $700,000 net of any cost of the sale. If you had taken no depreciation during that time (and you could have elected not to depreciate anything), your gain would be $200,000. However assume you took $20,000 of depreciation each year. Let's first look at what that did to your taxable revenue for each year in Table 32-3. Note that the current maximum tax for capital gains is 20 percent of the taxable gain. There are exemptions to the actual gain that may adjust downward the actual taxable gain. These exemptions apply to personal residences and not to investment property, which is the only kind of real estate investment that can use the IRC 1031 loophole. In any event, no capital gain tax can exceed your actual income tax rate. If, together with your gain, you are in an 8.5 percent tax bracket then that will be your capital gain rate. Most real estate gains, however, will throw the investor into a higher tax bracket, therefore I consider the minimum rate you will likely face will be the 20 percent gains rate.

As you can see from this example, depreciation has the beneficial effect of increasing the cash flow each year and returning a slightly higher grand total when all cash return has been added together. For many investors the spendable cash flow increase will be the most significant item to consider. As any debt cost must be met by the cash flow, the moment we add debt to the equation things begin to change dramatically. As I showed in the first chapter of this book, it will be debt, at fixed rates or at rates that are less than the appreciation of the property, that leverages your return.

T A B L E   32-3

	With Depreciation	Without Depreciation
Revenue before depreciation	$ 50,000	$ 50,000
Income tax on this at 35 percent	$ 17,500	
Net spendable after tax	$ 32,500	
Total spendable over 5 years	$162,500	
Depreciation taken for the year	$ 20,000	
Taxable income	$ 30,000	
Tax each year at 35 percent	$ 10,500	
Net spendable after tax	$ 40,500	
Total spendable over 5 years	$202,500	
Extra cash as a result of depreciation	$ 40,000	
BASIS CALCULATION		
Asset value	$500,000	$500,000
Annual depreciation taken	$ 20,000	0
Total depreciation over 5 years	$100,000	0
New basis	$400,000	$500,000
SALE CALCULATION		

	Sale with Depreciation	Sale without Depreciation
Net sale price	$700,000	$700,000
Less basis	$400,000	$500,000
Taxable gain	$300,000	$200,000
Tax rate on gain	× 20 percent	× 20 percent
Tax due	$ 60,000	$ 40,000
Sale net proceeds	$640,000	$660,000
Total spendable	$202,500	$162,500
Grand Total	$842,000	$822,000

How Exchanges Benefit the Transaction

In the above sale (with depreciation), there would be a $60,000 tax due. That would mean that the investor would have only $640,000 to reinvest if the property were owned free and clear. If there had been a first mortgage on the property of $340,000 still owed at the time of the sale, the actual cash to reinvest would be $300,000. If we could do away with that

$60,000 tax the investor would have $360,000 to reinvest. This is a 20 percent increase of investment potential. Had the first mortgage been $400,000 outstanding at the time of the sale, the after-tax funds to reinvest would be $700,000 less $400,000, less 60,000 or a total of $240,000. By eliminating the tax here the reinvestment potential has increased by 25 percent.

In an age when banks are paying less than 3 percent interest on deposits, these kinds of yield return increases are worth your effort.

What Role Does "Boot" Play?

"Boot" is the part of the exchange that will be taxable even in the best set-up 1031 exchange. Boot is anything other than real estate. If you get $10,000 cash, it is boot. If you get a gold watch, it is boot. A car, boat, airplane, diamond ring, all are boot and are taxable. You can qualify for a 1031 with receipt of boot, but you will still be taxed on the boot portion.

Watch Out for Net Mortgage Relief

Net mortgage relief is something else to look for. When you exchange one property for another and they are both free and clear of any mortgages throughout the exchange, there is no mortgage relief in that there are no mortgages given up. However when you deal with properties encumbered with mortgages, you need to look for the situation referred to as "net mortgage relief."

Assume you have a property worth $100,000 and you owe $55,000 against it. If you exchange for a property worth $45,000, making an even swap, your equity for theirs, you will be relieved of $55,000 of mortgage obligation. You now own a $45,000 property without mortgages. You have had an exchange without any boot, but you have a recognized gain of $55,000 (the amount of the mortgage). You will have a taxable exchange if the mortgage relief is greater than your realized gain by the amount of the mortgage relief. If there is any gain at all and you have net mortgage relief, you will have some tax in this exchange.

The reason for this should be simple to understand. Assume for a moment that today you own the same $100,000 property and it is free and clear. You go down to the local savings and loan and borrow $55,000 in cash, which you put into your pocket tax-free. A day later you make the exchange shown above, getting a free-and-clear $45,000 property. As you now have net mortgage relief, you may have a tax because you have already received the $55,000 cash without paying any tax on that revenue.

Calculating the Taxable Gain in Exchanges

I will borrow from my book *Real Estate Finance and Investment Manual.* In its chapter on how to use exchanges in financing real estate, there is a table showing the tax calculations of the following exchanges shown in Table 32-4.

Smyth and Greenbalm are our two owners. Smyth owns 100 acres of land. Its value is $200,000. He owns this land free and clear of any mortgages and his basis is the $100,000 he paid for the property. The other $100,000 in value is appreciation over 12 years of ownership. Greenbalm owns a 15-unit apartment house. Its value is also $200,000, and it, too, is free and clear. Greenbalm's basis is $140,000 (he paid $180,000 but has taken $40,000 in depreciation). Smyth and Greenbalm make a trade with no cash paid between them and no mortgages swapped or assumed. It is an even exchange.

In the second exchange, the two parties are Jones and Blackburn. Jones owns 100 acres of land valued at $200,000 with a first mortgage of $50,000. Jones's basis is $100,000. Blackburn owns a 15-unit apartment house valued at $300,000. His basis in the apartment house is $125,000 and he owes $200,000. Jones has equity of $150,000, while Blackburn has a $100,000 equity. In order to make the exchange, Blackburn must balance his equity with Jones's. He will do so with a $50,000 cash payment to Jones.

Table 32-4 shows the tax calculations in these two exchanges. In examining this table, you will notice that in the Smyth-Greenbalm exchange there will be no resulting tax, as the recognized gain for both Smyth and Greenbalm was zero. But look what happened to Jones and Blackburn.

You can use the numbers of your own exchange in place of those shown in Table 32-4 to see just where you will stand in the case of a potential tax. The tax, of course, will be calculated on the taxable-gain portion by using the current capital gains calculations. As these are apt to change from year to year, consult your tax accountant for the current method. In this example I am using a capital gains tax rate of 20 percent. As laws change, so might this rate as it would apply to you, so be sure to check the current rates.

T A B L E 32-4

Calculations of Taxable Gain in Exchanges

	Jones	Blackburn	Smyth	Greenbalm
Value of Property Received	$300,000	$200,000	$200,000	$200,000
ADD THE FOLLOWING:				
Cash Received .	$ 50,000	0	0	0
Other Boot Received	0	0	0	0
Mortgage Relief	$ 50,000	$200,000	0	0
SUBTOTAL	$400,000	$400,000	$200,000	$200,000
SUBTRACT FROM SUBTOTAL:	$100,000	$125,000	$100,000	$140,000
Basis at Time of Exchange	$200,000	$ 50,000	0	0
Amount of Mortgage				
Assumed	0	$ 50,000	0	0
Amount of Cash Paid	0	0	0	0
Amount of Other Boot Given				
GAIN REALIZED	$100,000	$175,000	$100,000	$ 60,000
TO COMPUTE AT THE TAXABLE GAIN:				
(1) Total Mortgages Relieved	$ 50,000	$200,000	0	0
(2) Less Total Mortgages				
Assumed	$200,000	$ 50,000	0	0
(If [2] is greater than [1] put 0				
Amount)	0	$150,000	0	0
Less Cash Paid	0	$ 50,000	0	0
Subtotal	0	$100,000	0	0
Plus Other Noncash Boot				
Received	0	0	0	0
Plus Cash Received	$ 50,000	0	0	0
RECOGNIZED GAIN	$ 50,000	$100,000	0	0

Taxable gain is the lower of gain realized or recognized gain. Note below calculation shows the gain that is not taxed by virtue of the exchange.

	Jones	Blackburn	Smyth	Greenbalm
GAIN REALIZED	$100,000	$175,000	$100,000	$ 60,000
Less Taxable Gain				
(Recognized)	$ 50,000	$100,000	0	0
GAIN SAVED:	$50,000	$75,000	$100,000	$60,000

GETTING INTO EXCHANGES

The only way to get into exchanges is to make exchange offers. You don't make exchanges by waiting for someone to come around and ask you if you want to exchange. The best way, I believe, is to find an exchange-minded salesman and then go through a learning process with him or her. All investors who expect to make profits over a long haul, and to reduce or eliminate as much risk as possible, will be continually learning. I know that I feel slighted if I don't learn something every week I am in business. Fortunately I never feel slighted. I usually learn something every day. All that learning doesn't always keep me out of trouble, but it sure keeps me from being bored.

THE PITFALLS OF EXCHANGES

Frustration is the enemy of the exchanger. There is a lot you can get frustrated about when it comes to exchanges. You will be dealing with people who think you are out to take them—or, at best, will pretend they don't understand anything. You will have to deal with double-pricing situations, with hotshot salesmen who will tell you that a five-story building is a seven-story high-rise. You will get turned on only to find that what was described as a beautiful home by the sea just washed out at high tide.

But, as Elbert Hubbard once said, "There is no failure except in no longer trying." When it comes to exchanges, you have to keep trying. Your day and the right deal will come along.

From an economic point of view, you need to watch your tax laws and your own tax situation when it comes to the exchange at hand. It is possible that you will be better off making a sale and then purchasing, accepting the tax liability in that year, rather than allowing your old basis to carry over to the new property. You see, if your old basis in that $200,000 property is only $25,000 you would have a $175,000 gain in that year. Even with a 20 percent maximum tax on capital gains, you would have a $35,000 tax to pay. However if you also had a major loss in the same year, say $175,000 worth, you might prefer a sale in which your losses would offset the gain. You could then step up your basis in a new property, beginning fresh rather than passing along a $200,000 value with only $25,000 of basis.

My suggestion is that you don't try to be an expert on tax ramifications (unless that is your business of course) and that you hire the services of a professional in tax law and taxes.

33
CHAPTER

The It's-Not-Mine-Will-You-Take-It? Exchange

This technique is useful when you don't have what the seller is willing to exchange for. What you do is find out what the seller wants or will take and then locate something similar to what the seller will agree to take in the exchange.

THE SOFT PAPER DEAL

Let's say you are interested in buying a small office building you have located in your town. The property is offered at $300,000 and has an existing first mortgage of $110,000 and second mortgage of $55,000. You know you can refinance the building, generating around $210,000 net after mortgage costs. The seller started the negotiations saying he wanted all cash to the existing financing, but in the endgame agreed to take a minimum of $100,000 cash and hold some paper. The seller confided to you (or your agent) that he needed the cash because he wants to buy some vacant land on which to build a rental apartment building.

Armed with this knowledge, you search around for a few days and find a tract of land that is zoned for business and commercial use, but you know the zoning will allow the development of apartments. The property has not sold as a business site because it is a poor site for that kind of use, but it's an ideal location for a rental apartment building. The owner will sell the land for $75,000 on easy terms.

The fact that the land is not labeled apartment property causes many investors to forget that labels in real estate mean very little. It is what you can do with the land that is important, not the specific category of the zoning. Most zoning comes in categories such as business, industrial, commercial, residential, and multifamily, in varying orders of density and intensity. For example multifamily might be subclassified as a duplex (2 units), up to 5 units, up to 15 units per acre, 25 units per acre, and so on. Each step in the zoning classification that allows a greater use of the property tends to increase the value of the property. In multifamily zoning an increase from 10 units to the acre to 20 units to the acre will usually increase the value substantially. Note that I say, "will usually increase the value." While this is true, you need to examine the area around that zoning. If the area is principally high-end single-family homes with a mix of luxury low-rise apartments, then an increase to a very high density multifamily use may not fit with the community and can end up lowering the values of the neighboring properties, and not necessarily increase the value of the property in question. But keep in mind that building codes usually allow a developer to downplay the zoning, and just because the zoning allows 60 units or more per acre does not mean that is a minimum density.

Let's say you have found an owner of some vacant business land who has been unsuccessful in selling it. You then offer him a soft deal that ties up the land so you can make your exchange on the small office building you want. Note that it is critical for you to tie up the land first. By that I mean put it under a binding contract. You must do this before mentioning the land to the owner of the office building. If you don't you run the risk of the office-building owner buying the land directly from its present owner.

You set this up by telling the land owner you will buy the land giving him $5000 down and a $70,000 second mortgage on the office building across town. (That's right, the very office building you are soon to buy.) You tell the owner you are about to refinance the office building and it will have a new first mortgage of $215,000. You set the interest on the second mortgage lower than the market rate because the seller of the vacant land would rather have some cash coming in than keep the cash-eating land. Just as you need not tell the office-building owner about your deal with the landowner, you do not tell the landowner you have not yet purchased the office building. You now go back to the seller of the small office building and tell him that you will do the following:

- Give him $25,000 cash.
- Take over his existing financing—subject to your obtaining the new financing mentioned.
- Give him the apartment land (which can also be used for commercial and business use as a bonus), which you value at $100,000.
- Give him a personal note signed by you in the amount of $10,000.

If he accepts this, you will then apply for the loan you want of $215,000, which, less $5000 in loan costs, will net you $210,000. You will use this to pay off the existing mortgages on the small office building, a total of $165,000 (a first of $110,000 and a second of $55,000). This will leave you with $45,000.

But wait, you have to pay the seller of the land $5000, so that also comes out of the $45,000, leaving you with $40,000. You then take another $25,000 from that and give it to the seller of the office building. You end up owning the small office building and have $15,000 left over for fix-up, or for further negotiations if this deal didn't fly on the above described offer. In short you have another $15,000 to play with to make your OPM deal work.

Even if you had not been able to increase the value of the vacant land, you were putting yourself in a far better economic position than by trying to buy the office building with the usual financing. The landowner, after all, was willing to take soft paper, which enabled you to maximize your leverage of the office building with some mortgage at below-market value.

THE FINE POINTS OF THE DEAL

Every time you buy real estate, there are four things you should do to ascertain whether the seller could be enticed into this kind of transaction.

1. Get to know the goals of the seller. In the previous example, knowing that the seller wanted to build apartments was what started you off on this tangent.
2. Take a quick look around the marketplace to see if you can help the seller meet the desired goal. Sometimes the seller has picked out exactly what he wants to buy. If you can find out what it is and then talk to the owner of that property, you might find you

can still do the soft paper deal shown in the previous example. You do not want to be hunting for pie in the sky however. Some sellers set unrealistic goals, and since even they won't find them, why should I spend my time looking for them?

3. Tie up the borrowed property before making the offer to the seller of what you want. You must have control of a property before offering it in an exchange. If you have only a loose deal based on a handshake, it may not survive to the closing. Remember many things offset good intentions, and greed is the number one cause of death of real estate deals.

4. Understand that the ideal doesn't exist, so don't overlook other alternatives. Perhaps the seller would build office buildings instead of apartments. If there aren't any apartment sites you can tie up to use in an exchange, try something else. Most property owners will take something in exchange. As long as you can buy a property on soft paper and move that paper onto the property you are going to buy or another property you own, you can have something to exchange. In this way you can generate a "cash" equivalent of property equity. You might tie up a North Carolina lot by agreeing to give the owner $20,000 (full price) in a soft mortgage on the $75,000 duplex you are buying. If you can give the seller of the office building the $20,000 lot as your total down payment, then you've just made another OPM deal.

PITFALLS OF THE DEAL

The most critical pitfall occurs when you do not first lock up the other property needed for the exchange. This happens in many transactions where the parties assume they are the only game in town. Never make the mistake of believing that no one else has thought of this kind of strategy or that property.

Another pitfall is that the opportunity to make this OPM transaction can move you into heavier debt than the property will support, but this is less of a danger here than in some of the other techniques we've examined. Using a soft mortgage may actually reduce the debt load and improve the economics of the transaction.

34
CHAPTER

Promise the Moon

I doubt many sellers ever thought of taking a future event as a down payment. But this technique might be just the thing to make your OPM investment work. This technique can be used when a buyer plans to have something in the future that can be offered to a seller now.

Suppose a developer is getting ready to build a condominium. He knows he is going to sell out quickly and will soon need another site on which to build another condominium. He can easily offer the owner of such a site a unit in the future building as a part of the down payment on that property. A homebuilder can do the same, giving the seller an opportunity to own a home in a project to be built. In a recent transaction I brokered there were two sellers. One owned the land under a hotel on the beach in Fort Lauderdale, and the other owned the 68-year leasehold. (A leasehold is the term for the rights of any tenant.)

In the case of a long-term lease most lenders and taxing authorities will take the position that a long-term lease is the same or nearly the same as a fee simple (outright ownership) interest. A lender may actually loan on a leasehold interest as long as the lease is for a greater duration than the loan (often 20 years longer than the loan term) and that the lease has no onerous terms and will allow unsubordinated debt on the property. (Subordination is a finance term that relates to a lender or lessor allowing the property that is security to their loan [or lease] to be pledged as security to a loan that is ahead of their lien rights.) In effect, if you enter into a long-term lease with a tenant and you subordinate your interest so that the tenant can pledge the property as security for a loan, then your rights will be subordinate to that of the lender. If you sell a property and take back a purchase money mortgage (first, second, or whatever the position) and have subordinated the mortgage you are holding to a new loan, your rights will be behind that new mortgage. This is a very common situation but does contain risk. If you are in a subordinated position and the borrower defaults on the loan payments then your rights have been compromised. Whenever the term "subordination" is used, or the contents of a document indicate the act of subordination even though the word is not used, be sure that your lawyer has discussed the situation with you in great detail.

The owner of the leasehold interest (the tenant), in this example, was operating the hotel, which needed a lot of work to be done to make it profitable. The landowner was collecting an annual rent of around $30,000 that had never changed from the start of the lease 31 years earlier. He chose to take several apartments in the new building. The deal was made three years ago, and only now are people moving into the just completed building.

As happens with many of the other techniques, the ability to move some of the purchase price (seller's equity, really) to another property enables the investor to get maximum use of cash generated in financing. Sometimes moving all or a portion of the seller's equity to this future event enables you to give him cash in addition to that future event.

THE FUTURE PRODUCT DEAL

Simone is a top builder in South Florida. She and her husband used to build high-rise condos; now, after her husband's death, she concentrates on low-rise, garden-type condominium apartments. Usually she has several projects going at the same time, and she has become successful offering owners of sites she likes future units in her developments as a part of the deal. Sometimes the future unit is in another project that is already completed and not 100 percent sold out; other times she lets the owner have first choice in a new project not even started yet. She and other developers who use this technique have long since recognized that sellers will frequently take a future unit on the site they are selling rather than an instant unit across town. They do so out of sentiment for the site they once owned.

One such deal looked like this: Morris needed a site for around 100 townhouse units. His broker located a nice site in the Tampa area at a price of $3,500,000. As this was only $35,000 per-unit land cost and the units were going to sell for an average of $450,000, the ratio of land price to selling price was well in the profit range for Morris' development. In fact for good locations like this, he has been known to pay as high as $50,000 per unit for his sites. Like most builders, however, Morris doesn't like to tie up cash in the land. The deal he would work out with the seller, then, would have to be as highly leveraged as possible.

The broker, knowing how Morris operated, structured the deal with a local lender to finance half of the acquisition price and all of the construction and development cost. That left Morris $1,750,000 short at the hardest time of the project, in the very beginning. However, since Morris had a respectable background and reputation, he was able to convince the seller to take $1,750,000 worth of units at a discount of 15 percent from the market price. The seller could choose the units right away based on the published prices or wait until units were selling. If the seller waited, he would have the advantage of knowing what the real market price was. But then, historically, developers would continue to increase the prices as development progressed. This seller placed his order immediately.

This kind of deal can work out nicely for both parties. The builder does not have to come up with the necessary cash, and the seller stands a good chance of obtaining a good profit in the new units. Giving a future product, then, is an ideal way to start out your negotiations if you are a builder or developer. Land developers turning farmland into residential subdivisions can frequently make the same kind of deal. Their future vacant residential lots, if tied up early enough by the tract seller, can prove to be excellent investments.

THE FINE POINTS OF THE DEAL

Nothing is better than resting on your laurels when it comes to making future deals work for you. The success of your past performance will give a seller some idea of what can be expected in the future. If you are just starting out, you can overcome the seller's objections by using the blanket mortgage approach to secure the seller's 100 percent mortgage. In this way you give a future benefit but secure the balance of the deal with a blanket mortgage. If you screw up and blow the future event, at least the seller has some other property to look to as security on what you owe him.

The presentation of this kind of deal is very important, so you must spend a lot of time in its preparation. If you are using a broker, you will be ahead of the game as the broker can tout your past performances, whereas, if you did so, you would sound like a braggart. Modesty is important for you to practice, because one thing that turns off a seller quicker than anything are people who tell everyone how important they are. So be careful how you sound.

If you have a good record of past performances, let your broker document them. Put together an information package that shows off your recent accomplishments. Include in that package some of your sales brochures, recent photographs of the properties you have developed, and a history of how you got into this business. Most importantly show the list prices of all the units on opening day and what those same units are selling for now, years, or months later. If you have made future deals before, it might be interesting to show how the sellers in those other transactions profited, assuming they came out on top of the game.

If you have to fall back on a blanket mortgage to cover a lack of past performance, then make sure you have well documented the property the seller is going to get as additional security. If as a developer you are in need of some land released from any mortgages to begin development, make sure you cover any needed releases of security from the mortgage documents. You are making an OPM transaction and need to cover all your bases.

THE SIX KEYS TO MAKING FUTURE DEALS WORK

1. Never offer the future deal until you have tested the seller's motivation. This means putting your toe into the water to see how cold it is and whether you really want to swim after all. When it comes to negotiating your deals, you must invest some time and entice the seller to invest some of his time as well or you will find the "no" given far too easily. It is possible that there are other forms of buying that will be better for you than this technique. If you want the property, you want to buy it at the best terms for you but the seller will never say yes until he is motivated to do so.

2. Get some press coverage on your past abilities. I don't mean you have to have actual media coverage, but if you have some past clippings from the newspaper, use them as part of the package your broker gives to the seller. Remember, never talk about

yourself—let others talk about you. Place an ad if you have to, however, to get into the paper.

3. Give yourself ample negotiating room in the future offering. You don't want to promise something in two years that you won't be able to deliver for five years. It's always possible to get caught in some delay so be sure you have covered yourself at the outset by having a buyout provision where you can substitute cash for the future event. It is a toss-up as to whether you should make that a unilateral event with the option going to either you or the seller.

4. Make sure your price or discount for the future event is fair to you and the seller. At this stage you aren't worrying about the seller; if you have a buyout provision and the seller wants to take cash, you can be trapped into losing on something you had planned on making a profit on. On the other hand if you are offering a future unit and set a price now for that unit and have delays in building, you might find the unit costs twice as much to build as you pre-sold it for. It's best to give a discount on the average of the first few sales to the public as a tie to actual market value at the time you actually start selling. The seller taking the future will, of course, want to have a fixed price set now.

5. Use the blanket mortgage technique to lock up wishy-washy sellers. Review Chapter 30 on blanket techniques to refresh your memory of how they are used. There are many other ways to bring the seller in line with your future deal by connecting the future to some other event such as an exchange or a pyramid of another mortgage.

6. Think options and alternatives. This is a must with every kind of technique you will work with. Your final deal and the technique you use may not resemble any of the examples I've shown in this book. Your own unique situation will require you to adapt the technique or techniques to fit the mood and motivations of the seller with your needs and abilities. Almost all the techniques in this book can be used in conjunction with each other.

PITFALLS OF THE DEAL

From the investor's point of view, there are only two real pitfalls to watch out for. The first is pre-fixing the value of the "future," and the second is giving too much of a blanket.

The first is simple. I've already discussed the importance of making sure you don't get caught giving the seller a future that ends up costing you far more than you anticipated. Keep in mind that some futures can come from other properties and not the one you are buying. If you are building across town, you can offer a unit there, or perhaps it isn't a unit at all but a percent of the profit when you sell something. Futures are anything that hasn't happened yet. Just be darned sure you don't have to reach into your savings later to cover something you didn't count on.

The second is a real danger if things go wrong. The blanket mortgage you may have to give the seller to entice him into the future deal will tie up some other property you own. In this way the seller is covered and if there never is a future (because he has foreclosed on your project and you, too), he will not be left holding the bag. You don't want to tie up a million-dollar property just to blanket a $500,000 property. Try to match the security requirement to the needs of the seller. If you feel you can make the deal fly with only a $100,000 additional security, then put one-tenth of the million-dollar property up as security. Always keep the release provision in tip-top shape in making your blanket mortgage. This provision enables you to release the extra security from the blanket when you do something spelled out in the mortgage. That something might be a payment of part of the money owed, or simply completion and delivery of the future event as promised. These release provisions are essential to you in working a wrap, so don't overlook them.

35

The Green
Thumb Transaction

"FOR SALE: Two oak trees, five elm trees, and 100 assorted bushes and shrubs. U'dig'em." The first time I heard of this technique I was in Jacksonville, Florida, giving a seminar on creative real estate investing. The investor who told me about this technique had apparently used it successfully half a dozen times.

"It's quite simple," he said. "I look around for properties in the older parts of town. You know, where the landscaping has matured and what trees that are there are full grown and valuable. I make sure the property is sound in value and that I can do something with the buildings on the site. I make as good a deal as I can, trying to keep the cash down as low as possible or the cash I need to close at a minimum. I then sell the landscaping for the cash I need, closing on the real estate at the same time."

His explanation of this technique was so simple and clear, I could think of no way better to give it to you. In the examination of the technique, however, there are many elements that need greater study, as this opportunity often slips by many investors. I've seen smart buyers who knew nothing about the value of plants end up having unwanted or unneeded trees removed at great cost when those same plants could have brought a profit.

Let's take a look at two examples of this technique, where each investor will use the plant sale for a different result.

THE LANDSCAPE DEAL

Harper was a house buyer who fixed houses up and then sold them. His whole philosophy was to find property that was run down but in a good part of town. He knew that most buyers associated small, young trees and shrubs with newness. He also knew that many properties in the older parts of town were so overgrown with older trees and shrubs that he would have to cut out a lot of them just to paint and fix up his newly purchased houses.

Knowing all of this, Harper gave high points to properties with landscaping that was removable and salable. Harper knew that at worst he might get a trade-off at the local plant nursery when it came time to re-landscape the refurbished property.

To make sure he didn't overlook any prime opportunities, Harper visited several leading landscapers in town. He selected them after phone conversations with about two dozen listed in the Yellow Pages. He wanted to be sure he was dealing with large-scale landscapers for major developers, hotels, hospitals, and airports—clients who wanted the finished job to look finished, not like something that would have to grow for 10 years to look good. Such landscapers would need larger, mature plants, not the potted houseplant variety.

In visiting these landscapers he found out what kind of plants they could use, making a list of them as well as taking a photo of the plant itself. He also got an idea of what the landscaper would pay for a matured plant. He was then ready to start looking for a property. Of course plants weren't the primary criterion for his real estate transactions: If he couldn't fix up a property and make a profit, he didn't buy it, plants or no plants. But the sale of the plants helped Harper make greater profits and that he liked.

Harper was able, on some occasions, to make OPM transactions because he recognized the value of the plants. He knew whom to call when he saw a tree that would look fantastic in the lobby of a hotel under construction across town.

Evan, on the other hand, was using every dime he had or earned to make ends meet. He was plowing rents from the homes and apartment buildings he was buying back into the fix-up of these properties, not with the idea of selling them but with the idea of increasing the rents on the properties. This was great, but it kept Evan property-poor and constantly out of cash.

His need, then, was to buy without cash, so OPM methods of investing were the most important part of his program. He wasn't interested in the fast turnover that Harper looked for, so Evan could take properties in less-than-prime areas and look for a longer-haul picture. If he could rent a property for enough to cover the mortgage, pay the expenses, and put a few dollars aside for the property's improvement, Evan would, more than likely, buy the property. The idea of getting some instant cash out of a property appealed to Evan. Any sudden income could be put to good use in upgrading the apartments he was purchasing.

He took a night course in landscaping at the local public high school and even took out a city occupational license as a landscape designer. This cost him about $100 a year, but it allowed him to buy supplies and plants to fix up his buildings at builders' and landscapers' wholesale prices, which were often well below the price the public would pay.

In going through this course, and in later dealings with the landscapers in town, he learned what plants the landscapers would pay premiums for and how to go about selling them. Now Evan was smarter about the value of landscaping. When he looks at property, the condition and make-up of the landscaping around prospective properties is one of his important criteria. He still is primarily concerned with the area and surrounding neighborhoods. His primary concern is the demographics of the immediate subdivision and the status of the rental market: If there were a lot of vacancies in the area at what he felt was market or below-market rent, then he didn't want to touch the area unless the price and terms of the property would allow him to grossly undercut the vacant rental offerings.

The next thing he looked for was plants. When Evan saw a property whose front and side yards were filled with salable plants, he knew he had a gold mine. He would use the promised cash from the landscaper as part of the down payment even if he had to split-fund the deal with some of his own cash upfront. Then he would repay himself when the plants had been sold.

THE FINE POINTS OF THE PLANT SALE

There are five key elements in this technique that you need to keep in mind.

1. **Know your plants.** When you start out in this technique, you will not be as familiar with the plant market as you will be later on. It will help if you cultivate (excuse the pun) the friendship of a landscaper and have him take a look at an intended purchase you think is full of valuable plants. Look also for local courses in horticulture and landscaping as additional ways to add to your knowledge of plants and the marketing of them.

2. **Learn what plants you can do without on the site.**
Unknowingly selling off valuable plants can cause your newly purchased property to go down in value, and that's cutting off your nose to spite your green thumb. In this age of high electric bills that well-placed shade tree might mean far more to the building you are buying than the cash you will get in selling it. However, thick trees blocking the cool summer breeze will have to go, and why not at a profit?

3. **Learn which landscapers you can trust.** This is sort of like finding out which heart specialist will have the highest success in your own open-heart operation in advance of the operation, but it can be done if you simply ask around. Make sure you are dealing with the guy who does a lot of expensive work, because he can afford the expensive plants.

4. **Don't overlook the grass.** Sod is expensive, and sod growers have machines that will pick up a whole yard in a few hours. If you are putting in wood decks and stonework and that sort of thing or if you anticipate that workmen going around the property for a few weeks while you fix it up will kill the grass, then sell the grass first. Granted this is sometimes more difficult than selling the plants, but it might mean another couple of thousand dollars and that might put you into the profit range earlier.

5. **Don't try to move plants yourself.** If you don't have the right tools and don't know what you are doing, you can easily kill a plant—dead plants don't bring in any cash.

The real finesse is in tying up the property so that you can get a price on the plants. You don't ever want to spend much time fooling around with any property you can't tie up first. Once you have made the seller an offer that both he and you can live with, you can move ahead. Your offer should have some provision permitting you to inspect the grounds to ascertain what plants must be moved to accomplish the needed repairs, remodeling, and improvements. It will take you about a week to ascertain the potential profit, if any, from the plants—or at least what a landscaper will do for you in exchange for the trees and plants you want to get rid of. Do not tell the seller that you need a week to find out how much you can get for the plants. The seller may have a sentimental attachment to the apple tree in the front yard (just where you want to put a new driveway) and if he thought you were going to sell it or cut it down, he might find some reason to object to a term or condition of the agreement. Remember, George Washington may have sold the cherry tree he cut down for the dollar he used to throw across the Potomac.

Step one is to tie up the property. Step two is to get a quote from two or more landscapers on buying the plants you want to sell. Step three is to tie the closings of both sales together so you can get the cash you need out of one for the other. If you don't need the cash to close then you can wait until after you own the property to deal with the sale of the plants.

Step three is often the most difficult part of this transaction. The seller doesn't want to give you the property until he has gotten his cash, and the landscaper doesn't want to give you cash until he gets the plants. If you can do what Evan does and simply not pay someone else that week to get the cash for the other, then that's okay—if you don't get caught on the short end of the stick. The best way, of course, is to tell the seller that you would like to start with the landscape work before closing. Naturally you will assure the seller that you will pay for the work done (that needs to be paid for). If the seller balks at this, then try to get the landscaper to put some cash up front. Once you have a working relationship with the landscapers, they will be more inclined to do this. The first deal is always the hardest. You might try a short-term loan to tide you over from the closing on the property to the closing on the plants.

THE PITFALLS OF THE PLANT SALE

There are only three pitfalls to watch out for, but they can hurt you if you're not careful.

1. **The mortgage that covers the plants.** Most mortgages do not cover landscaping, but as the plant sale technique gets around, you might find lenders getting smarter. Read the mortgage documents carefully to be sure they do not encumber all improvements to the buildings and land. If they do, you will have to get approval from the mortgagee to relandscape the property. Make a sketch showing what you are going to do to the site. As you will be planting new (but much smaller and cheaper) plants in the right kinds of locations, you don't have to worry about the sketch looking barren. The person who reviews the sketch and gives the final approval probably won't even look at

the property. A few photos showing how cluttered the existing landscaping looks won't hurt, though, just to make sure the guy doesn't drive by and fall in love with the live oak you are going to sell for $1500.

2. **The landscaper who digs a hole you fall into.** "I know I said I would give you $15,000 for all those trees and that yard of grass, but that was last week. Now I'm just not sure I can afford more than $3000. Take it or leave it." This kind of conversation can make your stomach turn over, and unfortunately it can happen. The bigger the landscaper, the better your chance of making a sale, but anyone can run into a tight situation and fail to live up to an agreement. A deposit from the landscaper at the time you agree to sell the plants to him might help, but you need some insurance. Your insurance is a quick closing and an out if something goes wrong. Since time works against you in these deals (the landscaper no longer needs the plants), you should be ready to move fast. There is no room for hesitation in this kind of deal, and if you are the softhearted kind, then it's best to move on to another technique.

3. **You have a black thumb and no plant smarts.** In selling anything of potential value, it is essential that you have some idea of that value. I went to a football game at the Orange Bowl in Miami. I went with a friend who had a ticket, and I was sure I could buy one at the stadium from a fan who had an extra one. Instead I found tickets being scalped for $175 and up, which were two and three times the stated price on the ticket. I decided to wait until the kickoff and positioned myself out in the VIP parking lot, away from the crowds. As people ran past, I asked, running alongside, if they had any extra tickets, holding the exact price in my hand ($56.00). One seller, anxious to get into the stadium and not miss the kickoff, was willing to take only half the price of the ticket (I gave him the full price as I knew I would be sitting next to him). The ticket was on the 50-yard line.

This is an example of knowing what was going on. I knew the market. They didn't. I was willing to wait until the last minute before the kickoff, at which point sellers were anxious to get into the game and didn't want to haggle.

You should not try to play the landscaping game until you invest some time in learning about plants—what they are good for, which are valuable, and which aren't. You don't want to be caught with extra tickets (plants) and the game (real estate closing) about to start and not have any room to negotiate. When you acquire some expertise, you can turn that black thumb green.

36

CHAPTER

The Home Loan Caper

When investing in real estate, you will find that the easiest mortgage to obtain is the home loan. This goes for new first mortgages as well as second mortgages. Because of this many investors find that when they need to generate cash to make a worthwhile investment, this cash can often be obtained through the financing, or refinancing, of their own homes. This is important, of course, if you have a home that you can refinance. But even if you don't, it is possible to include a home in your investment portfolio for this very purpose.

Therefore, I will approach this technique from the standpoint of both the investor who has a home to use and the investor who does not presently have a home to show how the technique can benefit both.

THE INVESTOR WITH A HOME

Ginger is a flight attendant for one of the international airlines. She loves her work and has enough seniority to pick and choose the flights she wants so that she can have sufficient time to work at fixing up her real estate purchases. She has a live-wire salesperson working on her behalf, scouting out properties for her to buy, and she is constantly making offers. Most of the time Ginger is able to make OPM transactions by using pyramiding and refinancing of the properties she buys. But sometimes she finds something that she wants to have and a seller who won't respond to her usual techniques.

One such example was an industrial complex that backed up to one of the local private airports. She realized it would be an ideal place for the many airline pilots she knew to store their small weekend aircraft. The seller, however, wouldn't take a pyramid, and the existing mortgages on the industrial building were at such low interest that it would not benefit Ginger to refinance them. So she looked over her portfolio to see if there were any other properties she could refinance. She found that the only property she owned that didn't already have a maximum loan-to-value ratio was her own home. She had never wanted to refinance her home because she had worked hard to pay off the mortgage on that property and had sworn to herself she would never have a mortgage on her own home. Many investors feel this way, and, for some, it is a sound strategy. But Ginger had a better use for the capital she had tied up in her home, and when she tried other ways to get the industrial building, she soon realized the only way to get the needed cash was to put the mortgage on the home.

She didn't need as much cash as she could generate from a new mortgage, so the loan-to-value ratio was going to be less than 60/40. This meant she would have some bargaining power with the lender to cut the right kind of mortgage. In essence she was able to make a better deal than she had anticipated at an interest rate several percentage points below any possible commercial loan.

The story, of course, has a happy ending. Once she owned the industrial building, paying the seller cash to the mortgage on that property, she was able to rent the building out to the airline pilots after she formed an aviation club especially for them. As the rent on the building was far more than the old tenant had paid, the value of the new property went up quite fast. The best part of the story is that Ginger was able to pay off the mortgage on her house in short order (in the loan negotiations, she had insisted on a clause permitting early payoff without penalty).

When you finance your home or obtain a new mortgage on the property, you want to gain as much leverage on the terms of the mortgage as possible. Savings and loan associations are, of course, your primary source of funds for this kind of loan. Your local savings and loan is a business much like any other except they have a lot of rules and regulations governing the way they act and controlling much of what they do. But one thing many investors overlook is the fact that these institutions are in a very competitive business and will thus make concessions and offer deals that the competition may not. Because of this it is essential that you shop your loans, going to at least three loan institutions in the attempt to get the best deal.

You should approach a savings and loan association with a clear understanding of what you want in the way of loan amount (net to you after loan costs), interest on the loan, and term of years. Your desire for prepayment rights without penalty must also be clearly stated in your loan request. This loan request should be presented to the loan officer of the savings and loan association. It should follow the outline provided for you in this chapter and must be brief and concise. The association will have its own loan-application forms and financial statements, which you must also have filled out and attached to the loan request.

THE INVESTOR WITHOUT A HOME

This gets a little more tricky, as you might imagine. First of all, if you are trying to buy a property such as a vacant lot or a vacant industrial building or some other difficult-to-finance property, you might want to tie that purchase to the purchase of a single-family home at the same time. This is one of those situations where it is sometimes easier to buy two properties at the same time than one.

Assume you want to buy a nice vacant lot as an investment. You know that, due to its commercial use and prime location in the path of growth, you will see a great rise in value over the next few years. The owner of the lot says he will take the price you have negotiated him down to, which is $50,000. However he will take this price only if he gets $25,000 cash and can hold the balance in a purchase-money mortgage on the lot. This is great, except you don't have the $25,000 cash.

So you look for a free-and-clear house that will fit into your investment portfolio. You find one and, after some preliminary negotiations, learn that the seller of the home will take $75,000 for the property and will hold some paper, but he must get at least $25,000 in cash. Of course, you don't have the $25,000 in cash, either, so do you give up? No. In fact, you've just made the deal go together, because:

- You know you can finance the house for an easy $60,000 through any of several savings and loan associations. You know this not because you are clairvoyant but because you have called some of your loan officer buddies and have picked their brains and have the up-to-date scoop on what their associations will do on this property.

- You have tied up the two properties with subject-to-financing agreements and have some control over the destiny of the property owners.

- The economics of the deal work if you make one change—which shouldn't be that hard to do. What you need to do is go back to the lot owner and ask him if instead of holding the $35,000 mortgage on the lot you are buying, would he prefer to hold a mortgage on the home you have (you don't add "under contract") across town. You show the lot owner a photo of the home, even drive him over and show him the place. You can say someone else is living in the home now but you will be moving in soon (or renting it to someone else). If the lot owner takes the switch, then you are all but set.

Next you go to the homeowner and tell him that you will give him a $50,000 mortgage on the vacant lot and since it will be a first mortgage, wouldn't he like that better?

If each of these sellers will allow this switch of security, you don't have to offer anything else and you still have some cash up your sleeve. You are going to borrow $60,000 on the house, so, even with $2000 of loan costs, you will have $58,000 to work with. So far you have to give the lot owner $15,000 and the homeowner $25,000, which is a total of $40,000. The remaining $18,000 will go into your pocket if you have made the mortgage swap without any further cash outlay. To make the swap, however, you might have to give the lot owner another $5000 cash, and the homeowner another $10,000 cash at closing. You still have made an OPM transaction deal and have $3000 in your pocket.

When you are making this type of deal, keep the following rules in mind:

- Never tell the other party that you have just contracted to buy this property and will give him the mortgage on it.

- Use a broker to do your negotiating so you won't be confronted with direct questions you don't want to answer.

- You can fall back on the blanket and give the remaining holdout a blanket mortgage on both properties.

GET TO KNOW YOUR LENDERS

It is helpful to develop a good relationship with a loan officer at each of the savings and loan associations you plan to deal with. This is best established well in advance of a need for their services, and I recommend that all investors, as well as real estate brokers and salesmen, maintain a good rapport with these lenders on a permanent basis. It doesn't take much effort on your part to stop by a loan association and meet some of these loan officers. Tell them that you are going into real estate investing and hope to use their services in the near future. In the meantime, you would appreciate their explaining the policy of their institution so you will be familiar with the applications and procedures for obtaining a loan. Loan officers will be pleased to have the opportunity to set up what might be a good account for them in the future. A frequent phone call or occasional visit to each will maintain that rapport until the time when you need their assistance. When you do make the professional call and present them with your loan request, they will have a personal stake in your success with the loan committee.

OUTLINE FOR MORTGAGE LOAN REQUEST

It is a good idea to use the following outline when you make any loan application. This outline is as effective for a multimillion-dollar loan as it is for a $10,000 loan. Remember, however, that the greater the loan amount requested, the more detailed the backup data should be.

I. Description of the Property
- A. General description with photos of buildings
- B. Legal description
- C. Location within the city
- D. Site plan or sketch
- E. Location benefits
- F. Aerial photo
- G. General statistics
   1. Demographics
   2. Comparable sales in the area
   3. Traffic count

H. General site data
 1. Size and square feet and land and site coverage
 2. Present use of site
 3. Zoning ordinances and allowed uses of the site
 4. Available utilities
 5. Access
 6. Sketch of buildings in the area and their uses
 7. Survey
 I. Site disadvantages and drawbacks (in soft understated terms)
 J. Land value
 1. Estimated value of site
 2. Comparable land sales and values
II. Description of the Improvements
 A. General description of the improvements
 B. General statistics
 1. Date built
 2. Year remodeled
 3. Type of construction
 4. Other structural and mechanical data
 5. Floor area: living, covered, garage, balcony, etc.
 6. Parking available
 7. Other general data
 C. Floor plans
 1. Show sketch for each floor
 2. Building plans if new construction
 D. Personal property in building
 1. Inventory of mechanical personal property
 2. Inventory of furniture and fixtures which are personal property
 3. Values of personal property
 E. General statement of condition of improvements and personal property
 F. Replacement cost of structure and combined land and buildings

     G. Comparable sales of improved property of similar nature

     H. The economics of any income-producing improvement

     I. Plans to increase present revenue

       1. New evaluation of value based on increased income

     J. General summary of value

  III. The Person Asking for the Loan

     A. Name

     B. Address

     C. Occupation

     D. General financials

     E. Net worth

     F. Supporting documents

  IV. The Loan Request

     A. The amount of the loan requested

     B. Terms desired

     C. Pay off provisions

     D. Other terms and conditions required

  V. A Completed Loan Application

When you use this outline, do not be tempted to expound in great, superfluous detail. Often this information will take little more than five or six neatly typed pages—not including the sketches and backup data, of course. If there is something in the outline that does not apply to your situation, leave it out. If you're not sure whether it applies, put it in.

Remember, all loans are different but they do share the same end result when they are not paid back. Thus while you should not refuse to consider financing your home, you should choose the option most economically beneficial to you. If you can borrow the needed cash at 5.5 percent on your home instead of 9 percent on the building you want to buy, the choice should be clear.

THE PITFALLS OF FINANCING THE DEAL

There are no more pitfalls than usual. In fact, if you find well-motivated sellers the deal is pretty easy to do. You usually don't have as great a variety of choice in any kind of OPM transaction that you will have when you walk in with all cash. These transactions are designed to generate cash to give you added flexibility of choice. Since this is the objective, use it to your benefit by buying something you want but can't get.

As with all borrowing, there are two major pitfalls: borrowing more than you can pay back, and getting locked into onerous terms for the payback of the loan. Avoiding the first of these two pitfalls will require buyers to review carefully their own financial situation. Is the investment going to take more money than was anticipated? Will that extra drain on existing or borrowed capital put the payback of the debt service in jeopardy of a default? Play this in a conservative way. Always overestimate expenses and anticipate vacancy when investing in any income properties.

If you are new to the borrowing game, the second of these two pitfalls is easy to fall into even when loans are easy to come by. The reason for this is because loan officers are in the business of making loans that return their employers the highest possible return while at the same time providing the greatest protection against risk for those same employers on their invested capital. This means you need to shop around with lenders and carefully read both the mortgage document and the mortgage note. The mortgage document spells out the rules and regulations of the security of the loan and the borrower's obligations. These rules and regulations will vary between lenders. The mortgage note spells out the method of repayment and penalties, if any, for late or early repayment of the amounts due. In each of these documents the print is generally small, and sometimes is printed on colored paper so it does not copy well.

You avoid the majority of problems by making comparisons between lenders' terms, asking questions about what you do not understand, and trusting what is in writing, not what is told to you. For the best chance of getting the best terms, always seek competent professional advice that is not connected to the transaction. Keep in mind that you may not recognize an onerous term because you may not anticipate how it can affect you in a changing market.

A very good example of this occurred with borrowers who got locked into long-term conduit loans in the mid-1990s through the early 2000s. These loans were offered at very attractive rates compared with the general market rate, and the catch that most people never thought would be a problem was that the lender locked in the loan for a period of time, often half the term or better. This meant that the borrower could not prepay the loan at all for the first period of years (each loan was different), and after that term there was a "yield maintenance" penalty. This meant that it was okay if the borrower wanted to prepay the loan after that first period;

however, if the general lending rate at the time of the prepayment, as determined by a formula in the loan document, had fallen below the contract rate (interest rate) of the mortgage, the borrower would have to "make up" the loss in income to the lender by virtue of getting paid off and then having to reinvest in new loans at a lower rate.

Here is an example: In 1999 you borrowed $1,000,000 with a conduit loan at 9 percent interest, say at interest only for 15 years (to make this example easy to follow), and it had a yield maintenance provision that ran until the end of the 15 years. Four years later you have a buyer ready to pay you cash if you get rid of the conduit loan—and you might be in for a shock. The general lending rate in 2003, following the formula in the mortgage, could easily be 5 percent. This means the lender will lose 4 percent per year on the $1,000,000 you owe. That would be $40,000 a year times the remaining 10 years. It could be that you might face a penalty of at least $400,000. This would likely kill your deal, and would be an event that no one in 1999 would have anticipated. Try to avoid loans with yield maintenance penalties for this easy-to-understand reason.

37 CHAPTER

Launch Your Craft

Long before money was invented, people did things in exchange for other benefits. Today, as in ancient times, the barter of one's craft is an ideal method of OPM investing. A craft, by the way, is a job you can perform for someone rather than some merchandise you might manufacture. The doctor or dentist has a craft that is frequently bartered within his own professions for like services. Because of the realty orientation of his profession—a plumber or, for that matter, anyone in the construction, fix-it, or handyman profession—might find many opportunities for OPM real estate investing in barter for their craft.

As you read this chapter you will find that not only can you barter your own craft, you can barter someone else's craft for your OPM real estate deals.

KNOW YOUR CRAFT

You don't have a craft to barter unless you can do something that other people cannot do or would rather have someone else do it for them. Take Doug, for example. He is a carpenter. He works about 45 hours a week at his job but is free on the weekends. He used to work from time to time for George, who bought property to be fixed up for a fast turnover. It was here that Doug got the idea of going into real estate investing for himself. However, as is frequently the case, Doug didn't have enough cash to make that move.

In a conversation with George, Doug learned that cash wasn't necessary. To prove the point, George told Doug he would sell him one of his properties. He would do so for a no cash, OPM deal. All Doug had to do was agree to work sufficient hours over the next year to pay the down payment. George would hold onto the title to the property until Doug had fulfilled the agreement, and then pass the title to him. Now any time you barter your craft you are, in a way, using money you would earn anyway, the only difference is that you often get to pick how you spend your time in the meanwhile.

Doug thus bartered his craft of carpentry to George for some real estate. And once Doug had the property, he could spend some more of his own time and effort to continue to improve the property and enhance its value.

A SERVICE CAN BE BARTERED, TOO

In an example of barter of a service, let's look at Margo's situation. Margo is a tax accountant. She had been renting her office from the same landlord for six years and wanted to buy her own building, but she just never had the cash she thought it would take to buy. Then a developer built a condo office building across the street from where she rented. This was the ideal moment for her: If she could scrape up the down payment, she could own for less than the monthly rent she had been paying. Better to make mortgage payments and build up equity than make rent payments. Besides, she had a strong working knowledge of the new tax laws and knew that she'd be better off owning than renting.

She was able to raise some cash, but in the final negotiations to buy she fell short by $6000 to meet the total payment. In desperation she told the developer she would have to bow out of the deal despite the fact that she wanted to buy very badly. The developer thought about it for a few moments and then told her that they would work something out. It seemed he needed a tax accountant to wrap up the year-end for several of his corporations, and if she would do that work for him and become his tax accountant on a consultant basis, he would let the $6000 shortage be the retainer against her future fees.

In this way Margo made her deal. And while it wasn't completely OPM, the important thing was that she bartered her craft and made her investment.

MAKE SIDE DEALS WITH YOUR CRAFT

If your craft isn't in demand with the local real estate sellers, look around for what is and make a swap with them. Let's say your expertise is in the field of hospital development and you want to make a barter deal with a condo developer. You might find that, while the condo developer has no use for that expertise, you can go to someone who uses your services and see if they will swap some of their services to the condo developer.

In this way a dentist might trade his services to the owner of a lumber company for credits on lumber and building materials for a housing developer. If you have a craft of any kind, you should be in a position to make some kind of barter, either direct or indirect. Sometimes you have to dig deep into your box of abilities to discover an unused value you can barter, like the cabdriver who couldn't think of what to barter until he discovered his talent as a weekend chauffeur or private driving instructor.

You might find it tough to find a barter, and if this technique looks like it will be harder to make it work for you than some of the others, then read the other chapters over for clues—or change crafts.

How to Barter the Craft of Someone Else

It is possible that you are still learning what will be a worthy and valuable craft in the future (safe-cracking, brain surgery, electronic eavesdropping, etc.), but right now you—and many young people without a truly barterable craft—might find it easier to barter with another person's craft. Remember the scrip transactions? Well, much like those, you can make a deal for someone's craft and then exchange that craft or service for what you want.

Sylvia was still a student at the University of Michigan when she decided to buy a duplex. She didn't have much cash and what cash she had she wanted to use to fix up the property. She negotiated with the owner of a nice property and got the seller to hold a major part of the sales price in the form of a purchase-money mortgage provided that Sylvia did actually spend the money on fixing up the duplex. However, the seller insisted on $5000 in cash.

Sylvia didn't have an extra $5000 in cash, so she did some homework. She discovered that the seller owned a company that built schools for various school boards in the state. Sylvia had no craft that would be of economic interest to the seller, but she knew of many jobs that the seller must utilize on a consultant basis.

She checked around and found a well-recommended structural engineer who had done some work on school projects from time to time, and she offered to buy some of his consulting time at a discount. In essence she was to get a commission on his time, only she was going to have to pay him back as a draftsman when she finished her schooling.

Essentially what Sylvia did was contract for a certain number of hours of consultant time at a rate equal to the usual payment the engineer was accustomed to receiving with a discount. From the engineer's point of view it made sense too. The business Sylvia would bring to him would more than likely be business he wouldn't get otherwise, and things were slow enough that he could use the opportunity to strike up new clients who would pay cash later on.

Clayton was negotiating with a builder to buy a model home and ran into trouble raising the cash to make the down payment. Clayton went out and "bought" some carpenter time from a local carpentry company and bartered that time to the builder. Clayton then paid the carpenters off with vacation time available from several time-share apartments his dad owned and was not using.

Bartering your own craft or the craft of others gives you the opportunity for maximum leverage in transactions where you have a minimum of cash.

Three Things to Keep in Mind When You Barter with Another's Craft

1. Never make your barter offer until you have tied up the craft. If you want to make a deal with a builder, go around to some of the building trades or suppliers. Tell them you want to use their services to buy real estate if they will sell you those services on soft paper. If they say yes, get that in writing before you go to the builder to make your offer to use that service as a part of a transaction to acquire the builder's property.

2. Make sure you have sufficient outs in both agreements. An "out" is an escape clause that gives you the right to call off the transaction. This escape provision generally will be binding once the party has delivered on their obligations. However, it

possible to have a few days for either party to back out of the deal. "I need five business days to check out your property, Mr. Seller. Is that okay?" The seller replies, "Sure, as long as I have the same time to check you out too." You don't want to have to spend money to supply the craft if the craftsman backs out of the deal. If the builder has agreed to sell you the property with the craft service as part or all of the down payment, and the tradesman or craftsman then goes belly-up and leaves you high and dry, you might have to dig into your pocket. You can protect yourself by having an agreement that you assign to the developer. In essence you have contracted for a craftsman's time, and the agreement between you and that craftsman is for a specific time in work. You assign that agreement to the seller of the real estate you are buying. If the work doesn't get done, you don't have to pay, and the seller has no claim against you—unless you somehow are also at default in the agreement.

3. Always do business with people you can trust or that you have some leverage with. After all, the seller of the duplex you are buying will look to you when the painter, you made a side deal with does not show up, or does a terrible job. Pick the people you deal with and make every effort possible to do what you said you would. You will owe the seller big time if you don't.

THE FINE POINTS OF BARTERING A CRAFT

When you barter your own craft, there are four things to keep in mind.

1. Never sell your craft short. If your usual wage is $30 per hour, then barter it at that same amount. If your services are profitable, then you are dealing at par with the seller. He also has a profit in what you are getting.

2. Don't barter time that you can easily convert to cash. It would be silly for you to give up actual paying time to barter for something else. If you can convert that time to cash, then negotiate with cash. You will get a discount when dealing with cash.

3. Do attempt to barter with persons who will need more of your craft than you are offering. In this way you will have room to

negotiate and the opportunity to develop a new client who will pay cash later on.

4. Don't be too anxious. It's unwise to take on something you don't want or don't feel comfortable with just to make a barter deal. Make your deals count.

38 CHAPTER

The Root Beer Float

People who own a business know all about the float. "Float" is the money owed to you from the normal course of your business enterprise. Whether through business or personal interactions, there are times when we owe other people. It might be the American Express bill at the end of the month, the gas company bill, or any of dozens of other monthly bills that come into your mailbox at various times of the month.

The normal outstanding bills many of us have each month add up to a great deal. If the would-be investor has a high monthly payable, it is possible that the needed cash to make investments can come from payments you would normally make on your bills.

Let me explain. It is all a matter of priorities and simple economics. If you need a couple of thousand dollars to complete a real estate transaction and you have several times that much in monthly payout on bills (both personal and business), you might be able to put some of these creditors off for a while and use that cash to make your deal.

THE FLOAT DEAL

Ella ran a nice publishing business. She was expanding her business each month and, while she wasn't making much money, she was paying off her equipment and could see that in a few years she would be on easy street.

Her monthly payables for supplies, services, rent, utilities, and miscellaneous payments totaled over $21,000 per month. Part of this was the $3000 monthly rent for the building she was occupying. Ella knew that she would be far better off if she could buy a building and move into it instead of paying rent.

She found a nice building and, applying some of the techniques shown in this book, nearly made it as an OPM deal. But hard as she tried, she just couldn't quite make the transaction go with the cash she had. She needed another $5000 of cold, hard cash to entice the seller into taking the other terms offered.

Ella studied her monthly payout and decided she could push several of her creditors to the tune of $5000 that month. In short she let the creditors carry the float of $5000 for a while longer instead of paying them on time.

Now before you cringe and think I've lost my mind about sound investment techniques, let me tell you that many people do far worse to their creditors. I've even known several noninvestors who stopped paying their creditors in favor of playing the horses. The idea isn't to get into the habit of pushing off creditors, only to know what to do if all else fails.

Sometimes the need to own some real estate, as in Ella's case, overshadows the temporary benefits of being an on-time payer of your bills. If the picture in the relatively near future seems to be beneficial and you have a promising economic year ahead, the chances are this technique can be useful to you.

HOW TO DETERMINE WHICH CREDITORS NOT TO PAY NOW

This is the tough part of this chapter because the answer is very simple: The creditor you will push will be the one who is least likely to press you when he isn't paid right away. It might be the creditor you have been using the longest. It might even be your best friend. But most certainly it won't be the guy who will slap a high interest rate and credit charges on your account if you are five minutes late with your payments.

Take a look at your monthly flow of bills. If you notice that there are several creditors who are regulars each month and one or more of them (on the monthly basis) will total up to the cash you need to make a deal go together, then consider these creditors as likely choices.

Do You Make a Mortgage Payment?

Sometimes you can find that the lender actually has a heart of semisoft matter. Savings and loan associations are well-known softies because they hate to foreclose. After your mortgage has gone close to the end of its grace period, you can always send them a check to meet the deadline. In this way you will never be in default and can get a month or so behind, using the savings and loan to carry your float.

If you need more than one month, or have a short grace period in your loan, you might want to call the loan officer and have a chat. "Frank, I've purchased a building across town and am going to be up against it for a couple of months. I won't be able to meet my payments during this time, but I promise I'll catch up later on. How can we work this out?"

TO TELL THEM OR NOT TO TELL THEM—THAT IS THE QUESTION

Should you level with the creditor or not? You could just call him up and say, "Bill I'm going to be a little short this month. In fact I won't be able to meet my payment to you at all. But I promise that I will before the end of next month." This is the tack some of you will take no matter what the reason for being short of cash at the end of the month. If, on the other hand, you are absolutely using the cash to buy something like the building you are to occupy—and to expand your business—then it is better to say, "Bill, we've made a big step this month and I wanted to let you know that we've bought the building over on Main Street. We will be growing bigger and bigger because of this, but we've extended ourselves a little much this month. We want you to know we appreciate your service over the years and hope you will be patient for about four weeks until we can catch up on our payments." Now doesn't that sound better?

When you decide that the creditor you need to push is the bank holding your mortgage, call the loan officer you originally dealt with and explain the situation. Offer a plan to pay back the amount you are going to have to defer for a month or three, and if you feel you do not have a sympathetic person across the desk from you, excuse yourself and the next day call the president of the lending association and ask if there is someone else you can talk to. Do not pick an argument with the loan officer. Remember that all lending institutions, even private sources of money, want to get paid, but they also do not want to run up extra cost while doing that. Generally they will work with you if you show them that this is not a habit of yours, and that you are sincere.

If you habitually make minimum payments on your bills, then this will show up in a quick credit check and will punch holes in all of your best efforts to convince the loan officer that you are sincere in working out something with them.

Getting in debt more than you can possibly handle is one of America's most debilitating illnesses. The ease of getting credit cards, and the "minimum payment" that many people make each month allows the total owed on a credit card to go out of sight. And if not out of sight, most certainly out of the realm of reasonable expectations in one's budget.

Getting an early hold on the problem is the key to the credit crunch. But this chapter is not really about that. What I am talking about is what you do when you need to buy some time.

The first step is not to ever make a minimum payment on a credit card unless you absolutely cannot afford to make the full payment. By keeping your credit card clean and not building up a "balance owed," you will be establishing sound and verifiable credit. This establishes a "line of credit," which is the amount the credit card company will let you charge. Later in this chapter I show you a far cheaper way to build a line of credit. However, having a good line of credit with card companies helps.

Don't Be Intimidated

Some creditors will be on the phone with you the instant your check is five minutes late. If your contract doesn't term minor lateness a default, there is little they can do except try to collect the amount due them. No creditor in his right mind is going to sue you without trying to collect the amount owed him on his own first. Collection companies and lawyers will take too much from the amount collected.

This brings up an interesting point. An investor is late with almost all of his creditors and has his brother-in-law (or someone like that) call up the creditor and offer to make the collection for the low cost of only 15 percent, guaranteeing collection within 30 days. This is a real neat game these guys have, as you can calculate. The only problem is that it doesn't allow one to build up any longevity in the community. Your good word is only as valuable as others say it is.

THE FINE POINTS OF THE FLOAT

Most investors I know run into cash flow problems from time to time. One of the best ways to ensure a "fall back" position is to develop a line of credit with a local commercial bank. A line of credit is not a loan, but a promise from the lender to give you money at predetermined terms, or under a formula that is set up in advance up to your "line of credit." All large corporations and investors have used this technique from time to time, and most have a standing line of credit against which they can draw needed funds when the occasion arises. The beauty of the "line of credit" is that the lender doesn't ask you what the funds are for. They have already determined you to be a good risk up to a certain point, and if you suddenly need money to acquire a property you know will be gone by tomorrow, the money is in the bank waiting for you to take it.

As with all loans, setting up a line of credit is much the same procedure as getting a loan in the first place. You will be asked to supply financial data and fill out forms and the like. Your past "repayment history" will be an important element to document because that establishes your overall credit rating. If you don't have a strong credit rating, then you should find out why. Often it is because of a mistake in the reporting system that establishes your credit. These errors happen all the time.

When all else fails and you have to push someone you owe money to, be sure you do everything possible to promptly make up the payment. If it is rent, or a loan to a personal friend, offer something to soften the blow, like use of your time-share next year, fishing in your boat, or just having lunch on you one day. Whatever you do, don't make a habit of pushing too far. Pushers fall off cliffs that way.

PITFALLS OF THE FLOAT

There are two important things that you may not have when you start out investing in real estate, but which you can build. Those two things are your word (your reputation) and good credit.

It takes a very long time to establish a reputation as the kind of person whose word is golden. This does not mean that people you do business with will not insist on a contract that is in writing and signed by you. What it means is that when people trust what you say, the contract becomes possible far more easily than otherwise. I am sure you have caught someone in a lie. I mean a lie that is important to your future trust in that person, and not a white lie about how nice you look today. Having a good word or reputation is like blowing up a king-sized mattress with your own lung power. It takes effort, you can get dizzy doing it, and in the end, all it takes is a single prick of a knife to deflate that mattress. Tell a lie like "the check is in the mail" too often and that becomes that knife prick. Your good credit is much the same, only it haunts you for far longer than you might like. I always recommend that people check their credit from time to time. I do, and just recently looked over my current credit rating from the major credit reporting companies. I noticed a statement from an out-of-state bank that reported that I was late for more than 15 succeeding months on a mortgage they said I owed. The mortgage amount was not a lot of money in relation to my annual expenses or lines of credit also published in the report, but the continual late payment history had brought my overall credit rating down to a level where I had been turned down for a new phone service and was told I had to send in a deposit before they would turn my phone on. That, of course, was what had prompted my obtaining an update on my credit report in the first place. What about the out-of-state bank? An error on their part. The mortgage was on an apartment I had sold over four years previously. The buyer has assumed the old loan (which was current when I sold it), and I was relieved from the obligations of the loan. However, the bank had not told the collection office that I was not the person they should punish.

Just remember, pitfalls in taking your reputation and credit out to the edge can be dangerous to your investment career. And besides, if you push the wrong guy too far you might end up with both arms and legs in a cast. I'm sure this has happened to some people who aren't around to talk about how well they almost played the game.

39 CHAPTER

The Syndication

What if I told you that you could make all the OPM investments you ever dreamed of anywhere in the world and own any kind of property you want? Would you be interested? You might be when you finish this chapter, or you might be turned off forever to dealing in syndicate territory.

Syndication is an event where you put an investment package together and get others to put up the money. Your reward can vary from a commission to a healthy percentage of the deal. Your ultimate profit depends on how the property was purchased, how your percentage was set up, and the time it takes to realize a profit.

THE SYNDICATE DEAL

Guy was from Canada and had been living in south Florida for about seven years. He went back to Canada from time to time, and each visit there brought new requests from his former business associates for Guy to locate an investment for them. When I met Guy, he was sure he had a gold mine at his fingertips, but he didn't know how to put the gold into his pockets.

I told him that the first rule of syndication is to have absolute control over the investment. This meant he would keep the whole thing secret until he was able to gain control over the property. To do this he would have to either already own the property or to have a firm option to purchase it prior to offering his friends and associates the opportunity to buy into the deal.

As it turned out Guy had already experienced the futility of trying to entice his friends into a deal where he had no control in property. What generally happens in this situation is the would-be syndicator goes to his friends and suggests they combine efforts to buy something he knows about. This sparks the "democratic rule," where each of the parties wants to give his opinion of how the deal should be structured, who is to take control and, as they are all equal in the venture, they want to ensure they all put in the same amount of investment capital and have an equal share of the profits.

The second rule of syndication is to forget this democratic rule stuff. If you are going to put a syndication together, you and you alone will establish the rules. You will also be entitled to a fee and a percentage of the profits as the syndicator. If the deal is a good one, you can also buy into the venture to increase your return but that is your option. There are other perks that, as the syndicator, you can give yourself, which will be discussed throughout this chapter.

Guy's Apartment Syndication

Following my suggestions, Guy located a small apartment complex near the Fort Lauderdale beach. I reviewed the economics of the property and suggested the property be converted from its current annual rental status to a seasonal property. Since Guy had a lot of friends and contacts in Canada, this connection could be ideal to keep the property full of high-paying Canadians.

Guy agreed with my analysis so he was ready to make an offer to tie up the property. I drafted an offer to buy the property, and Guy gave me a check for $5000 as a deposit on the apartments. He offered $650,000 for the property, which was $75,000 less than the seller was asking. Guy was surprised to see he could tie up a $650,000 property with only $5000 on deposit, and, on top of that, get the $5000 back if he was unable to syndicate the property within 45 business days. A few days later we had a signed agreement with the seller.

Guy flew up to Canada, taking a very detailed presentation of the property. It showed the location of the property, the projections for the future, and other data that was accurate, factual, and showed he was serious about his intent to buy this property. It also illustrated the terms of the deal that he was presenting to his friends. It carefully and in a very detailed way outlined exactly what they would have to pay, what ownership they would get, and the current income and projections for the future.

Guy then went to his friends and showed them the property he purchased. He let them know that he wouldn't be closing for a few months.
(The closing would be at least 90 days after his deadline to form the syndication.) Guy then presented his offer to his friends: "You have always
wanted to come in with me on something down in Florida, so here is your
opportunity. I've broken this down as shown in the data I've given you. If
you want in, let me know by the end of the week." The deal came together; he didn't use any of his own cash, and he ended up with a piece of
the action.

The Last Cavalry Deal

One of my syndications was a 60-acre tract of land in Delray Beach,
Florida. The land was purchased for $700,000. The seller, who happened
to be a survivor of the last cavalry charge of World War II (in Poland)
held a purchase-money mortgage for $600,000 at interest only for 10
years at 7 percent interest only. Just under two years later we sold the land
for $2,000,000 cash. There were 10 investors who each put up $12,000
for the down payment and other costs. There were two years of interest,
taxes, insurance, and my management fee, all of which totaled $6000 a
year. By the time we sold the property the investors had put in another
$1200 each. At the closing we collected $2,000,000, paid off the first
mortgage of $600,000, and then paid the real estate commission of
$200,000. Next was my syndicator's fee of $200,000 (10 percent of the
deal), and I divided up the remainder to the investors. Here is what that
looked like:

Land Syndication Deal

Sale price	$2,000,000
Less costs of	
Pay off mortgage	600,000
Brokerage	200,000
Syndicator's fee	200,000
Two years' carry	12,000
Total outlay	$1,012,000
Amount disbursed to investors	$ 988,000

This means each investor got $98,800 for his or her investment of
$13,200. Now that's a pretty good deal for the investors—and a very good
deal for the syndicator.

As the syndicator, my piece of the action was a simple 10 percent of the sale, provided that the investors made at least 20 percent on their investment. Not bad for a syndicator—and actually a conservative and modest piece. I've seen syndicators take 25 percent of the sales price right off the top, plus other goodies at the same time. Your ultimate benefit will be whatever the investors will pay, although my advice on this issue is to lean to the more-than-fair side of the deal.

Not All Syndications Are Rosy

Naturally, not every syndication has such a positive ending. I know a lot of syndicators who were into tax shelter deals and had some rather sour experiences. Those deals were pure and simple trade-offs of earned income to capital gains income. They occurred at a time when earned income rates were very high, and the tax shelter from depreciation was much higher than is allowed (by the IRS) these days. Those deals could lose money and the investors would still pocket a profit. Then the tax law changed and caught many of those investors on the wrong side of a new IRS regulation.

In my opinion those deals failed the most basic test of what is considered to be a good investment. What is the definition of a good investment? A good investment is one where the income or the appreciation will conservatively exceed the cost to carry the property and give the investor a rate of return that is at least 200 percent of the current prime rate charged at the major Wall Street banks.

Some syndications are the up and down of real estate investing. They put you into partnerships or other forms of legal ownership and can tie you down, or up, depending on your point of view. But you can make a fortune with them. The key to forming a syndicate is to invest in properties that are within your comfort zone and are located in your investment area. They should be properties you would want to own if you were the sole investor in the deal.

THE FINE POINTS OF THE SYNDICATE

The first thing to do when putting a syndicate together is to start with an objective. Simple you say? Not so in reality. Your future goals differ from mine and from those of just about everyone else you will meet. If you are profit motivated, you will (or should at least) have a healthy regard for money. By this I mean you should respect not just the effort that goes to earn it, but what it can buy, what it will cost to get, and what it will cost you once you have a lot of it.

Far too many people waste their energy on unworthy goals and misplaced priorities. Far too many successful people have beat their brains out to get a lot of money that once they end up with it, they find little satisfaction in having it. Therefore your objective is crucial to your application of any tool of investing. Use any tool wisely and you can build something. But will you like it when you're finished? In my opinion you will be satisfied (and generally happy) only if you chose the right objective.

Do you want to build equity, a bankroll, or income? These are just three of the many economic questions you have to answer prior to putting a syndicate of your own together. Whatever the property is that you decide to syndicate, you will find that your ability to make the deal fly will be increased a million fold if the investment fulfills your primary objective or moves you closer to it.

Another important point is never stray from your comfort zone or your investment area. Couple this concept with one more and you will see my point. Your comfort and investment zones should never be violated with syndication. In essence invest your partners' money just as though it were your own. That means don't experiment with their money by moving out of your own comfort zone. Remember your comfort zone is what you truly know well, and your investment area is where you apply that knowledge.

The Syndication Checklist

Now that you can see the foundation that will help you build sound and profitable syndications, take a look at the syndication checklist below.

1. Have you clearly identified your objective in doing syndication?
2. Write down what you want to accomplish through the pending investment. Remember, you are not writing a presentation for investors; this is for you, just as if you are the sole investor in the project. Do not try to kid yourself.
3. Is the pending investment within your investment area? If it is not, then you might be ready to make that fatal error and come down with the greener grass syndrome.
4. Is the pending investment one that fits your comfort zone? If you are comfortable with every fact about the property, your objective, and the future potential of the property and it fits with

your hard-earned knowledge about the area, the type of property, and the local market conditions, then you can move forward.

5. Are you able to convince an investor of your absolute confidence in the pending investment?

6. Other than time and effort, are you willing to invest money in the deal? This is an important step that you will want to consider, even if the amount of money is slight. If you have some extra cash, then it is likely a good idea to be one of the investors as well as a syndicator. It is especially a good idea if you are setting up an investment portfolio for your children and the investment is in their name. Putting some of your own money into a deal may be necessary in the first syndication you put together.

7. Do you have control over the property? If you have not negotiated for the very best price and terms that you could get and do not have a firm lock on the transaction for sufficient time to put the syndication together, then go back to the drawing boards. You are not ready yet. If you are comfortable with your control then get the package ready for the investors.

8. Do you know how many investors you want to invite into the deal? You need to keep it light and simple, so do not have more than a few. Be sure to get legal help at this stage of the game. You do not want to violate any securities laws. If you ascertain that you need to register the package as a security you will have added cost and time in the deal. Security registrations require absolute and total disclosure on just about everything you can think of that pertains to the deal. It is a good idea to read some Security and Exchange Commission (SEC) registrations to see what I mean by absolute. Remember, too, each state has its own SEC rules and regulations that pertain to a security offering within that state. Be sure to check those regulations as well as the Federal SEC. Ask your stockbroker to send you several offerings that relate to each of these sets of rules. Even if you do not have to register the syndication as a security it is a very good idea to give the same total disclosure to your investors as if you did.

9. The investment package should have hard-and-fast rules about how the syndicator is going to manage the investment and what decisions are pre-approved at the time the investor signs up. This is a critical element in any syndication. For example if the deal is

to buy land and build a new shopping center, the package should include all the cost to do just that, and the right to mortgage the property and building to a predetermined amount. If the goal is to rent up the building then sell it, a minimum price should be set together with who is to list the property for sale, what commissions will be paid and what the syndicator gets (over and above any return from an actual cash investment). The most important thing to include in any syndication is a hard penalty for any investor who does not promptly live up to the investor's obligations of the deal. If the investor is expected to meet his or her share of expenses for a predetermined time, and the investor fails to do that, then spell out that his or her share can be liquidated by the syndicator. I have never had an investor refuse to invest in a syndication for that reason, in fact, investors love such a tough approach because no investor expects to fail at his or her obligations, but all fear one or more of the others might. One good provision to include in syndication is to have a buyback from a disgruntled investor. In this situation you have the right to buyback any investor's interest at a formula of return. This would not be allowed if there was a pending deal cooking in the wings, and the buyback should be set up so that only the remaining investors can subscribe to the buyback.

10. Be highly conservative in projections for the future. It is best to limit your pro forma on what has happened in the past, what the current market indicates, and what income and/or profit can be reasonably expected.

11. Maintain constant contact with your investors. No one likes to be in the dark. It is best to have an investment newsletter that deals with each specific investment sent to the investors on a monthly basis. More frequent information can be e-mailed on a weekly basis with breaking news every time something occurs that is either positive or negative to the future of the investment.

12. Never make investment decisions on your own, as the syndicator, unless they are within the allowable decisions that are in the investment plan and objectives. Be sure that the package and terms of syndication spell out how decisions are to be made. Is it a simple majority vote? Is a 75 percent vote needed to sell or mortgage? Keep in mind that you must have these things written

down and that each kind of decision can vary as to the percentage of vote needed. In my opinion it is best to keep everything to
a simple majority vote. Why? Because not everyone will be
happy with whatever the situation is two years from now. No
matter how much money you make an investor, there are some
who will see what you are making and not like it. These people
can make your life difficult because they may have nothing but
time on their hands to disrupt the smooth operation of a syndication. This is another very good reason to have a buyback provision mentioned earlier.

Syndications do not have to be grand multimillion dollar ventures. In
fact, the best to begin with are simple investments with no more than five
or six people. Pick something that won't take more than $10,000 per in-
vestor for the down payment with the potential of another $10,000 per in-
vestor for fix-up money.

When you make your presentation to investors you are not asking
their opinion of the property, or of the way you have structured the investment package. You show everything of course, but the only reply you
need from them is yes or no. They should know that there are other
people who are being presented the same package but that you are limit-
ing the investment presentation to a very few people. Give them sufficient
time to make a decision and be ready to field questions from their lawyer,
accountant, or bartender. Let everyone know that when the time period is
up you are free to present to someone else.

THE LEGAL FORMS OF SYNDICATION

I won't go into a lot of detail on this matter for two reasons. First your state
might have different laws with respect to the legal forms of ownership
than Florida or the other states with which I am familiar. Second laws
change, and you need to be sure to get the most current data and apply it to
you and your objectives. However it is a good idea to know some of the
common forms of holding title and to have some conversational comfort
with them. What follows is a list of some of those forms.

- **Partnership.** You and I are partners. We are in this mess together,
  and if I screw up, it is your rear end just as much as mine. If we
  both pull it off, then we will reap the benefits on the percentages
  as stated in the partnership agreement.

- **General Partnership.** As in the regular partnership, you and I are general partners: We pull strings the same, speak the same language (to debtors and creditors), and have the same liability. We are brothers who will eat off the same plate if we have to in hopes of finding the rainbow on the other side of the mountain.

- **Limited Partnership.** A separation between general partners and other kinds of partners. The limited ones are just that limited in the scope of their liability. The general partner is God and will be held accountable for the bad and usually not given credit for the good. The limited partners do not have much say, if any, over what goes on in the partnership.

- **Trust.** I can hold title to your property in trust for you. If I form a land investment trust (legal in many places), then you have a beneficial interest in a form of joint venture but I hold the title to the land. Your interest as an investor is usually considered personal property, not real property, and that has some advantages as well as disadvantages. The transfer of a trust with many beneficiaries can be complicated if a dissenter wants to make life miserable for the others. On the other hand it is a very simple form of partnership with a minimum of exposure to the investors.

- **Corporation.** You and I form a corporation. We issue stock and take the money and buy a property. Remember, however, the person who holds 51 percent of the corporation controls the deal. If I'm the president because I own 51 percent of the stock, you can yell and scream all you want but you only own 49 percent.

    If you just want to put money into something and you have full faith in the future of the corporation, then this is the way to do it. Keep in mind that there are several different kinds of corporations. A "C" corporation, for example, is the normal corporation which is run by a board of directors and stockholders vote them in or out. A "S" corporation is really a Sub-"S" corporation, which functions much like a "C" corporation except that profits and expenses flow through to the individual stock holders. A Limited Liability Corporation (LLC) is a corporation that has limited liability to the stockholders.

- **Joint Venture.** A form of any of the above where two or more people get together to do something. Each party might be one of the above, joined together in one of the above forms, for example, a corporation formed by two corporations or by a partnership and a corporation. Most joint ventures are formed to accomplish one single limited purpose, which could be the construction of a shopping center, an industrial park, or a mountain cabin.

- **Real Estate Investment Trust.** This is a special kind of trust that has become very well liked by Wall Street. They are also called simply REITs and they enable individual investors to own shares in a corporate-like structure that owns real estate. Many of these trusts own mega portfolios of real estate. There are public and private REITs. It is not likely that you will start with this kind of ownership unless you are putting a large portfolio of a specific kind of real estate together with other people like yourself to receive some very specific tax benefits.

PITFALLS OF SYNDICATIONS

The main pitfalls are the law, the SEC, the state Security and Exchange Commission, and so on. The laws governing the formation of syndicates will vary from state to state, but all are overseen by the SEC. If you run into one of these agencies, you may wish you had never heard of the term "syndication," not because you have done anything wrong, but because they may treat you as though you have.

It is nearly impossible to do a syndication in full compliance with all of the laws and regulations that govern or restrict syndications unless you elect to go through a full-blown registration of the venture with the proper governing agencies. For most investments by small syndicators, this is not economically possible or feasible. Because of this, the laws generally offer some exemptions for the small syndicator. If you fall within one of these exemptions and adhere to the rules of that exemption, you may be okay. Then again you may not.

Still, don't avoid syndications out of fear of the law. The laws are basically designed to protect the investors. Take a look at some of the full-blown registrations (get them from your local stockbroker) and see how they are put together. The name of the game is honesty and full disclosure.

If you are sincere about what you are doing, and have invested some time (a couple of hours) with your local syndicating lawyer, you will know just where the thin ice lies. There are also some fine courses and seminars on forming syndicates, books on the topic, and accountants who will aid you willingly (if you use them later on). But remember, never buy a property for syndication that you would not buy for yourself (if you had the money, of course). And never run a syndicate according to the rules of a democracy. Dissenters will create anarchy in a hurry, and you will be the first they send to the guillotine. Make default rules tough so that if any investor doesn't live up to his or her obligations you can get rid of the person without problems. (By the way, in the beginning all investors like tough rules because they never believe they are the ones who will default.) Do your due diligence on the investors you want to bring into the deal. If there is any doubt in your mind about their ability to make the investment, do not let them do it. Avoid retired lawyers, no matter how much money they want to invest, as they tend to want to run the show. Be cautious about bringing family members and medical doctors into a syndication, as some of them tend to think they know more about everything than you do.

PERKS SYNDICATORS ARE ENTITLED TO GET

Just in case you would not think of them, the following is a list of a few of the perks I have seen syndicators build into their ventures. Not all of the following have ever appeared in any single syndication, but don't let that stop you from putting them into your next venture.

- **Syndicator's Fee.** This can be a stated percentage right off the top or a plateau kind of fee that increases as the investors' profit increases. The fee can be tied to a minimum yield that the investors earn.

- **Management Fee.** This is for the day-to-day operation of the venture, and the duties and obligations as manager should be clearly defined in the initial documentation. This is over and above the syndicator's fee.

- **Sales Commission.** If you are a broker or your state allows a party to the transaction to share a brokerage fee, then you would be entitled to that fee or part of it anyway.

- **Right to Sell.** Some syndicators have a formula that will allow them to sell the property anytime that formula can be met. For example, the formula might state a minimum price, say $1,000,000 provided the sale is within the first three years from the initial closing and the investors net return will be double their total invested capital. The importance of a specific right to sell is that sometimes strife will occur within the ranks of the investors. A war between the investors will eventually mean a war with you and as they outnumber you it can get messy. This happens to all syndicators who do enough syndications and the bailout sale is one good way to end the problem.

- **Right to Buy Out Investors.** You should never do this unless it is absolutely necessary and then only if the investor has asked to be bought out. My preference on this issue is to have a formula whereby a willing seller (of their share of the investment) must first offer the share to all other investors as a group. Any investor willing to buy can subscribe to their pro rata share of that position offered. For example in a 10-member syndication where each investor has one-tenth of the deal (after all fees have been satisfied) one individual's share could be taken by the remaining nine members if they would subscribe to at least one-ninth of the share offered. Naturally any member could oversubscribe to take up the slack if not all members wanted the share. As a syndicator your perk could be to buy all unsubscribed interest.

40
CHAPTER

The Corporation Deal

Why not form a corporation and issue stock? You then give some of the stock as your down payment to the seller of a property you want to own. After all, the idea of incorporation is like the American dream. IBM issues stock whenever they need to generate new capital, so why not you?

This technique is akin to the technique of syndication discussed in the previous chapter, in that a corporation is one of the forms of ownership that is used in that method of deal making. However, you should understand that incorporation and issuing stock as a part of a transaction is not syndication. Also be aware that although this chapter uses a corporation form, any legal entity that has shares of interest can be used.

THE INCORPORATION DEAL

Edwin was a single-family homebuilder who liked to build around a dozen expensive, custom-designed homes a year. This made for a comfortable life without many worries. Then along came the hot deal that Edwin didn't feel he could turn down. It was a great opportunity, if he could come up with $150,000 in cash within a few months.

Like many builders Edwin had a lot of his cash tied up in his building projects. He would have as many as nine homes under construction at any given time and that meant a lot of capital out in the field in the form of materials and labor.

Edwin knew he could bring a partner into his business and easily raise the $150,000. But if he did that he would forever have a partner. He did not want to take his whole business and dilute his and his family's interest in something that had taken him years to establish. But what about a part of that business that could be spun off and put into a package corporation?

What Edwin did was to package five of his homes into a corporation. He then sold 40 percent of the stock for the capital he needed to make his $150,000 investment. The stock that he sold was a preferred stock and cost the investors $160,000 with the extra $10,000 added to cover the legal cost of the deal. As preferred stock the investors would get the first $185,000 of the profit from the sale of the five homes no matter what the profit actually turned out to be. Edwin anticipated that the total profit from the homes would be around $525,000 to $660,000. Edwin knew that the investors were in safe hands. They were well protected for the first $185,000 and could earn up to $264,000. The homes were all within four to six months of being ready to be delivered and Edwin's marketing history suggested that they would all be sold and closed no later than 10 months from now.

The incorporation ate into Edwin's profits, of course, but the cost was well worthwhile as it enabled him to make the other investment without having to give away an even larger portion of his business. He liked the deal so much that he began to package other groups of homes in much the same way. Of course many of you reading this book won't have the opportunity to use this technique right now. You will have to build some past successes to allow those laurels to carry you on to other (and, with luck, more profitable) deals. But even if you are just starting out, you will still have some use for the incorporation techniques to nail down those deals where you can't quite close the gap in the OPM transaction you began with some other technique.

For example, assume for the moment that you are trying to buy a home in a nice part of town. Since you know the value of the area and feel you can fix up the property, even change its current use to a duplex (the zoning allows it). You have done your homework and you know you are in for a nice profit down the road. But first you have to buy it.

Here's the deal: price, $70,000 and first mortgage, $35,000. The seller tells you he wants a minimum of $15,000 in cash and will hold a second mortgage of $20,000. This looks like a simple pyramid job and a refinance of the existing mortgage. So you get him to hold a second mortgage on another property you own and discover you can borrow $56,000 on the property. That loan will cost you $2000, netting you $54,000 in new money. After you pay off the existing loan, you will have $19,000 cash left over. You can pay the seller his $15,000 and still have $4000 to make repairs and the like to the house.

This is fine, except that the remodeling and repairs you want to make turn out to be much more expensive than you thought they would be. By the time you get all the bids in, you find that if you close on this deal you will be short of cash. The work the contractor bids on will cost $12,500, and this is the very minimum remodeling you want to do.

If you incorporated the house into a single-event venture, you could then offer the seller $9000 in stock in the corporation as part of the cash offered earlier. I've added $500 to cover the cost of the incorporation, and the rest of the deal will balance out.

Your obligations in this deal are:

To pay off the existing mortgage of	$35,000
Give the seller some cash	6,000
Pay for incorporation	500
Have cash for remodeling	12,500
Pay for loan costs	2,000
Total cash obligations	$56,000

As the cash is generated out of the loan proceeds, you can easily see the deal made, provided the seller will take the $9000 in stock and the pyramid of $20,000 to some other property. Of course you now have a stockholder who is into you for a piece of the action. This stockholder is going to want to profit out of the deal so be ready to back up that obligation to him.

The percent of profit or piece of the action naturally will depend on the percent of the corporation you had to give up to make the deal work. That is between you and the seller and depends on the motivations of both of you.

THE FINE POINTS OF INCORPORATION DEALS

There is one single key to the use of this transaction: This deal will be far more palatable to some sellers than others. Remember we deal in a complicated society where some people seek the simplest way out. Here you find a seller who is motivated to make a sale. He isn't interested in some truly complicated situation and wants to do what is normal. There is nothing more normal than a stock deal. (Notice I said normal, and not usual.) Americans wake up in the morning and read the stock report; we live and profit by the stock market and the Dow Jones average of the top stock companies.

Use this familiarity when dealing with a non–real-estate, highly stock-oriented person, as it will be more comfortable to him than any other technique you can dream up. The seller's motivations are critical. If the situation is right the seller may actually ask for a piece of the action. This gives you a distinct edge in closing the deal as you wanted to in the first place.

How to Get the Seller to Suggest the Stock Deal

You've made your series of offers, each one slightly different from the last—different, but not necessarily better—to avoid direct comparison between your offers and to keep your ultimate highest offer hidden. As you progress in the attempt to buy the property, you might discover that you are unable to make an OPM transaction without some participation on the part of the seller. The thought of seller participation opens up several alternative forms of buying, of which the incorporation is one. Syndication, one of the formats shown in Chapter 39, is another way to offer participation, as would be the landlease technique.

Assume for the moment that you feel the best way for you to go with this seller is to give him a piece of the action in the way of some stock in the corporation you plan to form for the deal. If you came out and asked the seller, "Would you like some stock in this venture?" you might get a yes. "Sure," the seller might say, adding "about 50 percent of the deal, okay?" This is far more than you want to give. So instead you work on the seller, never giving any hint that you will take a partner into the deal. You build up effort points between you and the seller. These points might be scored directly between you and the seller or through the broker dealing on your behalf. (This is one of those times when you, the buyer, should be paying the broker, since you want to keep the entire edge in the deal.)

After you have made what looks like a firm deal, you later elect to terminate the deal through one of your outs in the contract; that is you simply didn't get the financing you had planned on. The fact of the matter is the deal isn't good enough for you the way it is structured and you can't close this deal on these terms. So you tell the seller, "Gee, Jeremy, I really wanted to make this deal. I've done a lot of work and have invested a lot of time and money into this project already. I'm confident of the profit potential once I've remodeled the building and quite frankly I'm disappointed that the financing fell through." This would be a good time for a third party, your broker, to say to you, "Mr. Buyer, if Mr. Seller was interested, would you give him a piece of the action if we could hold the deal together?" You look at the seller, he looks at you, you both smile, and you know you are on your way to making a deal.

I just introduced a technique called the take-away. It is a technique that many buyers use all the time. It can be effective, but if you use it a lot you will develop a nasty reputation. The technique is called the take-away because you have taken the seller into a new thought process. A seller that has a property for sale has one specific thought process that is to sell at the best price and terms as possible. In a long and drawn out negotiation process the seller goes through some give and take, often on the verge of walking away from the deal by rationalizing that the deal just was not meant to be. Then the deal comes together and it looks like the property has finally sold. Now the thought process changes. The seller no longer has a property to sell. He can start thinking about spending the money. They shift from "for sale" to "sold."

Then the buyer takes the deal away. If played carefully with sound and logical reasons why the deal did not work out, and there is an intermediary ready to jump in and try to hold the deal together, it is possible to renegotiate a new deal. There is danger in using the take-away. It is possible that all you do, as a buyer, is set up the deal for another buyer who has become interested in the deal.

PITFALLS OF STOCK DEALS

There are several pitfalls you have to watch out for:

1. **Laws of your state dealing with stock offers**. Never make this kind of an offer unless you are sure you know the ramifications. You can do it, but there are limitations. Learn what they are from your lawyer.
2. **Sharing the profit**. Never offer any participation unless you have examined alternative ways to make a deal without giving up a part of your hard-to-be-earned profit.
3. **Offering too much**. Don't offer too much of the action. Offer 15

percent even if you are ready to go to 45 percent. Keep in mind that you can balance the rest of the equity in mortgages and offer only a token piece of the action. Sometimes that is enough. Giving up a percentage of the income was one of the kickers that I discussed in an earlier chapter and does not require that you go through the corporation process at all.

4. **Loss of control**. Never give more than 49 percent. A 50-50 deal is nothing but headaches, and losing control is not fun either. Better to find another deal than give up too much.

5. **Too many partners**. Don't deal with a lot of stockholders. Don't give the lawyer a piece of the action, the broker a piece of the action, and the seller his piece, too, or you will be in for a lot of sleepless nights.

6. **Never let your insiders invest in your syndications**. I am sure you will relax this rule, but it is a mistake to do so. By insiders I mean the people who are your confidants: your lawyer, your accountant, your religious confessant, and so on. I would include some family members as well unless you are absolutely sure they can afford to lose the money they are going to invest. Best, however, to keep family out of the deal.

7. **Always be sure that you cover all the potential risks in this specific deal**. You don't want an investor to get a nasty surprise when he or she learns you forgot to tell them about the new highway that has been cancelled. If the property being purchased must go through any kind of zoning, ordinance change, modification, remodeling, or new addition to reap the benefits you and the other investors are counting on, make sure you have spelled out the full process to accomplish those elements of the deal, and the risk in getting turned down.

8. **Always have a back up plan to cover reverses in the ideal situation**. Don't wait for the dam to burst to plan for a flood. Anticipate potential problems and have solutions ready to be implemented.

41

CHAPTER

The Big Shot Move

Names are big business, as you can tell from television and radio commercials. The name of the guy who is drinking that beer is what's important, more so than the taste of the beer. Your name can be big business to you, if you have a recognized expertise in real estate. The degree of expertise is relative: All you have to do is be more lendable or more credible than the person who needs to use your name to make his deal work.

THE BIG SHOT DEAL

Emery had dabbled in real estate here and there. He owned his own home, a vacant lot he purchased on a contract for deed (a contract where you don't get a deed until you do something, such as pay off the seller-held mortgage), and a condo he inherited from his mother a few years ago. The condo was rented out, the mortgage on the lot did not cost much, and his house had tripled in value in the past five years. Emery was a real estate tycoon, however, in comparison to Jake. Jake had more theoretical knowledge about real estate investing (having read half a dozen books on real estate investing and being a great fix-it-up kind of person. However he didn't have a dime to his name. On the plus side Jake was one of those truly hard-working people who had more guts than brains (the making of many millionaires) and a determination to succeed. He also had a wife and three kids to support.

Emery liked Jake a lot for those hard-working attributes. So much so that when Jake found a small apartment building that he wanted to fix up and rent out for double the existing rents, Emery was receptive to going in on it with Jake.

Emery wasn't going to put up any money; he was only assisting in obtaining the financing. Emery took a 20 percent interest in the investment without putting up any cash. What Emery did was let Jake use his name in the deal. The seller of the property liked the fact that Emery was in the deal, the savings and loan liked Emery on the mortgage, and Jake liked the whole setup because he couldn't have done it without Emery—or someone like Emery.

The fact of the matter is that there are a lot of Emerys out in the world looking for Jakes. You, of course, can profit from either side of the coin. As an Emery you can pull the strings to put deals together, allowing the hardworking Jakes to make your fortunes even larger than they might now be. As a Jake you get your opportunity to become an Emery.

HOW TO GET TO BE IMPORTANT ENOUGH TO GET PAID FOR YOUR NAME

When I thought about this statement, the first factor I thought of was have a good credit rating. However when I gave this further thought, I was reminded of the many developers who had gone bankrupt only to spring back in good favor with lenders. Good credit is only one of several desirable assets and often not the most important one. I know many truly wealthy people whose credit went down the toilet, and many banks and sellers had to take back properties when those people could not make their mortgage payments. The following list will give you some idea of what makes for a good and valuable name in real estate participation. The list will guide you toward the things you can stress in your future real estate dealings.

Your name will be valued if:

- You have a net worth greater than the other partners to the deal.
- You have greater knowledge in the venture than the other partners.
- You have a record of success in similar ventures.
- You have a well-known and respected name in the area.
- You are politically in.

- You are very closely associated with the upper economic strata of the community.
- You speak out loudly, clearly, and not maliciously.
- You are the big cheese in town in what you do.
- You owe a lot of money to some of the best and biggest banks in town.

It doesn't take all of these elements to make your name worth a lot, any few of these together will do—and in some cases even just one will do the job.

How to Lend Your Name and Maximize Your Profits

"There is everything in a name. A rose by any other name would smell as sweet but would not cost half as much during the winter months."

George Ade

Your name will have its time, and if you don't take advantage of it, then shame on you. You see there is nothing wrong in capitalizing on what others need if they, too, will profit. The benefit is mutual. Of course the deal may not always be mutually beneficial from your point of view. This is the major area where people get into trouble in lending their name, and I will dwell on this when I discuss the pitfalls.

We'll assume for the moment that you have examined the proposition brought to you and have recognized that the deal, as presented, will increase your wealth and that of the other party, without causing you greater risk than you wish to accept. Risk, of course, is an ever-present, inescapable element whenever there is potential for profit. Never be led into believing there is no risk when you lend someone your name. Even if any financial loss from the venture will not come out of your pocket, the very fact that someone associated with you has lost money can be a black mark in your book of accomplishments.

Therefore, never lend your name unless you have examined the pitfalls so closely that you are positive that either they don't exist or that you are so slippery you can slip out of their sharp teeth.

PITFALLS IN LENDING YOUR NAME

1. **Avoid the would-be partner you have known forever but really not very well.** He may have gone to kindergarten with

you, and you've seen him a thousand times over the past 30 years but only to say hi to him. You are sure he has been doing well because he always drives a nice car, dresses well, and gives his regards to your wife when he bumps into you (even though he hasn't met her). To your embarrassment you frequently forget his name, and he prods you along with a statement like, "Remember when our English teacher used to single me out and say, 'Now you there, little Charlie Notsoworth, quit pulling those girls' hair.' " This is the person you should avoid since you really don't know his qualities and values. The problem is that this is the very person a lot of people end up having as partners. Why? Because they do not do any quality due diligence on that person. Never (and I speak from experience in not following my advice here) but never go into any business relationship with anyone without looking into his background.

This guy is a potential trap when he asks you for your name in a venture. He is a trap because you have been lulled into "remembering" him as a good guy, when in fact you hated his guts in school, and would now if you could see what was about to happen to you. It is far better to start a new relationship with someone you have never met, and to check him out with a fine-tooth comb.

2. **Walk away when you hear, "There isn't one ounce of risk here."** There is always risk, and if the would-be partner doesn't understand risk, then he's no businessperson. Take a close look and point out where the risk lies. If he counters unsatisfactorily, becomes argumentative, or takes it personally and tells you so, then back off for good.

3. **Shy away from any transaction that has no defined and limited liability that you can accept**. A general partnership in which it appears that all you have to do is to lend your name might put you into one heck of a mess later on when 500 limited partners come after you (they know your name, remember). All they want is to get their money back after the other general partner skips to Rio and your very deep pockets are the only thing in town. You avoid this simply by knowing what the liability is. See your lawyer to explain that to you if you aren't sure where your real risks lay.

4. **Skip the enormous profit deal that will make you a zillionaire overnight.** "Just put your name here, and we will own an entire island in the Bahamas (covered with cannabis) and we will charter flights to and fro (carrying illegal substances) and make millions (and do about 10 to 20)."

5. **Don't be dazzled by the just-too-glamorous everything.** You know what I mean by expensive everything: beautiful young women in the front office, sharp-looking guys moving around, and the would-be partner who says, "We like to bring local people into each of our many ventures." Be sure to count your fingers after you shake this guy's hand.

6. **Keep your comfort zone and investment area in front of you.** These two factors are your real protection. They are what you know and where you know it most. You should never invest out of your investment area, nor slide into a deal that is foreign to your comfort zone. Don't do it no matter how riskless the deal seems to be. The less you know about the venture, the less capable you are of recognizing the risk.

7. **Stay out of the crowd.** This is one of the easiest traps to fall into. "Say, Charlie, I've got a deal that is dynamite, I mean dynamite, and Brad Whatshisname and Phil Whomever are both putting up statements to make the venture look even stronger. You know what I mean? All you have to do is the same and we're home free, rolling in bread forever and ever." Of course he has just said the same thing to Brad and Phil, and when one signs, the others fall into line as the promoter hopes.

These traps won't usually stand out as clearly as I've presented them. They come sneaking in behind the mask of good intentions and well-meaning deals. Often the proposal comes from a person who simply hasn't thought out the deal as well as you should. Play the devil's advocate and question the deal to see the real deal out there. When you find the presentation to be well homeworked, the answers to your questions fairly given with the obvious attention to all sides of the risk reward aspects of the deal, then you may have found a deal worthy of your name. Just maybe.

There is one more pitfall, or trap, I've left out of the list: Your own good nature or generosity. There is little I can do to stop you, but you should at least recognize it, and maybe someday someone will find an organization like AA that will enable you to call in the middle of signing a deal and have three former name-lenders rush over and drag you off. I'm talking about the guy who will give his name out of compassion, pity, and sorrow. Compassion is a good quality to have, just don't sign your life over because of it.

42 CHAPTER

Keep Some and Sell Some

This technique is dependent on your ability to sell off part of what you want to buy in order to generate the cash needed to close. The degree of sell-off will determine the percentage of interest you retain in the original investment, as well as the future capital you might have to invest. You might, for example, sell only enough to give you the money for the down payment. Or you might sell enough to give you a fully paid interest in the remainder of the property without any cash investment on your part. Let's look at some of the variations.

THE KEEP-THE-POSITIVE, SELL-THE-NEGATIVE DEAL

You find it prudent and desirable to buy a tract of land consisting of 100 acres. You don't really need the entire 100 acres; it's the road frontage of about 40 acres that attracts you. You know, however, that the price you have negotiated of $5000 per acre for the whole 100 acres is well below the price for smaller tracts, and you can't pass up the bargain. Of the $500,000 total purchase price, the seller is willing to take only 10 percent down. And on top of that, at the closing, the seller will release five acres in the far rear of the property, farthest away from the road. The five acres, now released from the balance of the mortgage, will be yours and you can sell it. All you have to do, then, to generate the cash you need for the down payment is sell off these five acres at $10,000 per acre, closing on them at the same time you close on the 100 acres.

This transaction would work as long as an investor could be found at $10,000 per acre. However you might have to introduce another technique or two to solidify the deal and make it more secure. One way is to add the pyramid, if you have another property off which you can pyramid.

You contract to buy the above tract of 100 acres for $500,000. The contract calls for you to give the owner the $50,000 cash down, and, of the remaining balance, you give him part in the form of a mortgage on another property. Assume he took $100,000 in paper as a first mortgage on a rental property you own, $350,000 in a first mortgage on the property he sold you. In this deal he now agrees to release 15 acres instead of the original five, since he has only a $350,000 outstanding mortgage on this property and thus needs less security on the mortgage. This gives you more flexibility in selling off the land, as you can offer terms. Naturally, if you had to, you could drop the price to $8000 per acre on a bargain all-cash deal and generate a total of $120,000. This would give you the down payment you need at closing and could also reduce your debt even further. (Or you could have a ball with the extra $70,000.)

In this example if you sold the rear acreage, you have sold off some of the negative property. This back land was of no real use to you, but, since the package deal came in the form of 100 acres, you had to make the bulk purchase. This allows you to keep the prime location for development or later resale at a much higher profit.

Keep the Negative, Sell the Positive

What would have happened if you had sold the 40 acres fronting the road for the full price of $500,000 and ended up with the remaining 60 acres free and clear and without any capital investment on your part? This is called coming out smelling like money—to heck with a rose.

You might have sold that front 40 acres in 5-acre increments at $62,500 each (8 tracts multiplied by $62,500 equals $500,000). This might have been very possible had you introduced another investment technique into your bag of tricks: the time delay. If you had tied up the property with a long option, or even leased it with an option to buy, you could have capitalized on some event you knew was coming. Any pending improvement or development in the area can trigger sudden value increases. How do you find out before the owner? Easy, be observant at what is going on in the planning and zoning department of the city or cities where the property is located. Even mammoth projects are discussed there long before the general public hears about them. It is entirely possible the land or property you want to buy is outside the legal notice zone. This zone is set by local ordinance and is usually only 300 feet distance from the actual site of a proposed project. Property owners within that zone are supposed to get a notice of pending changes or proposed developments going before a public hearing. Few property owners ever see a notice or even hear about the meetings if they are outside of the zone. A beneficial event such as a new shopping center, or regional headquarters for a multi-national insurance company could increase the value of all the property nearby. It is a good feeling to watch something you don't own yet going up in value when you have locked in the price at a much lower level.

It should be obvious that it is often far easier to sell off what is presumed to be the positive than to sell the negative. Because of this you might look for investments that have a positive that isn't (for you) and a negative that is your positive. Sound confusing? Here's an example. You are buying a home in a New England ski area. You don't actually like to ski but you'd enjoy the place in the summer. This is an ideal situation because you can sell the positive and end up with your own summer place without spending a dime of your own money. The summer is your positive and the winter your negative, but the money people see it the other way around.

Selling Just Enough for the Down Payment

Let's say you are buying a place in the Florida Keys and you don't want or need 100 percent of the use of the facility. It is a simple matter of selling off part of the time in the property to make your initial down payment.

Assume that your villa in the Keys is priced at $120,000 and can be purchased for $30,000 down. You will owe $90,000 in mortgages and have an estimated annual cost of $7186.45 in debt service (30 years at 7 percent interest) and another $12,000 in estimated taxes, insurance, and maintenance on the property. Total carrying cost is $19,186.45 per year.

In this example you just need the down payment of $30,000 and you decide to do a private time-share. You will take this property and divide it into time increments, which can then be sold to others. In this format you can actually sell ownership (rather than rights to use) and you divide the total time up into 11 months of use. The twelfth month you set aside for repair and maintenance or rent-out time. However as you are going to get some time for your effort, you will actually divide all the cost of the facility over 10 months. The total price of buying a one-month share is now a total of $14,000. If each investor put up the $14,000 you would collect $140,000 out of which you could pay off the entire deal, and have a bonus of $20,000 for your trouble and still have a piece of the action. But you decide to pass on to the investors the opportunity to purchase with a mortgage in place. To close on the deal you need the following:

Cash to seller	$30,000
Cash to you	<u>$20,000</u>
Total	$50,000
Cash per investor	$ 5,000

In the final breakdown, that means a buyer will make a down payment of only $5000 and pay an estimated $2000 in annual cost of the seller held debt and the operating expenses.

When you sell all 10 months of time, you will end up with the eleventh free, and still have an extra month for income to the venture. You should be sure to include all costs of upkeep, and include a reserve (that goes into a savings account) for future replacement of furniture and fixtures.

THE FINE POINTS OF THE DEAL

You cannot haphazardly make effective use of the techniques we are discussing in this chapter. You will have to plan carefully the kind of investment that will lend itself to a partial sale at sufficient return to carry the total purchase, or provide the desired up-front capital. In selecting a property there are five things you need to look for:

1. **A forced purchase of excess property.** If a seller is forcing you to buy more property than you want, examine the possibility of a partial sale to increase the investment potential of this purchase. It is far better for the seller to require the additional purchase than for you to try to negotiate for the additional property. The reason for this is that you can frequently reduce the price and soften the terms, usually gaining some edge at least on the down payment. The seller may want out of the property, but will not sell by breaking up the tract. Use that as an edge to gain time or

get a reduced down payment or reduce the interest costs. Make sure, however, that the property meets other criteria for a potential investment.

2. **New roadwork on its way.** You should be on the ball gaining knowledge of your backyard and thus broadening your comfort zone. If you haven't contacted the road department (called Department of Transportation, or D.O.T. for short, and often by city, county, and state departments, depending on who has jurisdiction on the specific road in question) in the last three months, then you are losing your edge and should go back to selling encyclopedias. Don't limit your research of future events to road departments, either; any government office is a potential source of interesting data. If you hear of something about to happen that will make the property more valuable, verify it. If you can't verify right away, then tie up the property until you can. Once you are sure of the upcoming event, capitalize on that by selling off some of the property to cover your investment.

3. **Sales of similar properties in smaller chunks at multiples of the value.** If five-acre tracts are selling at three to four times the price of the 100-acre tract you're considering, then you have a potential to sell the property at a large profit. This can be mitigated by the costs of making those sales and the time elements involved; however, if you can make a fast turnover at triple the price, and the cost is small, then you are all right. But don't be misled by simple multiples of values. If you have to put in asphalt or concrete roads, water, sewers, and electricity, and provide fire protection or give the state or county some of the land for hospitals, parks, and schools, then you must sell in multiples of four to six times the raw land to come out with a healthy profit to offset the risk. Learn of the costs and go from there.

4. **Property that has no governmental restrictions against subdividing.** Such a property might be a gold mine, since many "in vogue" areas are cluttered with regulations and restrictions that make it impossible or very costly to subdivide. The environmentalists have tied up so much of the desirable land that in some places development simply is not economically feasible. I'm a realist when it comes to nature. Cities like Fort Lauderdale, Miami, New Orleans, San Diego, San Francisco, St.

Louis, and New York would have had a very difficult time becoming what they are (for good or bad) if they had to live up to the environmentalists' procedures and regulations of today. So look out for restrictions and look for property that is unique to the area because it has few or no restrictions governing its use.

5. **A plus factor you can sell off.** This plus factor, as I've mentioned, is ideal if the other side of the coin appeals to you more. In this way you get to keep what you wanted in the first instance and sell off at a profit the unwanted portions.

PITFALLS OF THE DEAL

The biggest pitfall you need to look out for is the form of ownership and the method of accounting of expenses and sharing of costs. Friends will become enemies and relatives will stop talking to each other in the dispute over who broke and must now pay for the water heater.

I've found that the tighter you make the deal from the standpoint of expenses, mortgage payments, taxes, and replacements, the better everyone will like it in the beginning. Be sure to cover your cost, or supervision expenses by others to oversee and manage the affairs of this property. Personally I would recommend a local realtor who would manage the property, look after rentals and maintenance, and so on. That extra month for income will come on handy, and you can be sure that there will be a lot of time when no one plans to use their allotted time. Rent it out and give them a percentage of the revenue, keep some for repairs, and keep the rest as management fees. If you have tied up a bargain and you offer out part of the deal for a percent of the action or to cover your down payment, then there is little risk on your part. However you might have a gold mine that you're ready to give away for too little. Keep your values up and don't let anyone try to get too much of a good thing unless you truly have no other option open to you.

43

CHAPTER

The Sliding Mortgage Trick

In the sliding-mortgage technique, you will move the mortgage from one security to another not without a slight of hand but with the smart ability of moving debt to another property. In doing this you maintain, or only slightly alter, the format of the existing financing. You thereby ease the total debt as it pertains to the property to be purchased, creating greater equity in the new property and enhancing its ability to support new and greater financing. At the same time you decrease equity in the other property, which now serves as security for the mortgage.

THE SLIDE DEAL

Robin, for example, owned several interesting properties and was constantly on the lookout for other investments. She found a nice duplex that was built on a lot that the existing zoning permitted up to six apartment units. Robin knew this because this property was in her investment zone as well as her comfort zone. She was confident in what she was about to do.

Robin had a builder friend of hers look at the property. They decided that at a cost of $30,000 they could convert the two garages in the duplex into four additional units and could add onto the existing building, bringing the property up to six units in total.

The seller of the property wanted $70,000 for the building and still owed $10,000 at 8 percent on a very old first mortgage with five years to go and $40,000 on a second mortgage at 9.5 percent interest-only. The second mortgage would balloon in seven years. The second mortgagee was the previous owner of the duplex who a few years earlier had sold it to the seller, who Robin was now dealing with.

Robin negotiated the following deal:

She would give the seller a cash payment at closing of	$ 20,000
Assume the existing first mortgage	10,000
Assume the existing second mortgage	40,000
Matching the full asking price of	$70,000

The interest rates and terms on the unsecured note were agreed to by the seller. The deal had one further condition: Robin had a period of 15 days to negotiate with the holder of the second mortgage to slide it to another property.

Robin didn't want to pay off the second mortgage; she wished only to transfer it to another property. If the mortgagee (the person who was owed the mortgage amount) would agree to replace the security of the duplex with one or more of Robin's other properties, then Robin could effectively remove the mortgage from the property. She would therefore increase her equity in that property by the amount of the mortgage. Remember Robin needed $30,000 to accomplish all her remodeling and another $20,000 to give the seller at the closing. Knowing the outcome of the ultimate deal and the agreement of the second mortgagee to transfer the mortgage over to another property by modifying the mortgage itself, Robin could easily borrow more cash than she needed to accomplish the OPM transaction intended.

Robin and her accountant worked out a pro forma showing the duplex as it would be when the conversion was completed: a seven-unit apartment building. The income potential and final estimated value would support an appraised value of $210,000. Based on this assumption, Robin (before she closed on the deal, of course) went to several lenders and made the best deal to borrow all the cash needed. She would have to pay off the existing mortgage. So she needed a minimum of $60,000 to go forward. ($30,000 + $20,000 + $10,000 = $60,000). Since Robin knew there would be other costs along the way, she asked for and got $70,000 in new loan proceeds, net of the loan costs. With this money, the deal was closed and everyone was happy.

The sliding-mortgage technique is often used in exchanges where one property in the exchange has a mortgage that can be slid over to another not involved in the exchange. Let's take a look at how this might work.

Ben wanted to exchange his equity of $50,000 in a vacant lot he owned for a small office building. He figured that if he spent $20,000 on some cosmetic improvements he could quickly increase the income from the building. The other party had agreed to sell for $155,000. However, he had $70,000 in equity in the office building subject to a first mortgage of $30,000 and a second mortgage of $55,000. In making the deal, Ben worked out a slide of that $55,000 mortgage over to become a first mortgage on his home.

Ben had no problem getting a new first mortgage loan commitment for $100,000 on the building. Here is how the deal ended up:

Takes out new loan of	<u>$70,000</u>
Pays off the existing first of	30,000
Pays seller the balance owed to him	5,000
Spends needed funds on fix up	20,000
Has funds left over for emergencies	10,000
Gives to seller the vacant lot worth	50,000
Slides the second mortgage to his home	$55,000

Ben got rid of the vacant lot, moved the second mortgage to his home, which he intended on selling anyway, and was able to borrow more than enough to make the improvements. Thus you have created a 100 percent OPM transaction and have cash left over.

Something to keep in mind is that pyramid transactions work nicely with sliding mortgages. If you review the pyramid transactions throughout this book, you will see great flexibility in that technique. The sliding mortgage technique is much the same, except the mortgage you transfer over to another property isn't made by you. There will be some other mortgagee and the ultimate payments for that mortgage will be paid by you to someone else. However anytime you are going to sell or exchange a property, you will increase the potential by sliding a mortgage onto that property from a property you are buying, prior to the sale or exchange, removing some of your equity in advance of the sale.

THE FINE POINTS OF THE SLIDE

An open mind, wide selection of alternatives, and creative thinking will show you much more variation than you might assume in the first glance at this technique. When you look at any property you are about to buy and see one or more mortgages, you should ask yourself this question: "Is there any benefit to me or to the deal in sliding any of these mortgages to some other property?" You will be better able to answer this question if you understand the five instances when you should consider mortgage sliding.

1. **When you need to generate cash for the down payment.** Robin did just this in the earlier example in this chapter. When you move debt from a newly acquired property to another property, you decrease your equity in the newly encumbered property, but you increase it in the newly acquired property. This greater equity and absence of debt now allows you to refinance for additional funds to allow the purchase of that property. In the right situation, you can actually walk away from the deal with cash.

2. **When you are attempting to reduce equity in another property for sale or exchange.** You might own a $70,000 vacant lot and want to sell that lot. If you are buying a home that has a $50,000 second mortgage that you can slide over to the $70,000 lot (now a first mortgage for the mortgagee, so there is some motivation on their part), you have increased your ability to sell that lot. Sliding this mortgage gives you the same benefit as receiving cash at the closing.

3. **When you want to refinance the first without changing the second.** Assume that the property you are about to purchase has both a first and second mortgage. If you refinance the first mortgage for any reason, you will have to pay off the second (except in the unlikely event that the second is subordinated to permit a new mortgage). The payoff of the second mortgage might make the refinancing too costly and not worthwhile, unless you can maintain the total debt level with that second by sliding it over to another property.

4. **When you want to get some other edge from the mortgage.** There are times when you will slide a mortgage for the benefit of the mortgagee. Perhaps the lender has told you, "Jack if you sell this property, I want you to transfer the security to another of your properties. I don't want to be owed this money by someone else. You are the person I lent the money to." In this kind of situation, you probably had set the loan up this way.

However, there will be times when you want to keep the lender in your back pocket, so you will go to him and ask if he will transfer over to another property. This will enable you to sell, exchange, or otherwise dispose of a property with greater equity if that is both possible and to your benefit. Let's say, for example, a buyer comes to one of your properties and you try to sell him on the advantages of your low-interest second mortgage, but he tells you it doesn't matter as he is going to refinance anyway. This means all the existing mortgages will be paid off. It would be a pity to pay off a low-interest mortgage if you can keep it; and you can keep it, by sliding it over to another property. You get the cash out of the sale as your equity has increased in the property you are now selling.

5. **Whenever you want to keep intact a low-interest or favorable-term mortgage.** If you are buying a property that has a 7 percent mortgage, why not try to transfer it to another property if the alternative is to refinance the property? If the new property is to be turned over fast after a fix-up, always attempt to slide the mortgage to a property you want to keep for a longer time. In this way you can hold new paper at a higher rate of interest on the turnover of the property.

Not All Mortgages Are Slippery

There are some mortgages that are difficult to slide. These will be any institutional mortgages made by banks, insurance companies, savings and loans to name a few. The easiest will be purchase-money mortgages where the mortgage is held by a former owner of the property. Second easiest will be convenience loans made by creditors, real estate brokers (for commissions), and family members.

In the sliding methods mentioned so far, you have transferred a mortgage from a property you were buying to another of your properties. There will be times when you will want the seller to slide a mortgage to another of his own properties. If, for example, the seller had a 20 percent mortgage with a three-year balloon, you would want that unattractive mortgage removed from a property you were buying and would ask if the seller could slide it over to another of his own properties. If you found that you were going to refinance a property that had a mortgage with penalties for payout, then the seller might move that mortgage for you, getting cash himself rather than paying off the mortgage. If you wanted to make an exchange into a free-and-clear property that was currently encumbered, you could "entice" the owner to slide the debt off to other property or stand the chance of losing the deal.

PITFALLS OF THE SLIDE

There are no pitfalls in this technique other than the potential risk the mortgagee might be taking by removing one security in lieu of another. Your investment risk as a buyer is highly leveraged, of course, in that you are developing another way to do an OPM transaction and you have a greater debt service because of the technique than you would have had otherwise.

However, the use of this technique will astound those around you with its simplicity and function. It will work when you can convince the mortgagees on the to-be-purchased property that the move you contemplate for them is not only safe but good business, in that their position will be improved. And you will have to document their position is in fact improved. You can enhance this by adding interest, reducing the number of years, or just moving them up in rank from a second mortgage to a first mortgage.

A P P E N D I X

Use of the Constant Interest Rate Table

Table A at the end of this Appendix may be used for many different short-cuts in calculating different mortgage payments and discounts. Once you understand how the constants work, you can, with any simple handheld calculator, ascertain a great deal of financial data.

The first step is to understand how to read Table A, which is to be used for the usual mortgage calculation where the mortgage provides for monthly payments. When using this table you must be sure that the mortgage in question is an amortization of the debt owed over equal monthly payments for the entire term of the mortgage. This table will not work with adjustable rate mortgages (where the interest rate is subject to changes during the term) or any other mortgage that has variable payments during the term. In the amortizing mortgage the monthly payment will be the same throughout the life of the mortgage. Yet within that payment the amount allocated to principal and the amount charged, as interest will change each month. This occurs because in the early years of the mortgage the amount of interest charged against the amount owed is much greater than in the later years since the mortgage is continually reduced.

As is the case with most tables and calculators, it is common to get slightly different answers. The number will depend on how many decimals the formula has and whether or not the calculator or table has rounded off too soon. For example, if the loan were $100,000 for a 25-year period at 12 percent and then amortized over a total of 300 payments, the monthly payment would be $1053.33 per month. Of this payment the amount of interest for the first payment would be $1000 and only the balance of $53.33 would be principal. On the other hand, the very last payment would also be a total of $1053.33, but the allocation to interest would be only $10.43 and the amount of principal reduction to the mortgage would be $1042.82. At some point during this 25-year term, the amount charged against interest and the allocation to principal was equal. This example was put to the test using several different calculators, and the range ran between $1053.25 and $1053.33 per month. A slight difference such as this should not worry you. Just keep in mind that when you go to the bank or a closing agent, amortization schedules may vary from these tables.

In a mortgage of 25 years at 12 percent where the amount borrowed is $100,000, the loan officer of the lending institution would ascertain the monthly payment you would have to pay by using a table such as Table A. The loan officer would look under the interest column (12 percent) and move down the page to the year row of 25 years. At the junction of these two items you will find the number 12.64, which would be the constant rate for that mortgage at the day it was to begin. The interest rate is 12 percent as shown earlier, but the charge that would reflect both interest and principal payback would be this slightly higher amount of 12.64 percent. By multiplying the gross loan outstanding by the constant rate ($100,000 × 0.1264), we would end up with an annual amount of $12,640. To get the monthly payment, simply divide that amount ($12,640) by 12 to end up with $1053.33 per month. Remember that when you use a percentage in any mathematical equation you must convert it to its mathematical equivalent by moving the decimal two places to the left. So 12.64 percent becomes 0.1265 when used in the actual formula and 9.50 percent becomes 0.0950. It is critical to remember that these constant tables are an annual percentage figure. To get the monthly payment you would divide the annual payment by 12 to end up with the correct monthly payment of principal and interest.

If you have a calculator that will multiply by percentages, then you would not have to move the decimal over to the left. If you aren't sure about your calculator then do the following:

1. Make sure your calculator is cleared.
2. Multiply $100,000 by 0.1264.

3. Check the results. The outcome should be 12,640 (or $12,640.00). If it is, then you don't have to worry.

To check out the table, try this exercise. Find the constant rate for a mortgage that is 30 years long at 7 percent interest, with monthly payments. Follow these steps.

1. Look for the 30-year row in Table A.
2. Go across the page until you come to the column for 7 percent interest.
3. Make note of the constant rate: 8.48 percent

With this information you could multiply 0.0848 times any loan amount (for that rate and duration) and divide the annual amount by 12 to get the monthly rate. For example:

$$\$100,000 \text{ loan} \times 0.0848 = \$8,480 \div 12 = \$706.66$$

LOOK FOR UNKNOWN INTEREST RATE

You can find the interest rate when you know years, amount owed, and amount of payment. For example, you can find the interest rate for a mortgage of $80,000 over 22 years, with 12 payments per year with a payment of $805.80 per month. In this situation you will use the table to help you establish terms on a mortgage to suit a transaction you are working on. You might discover there are existing mortgages on a property you want to buy that will be fully paid off in 22 years. You want the seller to hold a mortgage for the balance of the deal for that term. He wants $80,000 to make the deal. You only can afford a monthly payment of $805.80. What's the interest rate?

1 Arrive at the annual payment by multiplying the monthly payment by 12 ($805.80 × 12 = $9,669.60).
2 Divide the annual payment by the loan amount owed that day ($9,669.60 [division sign] $80,000 = 0.12087) It is important here that you make sure your calculator will write at least three numbers to the right of the decimal point. If you round off at 12.01 then you will not have an accurate number to work with. Either get a new calculator or divide by a smaller number and omit the next step.

3. Take the number you end up with (Step 2) and move the decimal over two places to the right so that 0.12087 will become 12.087.

4. Go to Table A and find the 22-year row.

5. Go across that row until you find the constant rate of 12.087 percent or the closest possible rate. You will notice that 12.09 percent is a constant rate for 11 percent interest. This will be as close as you can get with this table.

LOOK FOR THE UNKNOWN MORTGAGE AMOUNT

How can you find the mortgage amount outstanding when you know the term of years, the interest rate, and the monthly payment? This is a rather common problem that comes from different circumstances. You may be working with a seller who doesn't know the amount he owes on his mortgage. He can tell you the payment (make sure it is principal and interest only and that it does not include taxes and insurance, etc.), he knows how long it has to run, and he even knows the interest rate. For example it has 20 years to go, the monthly payment is $805, and the interest rate is 10.5 percent. Let's take a look at how it works:

1. Get annual payment again ($805 $\times$ 12 = $9,660.00).

2. Go to the 20-year row at the 10.5 percent interest column and see the constant rate, which is 11.67 percent.

3. Divide the annual payment by the constant ($9,660.00 divided by 0.11670 = $82,776.35, rounded up from a slightly larger number). The amount of the mortgage still outstanding is $82,776.35.

LOOK FOR THE UNKNOWN MORTGAGE TERMS

Here's how to find the term of years for a mortgage when you know the amount to be owed, the interest rate, and the monthly payment. When you are negotiating on a deal you may find that the flexibility of a mortgage term might bring the payment into reach. In this situation you might be fixed at having to pay off a $90,000 mortgage at 12 percent interest, with only $970 per month available from the current income of the property to support the added debt service. You and the seller agree to set the mortgage so that the $970 will pay out the mortgage. But what is the term?

1. Get the annual payment again ($970 times 12 = $11,640)
2. Divide the annual payment by the amount of the loan owned that day ($11,640 divided by $90,000 = 0.12933).
3. Move the decimal place over to the right two places (0.12933 then will become 12.933). (12.933 is the rate you will try to match. However, you will not find that rate exactly.) In the 22-year column you will find 12.94 constant at the 12 percent interest rate. That is as close as you will get.

USING CONSTANTS AS A SHORTCUT

When you deal with mortgages at a discount, you will find that any problem that you can think of for dealing with mortgage discounts (constant rate payment mortgages of course) can be ascertained using the constants. Let's say I sell my property, and take back a second mortgage for $50,000 payable over 10 years in equal monthly payments calculated at an amortization of principal and interest, with interest at 10 percent, and I want to sell the mortgage, what price will I get? A $50,000 second mortgage with 10 years in monthly payments at 10 percent.

Buyers of mortgages usually want a discount to increase the yield of the mortgage for that buyer. If the buyer of the above-mentioned mortgage wanted a 15 percent return rather than the 10 percent rate on the mortgage, he would have to buy the mortgage at a discount price that would accurately provide that yield.

To start, find the constant rate for the mortgage as it now stands. To do this, look in the 10-year row of Table A and go across to the 10 percent interest rate column. You will find a constant rate of 15.858 percent. This indicates an annual payment (the total of 12 monthly payments) of $50,000 times 0.15858 or $7929. This relates to a monthly payment of $660.75.

Now find the constant rate the buyer of the mortgage (at a discount) requires. The same number of years is in effect, so go to the 10-year row and go across to the 15 percent column. The constant rate for this yield is 19.360 percent.

The relationship between these constants is as follows: If you take the constant of the existing contract rate (10 percent interest and a constant of 15.858 percent) and divide that by the constant for the desired rate (15 percent interest desired and a constant rate of 19.360 percent) and move the decimal two places to the right, you will end up with the percent of discount needed to discount the mortgage to permit the desired yield. Take the existing constant, which is 15.868, and divide by the desired constant of 19.360 = 0.8197 and then convert to a percent would then be 81.97 percent. This is the discount percentage.

Now how much would you need to pay to get the desired return? To find out, multiply this percent of discount by the face amount of the mortgage at the day of the discount, and you will have the amount the buyer would pay under these circumstances to obtain a yield of 15 percent on a mortgage that has a contract rate of only 10 percent interest. So the amount of the mortgage ($50,000) multiplied by the discount percentage (0.8197) equals the discounted price. Thus you would pay $40,985 to earn your desired 15 percent per annum.

This same mathematical sequence can be turned around to find any part of this type of problem as long as you have sufficient data to close the circle. For example, Barry may own a mortgage with six years to go of $35,000 payable monthly at an interest rate of 11 percent interest per annum. He might just offer it to you at a price of $25,000. Would it be a good deal? You would want to know your yield as well as much more about the security and the mortgagor.

Here's how to find the solution to this problem:

1. Find the constant at the contract rate in Table A. Go to the six-year column at 11 percent interest. You will find a constant rate of 22.841 percent.

2. Find the discount percentage. To find this, divide the price of the mortgage ($25,000) by the face amount owed at the day of the discount ($35,000).

3. Price of mortgage or $25,000 divided by the face amount owed at the day of the discount ($35,000). So $25,000 divided by $35,000 equals 0.7143, or 71.43 percent.

4. Now take the constant rate found in step one (22.841 percent) and divide that by the discount percent (71.43 percent). Then take the existing constant rate, 22.841, divided by 71.43 percent to get the new constant rate of 31.98 percent.

5. This new percentage (31.98 percent) is the new constant rate for the discounted mortgage. If you then look across the six-year column until you find a rate equal to or close to this new rate, it will correspond to the yield on that mortgage. In this case you will find 31.958 percent under the six-year column at 24.5

percent interest. In essence, at $25,000 the purchase of this $35,000 mortgage would yield you over 24.5 percent interest should the mortgage go to its full term.

Mortgages rarely go the full term, however, and whenever you have purchased a mortgage at a discount, and that mortgage pays off sooner than the contracted term, a bonus will be in your pocket. If you paid $25,000 for that mortgage which has a face value of $35,000 and you held the mortgage for one year and the mortgagor then paid the mortgage off, you would get the following:

- One year's payments of $7994.35.
- At the end of the year there is still an outstanding balance on the mortgage of $30,640.26. This is found by taking the constant rate for the mortgage for the remaining term (five years) at 11 percent interest (26.091 percent) and dividing that into the annual total payment ($7994.35). $7994.35 divided by 0.26091 = $30,640.25, which is the payoff amount at the end of year one. This little step can be most useful in other financing problems as well.
- Add the total payments gained, and the payoff. $7994.35 + $30,640.25 = $38,634.60
- Subtract the amount paid to buy the mortgage: $25,000 Return of other than principal: $13,634.60
- Divide by the number of years you held this mortgage. $13,634.60 divided by 1 (in this case) = $13,634.60. This amount is your average return of interest per year.
- Divide the average return ($13,634.60) by the price you paid for the mortgage to get the average yield actually earned. Average return, or $13,634.60, divided by $25,000 = 0.5454, or 54.54 percent.

This indicates that you have actually averaged a 54.54 percent yield on this mortgage. Remember the contract rate is still only 11 percent.

TABLE A

Constant Annual Percent Expressing the Sum of 12 Equal Monthly Payments Needed to Amortize a Principal Amount

	Interest Rate								
Years	5½%	5¾%	6%	6¼%	6½%	6¾%	7%	7¼%	7½%
0.5	203.26	203.38	203.55	203.67	203.84	203.96	204.13	204.26	204.42
1.0	103.02	103.15	103.3	103.42	103.57	103.7	103.84	103.97	104.12
1.5	69.62	69.75	69.89	70.02	70.16	70.29	70.43	70.56	70.70
2.0	52.92	53.05	53.19	53.32	53.46	53.59	53.73	53.86	54.00
2.5	42.91	43.04	43.18	43.31	43.45	43.58	43.72	43.86	44.00
3.0	36.24	36.37	36.51	36.64	36.78	36.92	37.06	37.19	37.33
3.5	31.48	31.61	31.75	31.89	32.03	32.16	32.30	32.44	32.58
4.0	27.91	28.05	28.19	28.32	28.46	28.60	28.74	28.88	29.02
4.5	25.14	25.28	25.42	25.55	25.69	25.83	25.97	26.11	26.25
5.0	22.93	23.06	23.20	23.34	23.48	23.62	33.76	23.90	24.05
5.5	21.12	21.25	21.39	21.53	21.68	21.82	21.96	22.10	22.25
6.0	19.61	19.75	19.89	20.03	20.17	20.32	20.46	20.60	20.75
6.5	18.34	18.48	18.62	18.76	18.91	19.05	19.19	19.34	19.49
7.0	17.25	17.39	17.53	17.68	17.82	17.97	18.11	18.26	18.41
7.5	16.30	16.45	16.59	16.74	16.88	17.03	17.18	17.32	17.47
8.0	15.48	15.63	15.77	15.92	16.07	16.21	16.36	16.51	16.66
8.5	14.76	14.90	15.05	15.20	15.35	15.49	15.64	15.79	15.95
9.0	14.11	14.26	14.41	14.56	14.71	14.86	15.01	15.16	15.31
9.5	13.54	13.69	13.84	13.99	14.14	14.29	14.44	14.59	14.75
10.0	13.03	13.17	13.32	13.47	13.63	13.78	13.93	14.09	14.25
10.5	12.56	12.71	12.86	13.01	13.17	13.32	13.48	13.63	13.79
11.0	12.14	12.29	12.44	12.59	12.75	12.90	13.06	13.22	13.38
11.5	11.75	11.91	12.06	12.21	12.37	12.53	12.69	12.84	13.00
12.0	11.40	11.56	11.71	11.87	12.02	12.18	12.34	12.30	12.66
12.5	11.08	11.24	11.39	11.35	11.71	11.87	12.03	12.19	12.35
13.0	10.79	10.96	11.10	11.26	11.42	11.58	11.74	11.90	12.07
13.5	10.51	10.67	10.83	10.90	11.15	11.31	11.47	11.64	11.80
14.0	10.26	10.42	10.58	10.74	10.90	11.06	11.23	11.39	11.36
14.5	10.02	10.18	10.34	10.50	10.67	10.83	11.00	11.16	11.33
15.0	9.81	9.97	10.13	10.29	10.45	10.62	10.79	10.95	11.12
15.5	9.60	9.76	9.93	10.09	10.26	10.42	10.59	10.76	10.93
16.0	9.41	9.57	9.74	9.90	10.07	10.24	10.41	10.38	10.75
16.5	9.24	9.40	9.56	9.73	9.9	10.07	10.24	10.41	10.58
17.0	9.07	9.23	9.40	9.56	9.73	9.90	10.08	10.25	10.42
17.5	8.91	9.08	9.24	9.41	9.58	9.75	9.93	10.10	10.28

				Interest Rate					
Years	5½%	5¾%	6%	6¼%	6½%	6¾%	7%	7¼%	7½%
18.0	8.76	8.93	9.10	9.27	9.44	9.61	9.79	9.96	10.14
18.5	8.63	8.79	8.96	9.13	9.31	9.48	9.65	9.83	10.01
19.0	8.50	8.66	8.83	9.01	9.18	9.35	9.33	9.71	9.89
19.5	8.37	8.54	8.71	8.88	9.06	9.24	9.41	9.39	9.78
20.0	8.26	8.43	8.60	8.77	8.95	9.12	9.30	9.48	9.67
20.5	8.15	8.32	8.49	8.66	8.84	9.02	9.20	9.38	9.57
21.0	8.04	8.21	8.39	8.56	8.74	8.92	9.10	9.29	9.47
21.5	7.94	8.11	8.29	8.47	8.65	8.83	9.01	9.19	9.38
22.0	7.85	8.02	8.20	8.38	8.56	8.74	8.92	9.11	9.29
22.5	7.76	7.93	8.11	8.29	8.47	8.65	8.84	9.02	9.21
23.0	7.67	7.85	8.03	8.21	8.39	8.57	8.76	8.95	9.14
23.5	7.59	7.77	7.95'	8.13	8.31	8.50	8.68	8.87	9.06
24.0	7.51	7.69	7.87	9.05	8.24	8.42	8.61	8.80	9.00
24.5	7.44	7.62	7.80	7.98	8.17	8.36	8.55	8.74	8.93
25.0	7.37	7.55	7.73	7.92	8.10	8.29	8.48	8.67	8.87
25.5	7.30	7.48	7.67	7.85	8.04	8.23	8.42	8.61	8.81
26.0	7.24	7.42	7.60	7.79	7.98	8.17	8.36	8.56	8.75
26.5	7.18	7.36	7.55	7.73	7.92	8.11	8.31	8.50	8.70
27.0	7.12	7.30	7.49	7.68	7.87	8.06	8.25	8.45	8.65
27.5	7.06	7.25	7.43	7.62	7.81	8.01	8.20	8.40	8.60
28.0	7.01	7.19	7.38	7.57	7.76	7.96	8.16	8.35	8.55
28.5	6.96	7.14	7.33	7.52	7.72	7.91	8.11	8.31	9.51
29.0	6.91	7.09	7.28	7.48	7.67	7.87	8.07	8.27	8.47
29.5	6.86	7.05	7.24	7.43	7.63	7.82	8.02	8.23	8.43
30.0	6.81	7.00	7.20	7.39	7.59	7.78	7.98	8.19	8.39
35.0	6.44	6.64	6.84	7.05	7.25	7.46	7.67	7.88	8.09
40.0	6.19	6.39	6.60	6.81	7.03	7.24	7.46	7.68	7.90

				Interest Rate					
Years	7¾%	8%	8¼%	8½%	8¾%	9%	9¼%	9½%	9¾%
0.5	204.33	204.71	204.87	205.00	205.16	205.29	205.45	205.38	205.74
1.0	104.23	104.39	104.34	104.67	104.81	104.95	105.09	105.22	103.37
1.5	70.83	70.97	71.11	71.23	71.39	71.32	71.66	71.79	71.94
2.0	54.14	54.28	54.42	34.35	54.69	54.82	54.96	55.1	55.24
2.5	44.13	44.27	44.41	44.54	44.68	44.82	44.96	43.10	23.24
3.0	37.47	37.61	37.73	37.88	38.02	38.16	38.30	38.44	38.58
3.5	32.71	32.85	33.00	33.13	33.28	33.41	33.36	33.70	33.84
4.0	29.16	29.30	29.44	29.38	29.72	29.86	30.01	30.15	30.29

T A B L E A *(continued)*

					Interest Rate				
Years	7¾%	8%	8¼%	8½%	8¾%	9%	9¼%	9½%	9¾%
4.5	26.39	26.54	26.68	26.82	26.97	27.11	27.23	27.40	27.34
5.0	24.19	24.33	24.48	24.62	24.77	24.91	25.06	25. 2	25.35
5.5	22.39	22.54	22.68	22.83	22.97	23.12	23.21	23.41	23.36
6.0	20.89	21.04	21.19	21.33	21.48	21.63	21.78	21.93	22.06
6.5	19.63	19.78	19.93	20.08	20.23	20.38	20.53	20.68	20.83
7.0	18.55	18.70	18.86	19.00	19.16	19.31	19.46	19.61	19.77
7.5	17.62	17.77	17.93	18.08	18.23	18.38	18.54	18.69	18.85
8.0	16.81	16.96	17.12	17.27	17.43	17.58	17.74	17.89	18.03
8.5	16.10	16.25	16.41	16.36	16.72	16.88	17.03	17.19	17.35
9.0	15.47	15.62	13.78	15.94	16.09	16.25	16.41	16.37	16.73
9.5	14.91	15.06	15.22	15.38	15.54	15.70	15.86	16.02	16.18
10.0	14.40	14.36	14.72	14.88	15.04	15.20	15.56	15.53	15.69
10.5	13.95	14.11	14.27	14.43	14.59	14.76	14.92	15.09	15.25
11.0	13.54	13.70	13.86	14.02	14.19	14.35	14.32	14.69	14.86
11.5	13.17	13.33	13.49	13.66	13.82	13.99	14.16	14.33	14.50
12.0	12.83	12.99	13.16	13.32	13.49	13.66	13.83	14.00	14.17
12.5	12.52	12.68	12.85	13.02	13.18	13.35	13.53	13.70	13.87
13.0	12.23	12.40	12.57	12.73	12.91	13.08	13.25	13.42	13.6
13.5	11.97	12.14	12.31	12.48	12.65	12.82	13.00	13.17	13.35
14.0	11.73	11.90	12.07	12.24	12.41	12.39	12.76	12.94	13.12
14.5	11.50	11.67	11.85	12.02	12.20	12.37	12.55	12.73	12.91
15.0	11.30	11.47	11.64	11.82	11.99	12.17	12.35	12.53	12.71
15.3	11.10	11.28	11.45	11.63	11.81	11.99	12.17	12.35	12.53
16.0	10.92	11.10	11.28	11.45	11.63	11.81	12.00	12.18	12.37
16.5	10.76	10.93	11.11	11.29	11.47	11.65	11.84	12.02	12.21
17.0	10.60	10.78	10.96	11.14	11.32	11.51	11.69	11.88	12.07
17.5	10.46	10.64	10.82	11.00	11.18	11.37	11.55	11.74	11.93
18.0	10.32	10.50	10.68	10.87	11.05	11.24	11.43	11.62	11.61
18.5	10.19	10.37	10.56	10.74	10.93	11.12	11.31	11.50	11.69
19.0	10.07	10.25	10.44	10.63	10.81	11.00	11.19	11.39	11.59
19.5	9.96	10.14	10.33	10.52	10.71	10.90	11.09	11.28	11.48
20.0	9.85	10.04	10.23	10.41	10.60	10.80	10.99	11.19	11.38
20.5	9.75	9.94	10.13	10.32	10.51	10.70	10.90	11.09	11.29
21.0	9.66	9.85	10.04	10.23	10.42	10.62	10.81	11.01	11.21
21.5	9.57	9.76	9.95	10.14	10.34	10.53	10.73	10.93	11.13
22.0	9.48	9.67	9.87	10.06	10.26	10.45	10.65	10.85	11.06
22.5	9.40	9.60	9.79	9.99	10.18	10.38	10.58	10.78	10.99
23.0	9.33	9.52	9.72	9.91	10.11	10.31	10.51	10.72	10.92

Interest Rate

Years	7¾%	8%	8¼%	8½%	8¾%	9%	9¼%	9½%	9¾%
23.5	9.26	9.45	9.65	9.85	10.05	10.25	10.45	10.65	10.86
24.0	9.19	9.38	9.58	9.78	9.98	10.18	10.39	10.59	10.80
24.5	9.12	9.32	9.52	9.72	9.92	10.13	10.33	10.54	10.75
25.0	9.06	9.26	9.46	9.66	9.87	10.07	10.28	10.48	10.69
25.5	9.01	9.21	9.41	9.61	9.81	10.02	10.23	10.43	10.63
26.0	8.95	9.15	9.35	9.56	9.76	9.97	10.18	10.39	10.60
26.5	8.90	9.10	9.30	9.51	9.71	9.92	10.13	10.34	10.56
27.0	8.85	9.05	9.26	9.46	9.67	9.88	10.09	10.30	10.51
27.5	8.8	9.01	9.21	9.42	9.63	9.84	10.05	10.26	10.48
28.0	8.76	8.96	9.17	9.38	9.58	9.80	10.01	10.22	10.44
28.5	8.71	8.92	9.13	9.34	9.53	9.76	9.97	10.19	10.40
29.0	8.67	8.88	9.09	9.30	9.51	9.72	9.94	10.15	10.37
29.5	8.63	8.84	9.05	9.26	9.47	9.69	9.90	10.12	10.34
30.0	8.60	8.81	9.02	9.23	9.44	9.66	9.87	10.09	10.31
35.0	8.31	8.52	8.74	8.96	9.18	9.41	9.63	9.86	10.09
40.0	8.12	8.34	8.57	8.80	9.03	9.26	9.49	9.72	9.93

Interest Rate

Years	10%	11%	12%	13%	14%	15%	16%	17%	18%
0.5	205.88	206.49	207.07	207.66	208.25	208.84	209.44	210.04	210.64
1.0	105. 5	106.07	106.63	107.19	107.75	108.31	108.88	109.45	110.02
1.5	72.07	72.63	73.18	73.74	74.30	74.86	75.43	76.00	76.57
2.0	55.37	55.93	56.49	57.05	57.62	58.18	58.76	59.33	59.91
2.5	45.37	45.94	46.50	47.07	47.64	48.21	48.79	49.38	49.87
3.0	38.72	39.29	39.86	40.43	41.01	41.60	42.19	42.79	43.36
3.5	33.98	34.56	35.13	35.72	36.30	36. 9	37.50	38.11	38.72
4.0	30.44	31.02	31.60	32.19	32.79	33.40	34.01	34.63	35.25
4.5	27.69	28.28	28.87	29.47	30.08	30.69	31.32	31.95	32.58
5.0	25.50	26.09	26.69	27.30	27.92	28.55	29.18	29.82	30.47
5.5	23.71	24.32	24.93	25.54	26.17	26.81	27.45	28.11	28.77
6.0	22.23	22.84	23.46	24.09	24.73	25.37	26.03	26.70	27.37
6.5	20.98	21.6	22.23	22.87	23.52	24.17	24.84	25.52	26.20
7.0	19.92	20.55	21.18	21.83	22.49	23.16	23.83	24.52	25.22
7.5	19.01	19.64	20.28	20.94	21.61	22.29	22.98	23.68	24.39
8.0	18.21	18.85	19.50	20.17	20.85	21.53	22.23	22.95	23.67
8.5	17.51	18.16	18.82	19.50	20.18	20.88	21.59	22.31	23.05
9.0	16.89	17.55	18.22	18.90	19.60	20.31	21.03	21.76	22.51
9.5	16.35	17.01	17.69	18.38	19.09	19.81	20.54	21.28	22.04

T A B L E   A   *(continued)*

| | Interest Rate | | | | | | | | |
Years	10%	11%	12%	13%	14%	15%	16%	17%	18%
10.0	15.86	16.53	17.22	17.92	18.63	19.36	20.1	20.86	21.62
10.5	15.42	16.10	16.79	17.50	18.23	18.96	19.72	20.48	21.26
11.0	15.02	15.71	16.41	17.13	17.86	18.61	19.37	20.15	20.93
11.5	14.67	15.36	16.07	16.80	17.54	18.29	19.06	19.85	20.65
12.0	14.34	15.04	13.76	16.50	17.25	18.01	18.79	19.58	20.39
12.5	14.04	14.75	15.48	16.22	16.98	17.75	18.54	19.35	20.16
13.0	13.77	14.49	15.22	15.97	16.74	17.52	18.32	19.13	19.96
13.5	13.53	14.25	14.99	15.75	16.52	17.31	18.12	19.94	19.77
14.0	13.30	14.03	14.78	15.54	16.33	17.12	17.94	18.77	19.61
14.5	13.09	13.93	14.58	15.36	16.15	16.95	17.77	18.61	19.46
15.0	12.90	13.64	14.40	15.18	15.98	16.80	17.62	18.47	19.33
15.5	12.72	13.47	14.24	15.03	15.83	16.65	17.49	18.34	19.20
16.0	12.55	13.31	14.09	14.88	15.69	16.52	17.37	18.22	19.10
16.5	12.40	13.16	13.94	14.75	15.57	16.40	17.25	18.12	19.00
17.0	12.25	13.03	13.81	14.62	15.45	16.29	17.15	18.02	18.91
17.5	12.12	12.90	13.69	14.51	15.34	16.19	17.06	17.93	18.83
18.0	12.00	12.78	13.58	14.41	15.24	16.10	16.97	17.86	18.75
18.5	11.88	12.67	13.48	14.31	15.15	16.02	16.89	17.78	18.69
19.0	11.78	12.57	13.39	14.22	15.07	15.94	16.82	17.72	18.63
19.5	11.67	12.48	13.30	14.14	14.99	15.87	16.76	17.66	18.57
20.0	11.58	12.39	13.21	14.06	14.92	15.80	16.70	17.60	18.52
20.5	11.49	12.30	13.14	13.99	14.86	15.74	16.64	17.55	18.47
21.0	11.41	12.23	13.06	13.92	14.80	15.69	16.59	17.51	18.43
21.5	11.33	12.15	13.00	13.86	14.74	15.63	16.54	17.46	18.39
22.0	11.26	12.09	12.94	13.80	14.69	15.59	16. 5	17.43	18.36
22.5	11.19	12.02	12.88	13.75	14.64	15.54	16.46	17.39	18.33
23.0	11.13	11.96	12.82	13.70	14.59	15.5	16.42	17.36	18.30
23.5	11.07	11.91	12.77	13.65	14.55	15.47	16.39	17.33	18.27
24.0	11.01	11.86	12.72	13.61	14.51	15.43	16.36	17.30	18.25
24.5	10.96	11.81	12.6&	13.57	14.48	15.40	16.33	17.28	18.23
25.0	10.90	11.76	12.64	13.53	14.45	15.37	16.31	17.25	18.21
25.5	10.86	11.72	12.60	13.50	14.41	15.34	16.28	17.23	18.19
26.0	10.81	11.68	12.56	13.47	14.39	15.32	16.26	17.21	18.17
26.5	10.77	11.64	12.33	13.44	14.36	15.29	16.24	17.20	18.16
27.0	10.73	11.60	12.50	13.41	14.33	15.27	16.22	17.18	18.15
27.5	10.69	11.57	12.47	13.38	14.31	15.25	16.20	17.17	18.13

Years	Interest Rate								
	10%	11%	12%	13%	14%	15%	16%	17%	18%
28.0	10.66	11.54	12.44	13.36	14.29	15.23	16.19	17.15	18.12
28.5	10.62	11.51	12.41	13.33	14.27	15.22	16.17	17.14	18.11
29.0	10.59	11.48	12.39	13.31	14.25	15.20	16.16	17.13	18.10
29.5	10.56	11.45	12.37	13.29	14.23	15.19	16.15	17.12	18.09
30.0	10.53	11.43	12.34	13.27	14.22	15.17	16.14	17.11	18.09
30.5	10.32	11.24	12.19	13.14	14.11	15.08	16.06	17.05	18.03
40.0	10.19	11.14	12.10	13.07	14.05	15.04	16.03	17.02	18.01

INDEX

ABOUT THE AUTHOR

Jack Cummings is a highly successful real estate investor, broker, and developer with nearly 40 years of hands-on experience. The author of numerous books, including *The McGraw-Hill 36-Hour Real Estate Course,* Cummings is a popular international speaker who also makes regular television and radio appearances.